D1616846

The Politics
of Social
Administration

BURTON GUMMER
The University at Albany
State University of New York

The Politics of Social Administration

Managing Organizational Politics in Social Agencies

HV
40
.G94
1990
West

Prentice Hall
Englewood Cliffs, New Jersey 07632

Library of Congress Cataloging-in-Publication Data

Gummer, Burton.
    The politics of social administration : managing organizational
politics in social agencies / Burton Gummer.
        p.   cm.
    Includes bibliographical references.
    ISBN 0-13-684978-4
    1. Social work administration--Political aspects.   I. Title.
HV40.G94   1990
361'.0068--dc20   89-16402
                                                                      CIP

Editorial/production supervision: Betsy Keefer
Cover design: Suzanne Bennett and Associates
Manufacturing buyer: Carol Bystrom

© 1990 by Prentice-Hall, Inc.
A Division of Simon & Schuster
Englewood Cliffs, New Jersey 07632

Printed in the United States of America
10 9 8 7 6 5 4 3 2 1

ISBN 0-13-684978-4

Prentice-Hall International (UK) Limited, *London*
Prentice-Hall of Australia Pty. Limited, *Sydney*
Prentice-Hall Canada, Inc., *Toronto*
Prentice-Hall Hispanoamericana, S.A., *Mexico*
Prentice-Hall of India Private Limited, *New Delhi*
Prentice-Hall of Japan, Inc., *Tokyo*
Simon & Schuster Asia Pte. Ltd., *Singapore*
Editora Prentice-Hall do Brasil, Ltda., *Rio de Janeiro*

To Abby, Charlie, and Max
Here's looking at you, kids

Contents

8
Managing Organizational Politics II:
Negotiating and Bargaining 153

9
The Ethics of Organizational Politics 186

Bibliography 203

Index 217

Foreword

The practice of administration in social work is as old as the profession itself, and yet, until quite recently, relatively little theory and empirical research was available in the field to explain organizational behavior in social agencies or to provide guidance to those with managerial responsibility. There were, of course, significant contributors to the theory and practice of administration in social work in the early years of the profession (e.g., Elwood Street, Ordway Tead, Harleigh Trecker, John Kidneigh), but for the most part their work was a sidebar to that of direct practice theorists whose primary concern was services to individuals, families, and groups.

This situation began to shift significantly in the 1970s, when in response to the burgeoning scope and size of social welfare, and its growing political importance, officials in legislative and executive branches at both state and federal levels began to look critically at the organization and administration of social programs. In the nearly two decades since then, social work scholars have worked assiduously to build an intellectual foundation for administrative practice in social agencies. As might be expected, given the impoverished state of administrative theory in social work, much of this work followed the dominant theoretical and technical propositions found in the more mature fields of public and business administration. Consequently, much that has been transferred to social work and social welfare is rooted in rational or human-relations theories of organizations and the technologies that flow from them. Our conceptions of how to plan, organize, lead, evaluate, budget, communicate, and so on, are informed primarily by the assumptions implicit in one or the other of these theories. While there is nothing inherently "wrong" with these explanations of organizational behavior, or the technologies that follow from them, practitioners and scholars have become increasingly aware that neither theory provides us with a complete picture of why things happen in organizations, or how best to manage them. Indeed, there is now wide agreement that organizational phenomena are too varied and complex to be captured by any single perspective.

The political perspective on organizations and administration developed in this book significantly expands the theoretical foundation of administrative practice in social work. In clear and uncomplicated language, Gummer traces the forces that have contributed to the increased politicization of social agencies, sets out the elements of a political framework, and shows how it can be used to help us understand and work effectively with problems and issues that are commonly encountered in human service organizations. Of course, the political theory of organizations is not new. Gummer's distinctive contribution is to render a sophisticated synthesis of the extant work in this area without sacrifice to its subtlety and substance and to join it with a sensitive, far-reaching analysis of both social work and the institutions in which it practices. The application of the political perspective to social welfare has rarely been done so effectively. Armed with this perspective, the reader is able to view in new light persistent problems that occur in resource allocation, treatment of women and minority employees, evaluation of subordinates, and program implementation. Problems ordinarily attributed to irrationality, incompetence, interpersonal failures, or personal pathology, when seen through the lens of political theory, can often be better understood as the product of individuals and groups with conflicting political interests who are attempting to achieve their objectives in the context of scarce resources.

Several features of this book make it especially commendable. First, Gummer places the political dynamics of organizations squarely in the context of larger political and economic conditions and demonstrates how the long arm of the environment reaches into every nook and cranny of the social agency to shape and condition the terms and nature of the political processes that occur there. This is no easy accomplishment because it requires of the author a broad understanding of social policy and history as well as organizational and administrative theory. In any case, this integrated look at the interaction between the policy environment and organizations provides a much fuller understanding of how problems arise in human service agencies and where to look for change.

Second, Gummer takes power out of the shadowy recesses of professional discourse and resurrects it as a ubiquitous, normal, and necessary element of organizational life. He is not an apologist for the unbridled, unprincipled use of power (in fact, he is wary of its excesses), but neither does he shrink from the recognition that in order for professionals to achieve their legitimate purposes they must become skilled in its acquisition and use. While Gummer speaks most directly to administrators of social agencies, he is not concerned with empowering them in order to subjugate others. Indeed, his concept of the politically effective administrator is one who creates conditions that enable all the actors to recognize political issues when they arise and participate in their solution. The reader, administrator or clinician, will come away with a fuller understanding of how power is developed and how it can be effectively used to promote agency purposes.

Finally, it is relatively rare to find a book that succeeds equally well at explanation and prescription. The student of social welfare organizations will find fresh and stimulating insights about why and how political processes occur in social agencies. The practitioner concerned with shaping and managing those processes will also find practical ideas about how to assess their orientations to power, how to use power to influence others, how to bargain and negotiate, and how to examine the ethicality of one's political behavior.

We are in an era when politics permeate every aspect of organizational life. Social workers and other human service professionals have been slow to realize that political acumen is as necessary to building effective organizations as good human relations and sound administrative practices. This book can help us to become more informed and effective participants in organizational polities.

Rino Patti
Dean
School of Social Work
University of Southern
  California
Los Angeles, California

1

Introduction

We live in paradoxical times. More accurately, we live in *seemingly* paradoxical times because of the way we tend to think about the world around us, especially how we think about progress. We often confine our thinking about progress to one or two areas, ignoring the fact that developments are taking place in many areas. Moreover, we tend to restrict our notions of progress to tangible, material things like automobiles and computers and are less aware of progress in nonmaterial spheres like social and political behavior.

We think this way for a number of reasons. It's easier to think about concrete, visible things than about abstract entities. Also, it's easier to think about things that have clear guidelines for making sense of them. Few people would dispute the claim that there has been progress in the automobile and computer industries; a car that gets 40 miles to the gallon is four times better than one that gets 10, as is a computer with 256 kilobytes of memory compared to one with 64. Such agreement, however, rarely extends to the social and political worlds. Is the child who is placed in a day care center at the age of six months better off than the child who remains at home with his or her mother for four or five years? Is the employee who insists on having lengthy explanations for directives issued by duly authorized superiors a better employee than one who automatically complies?

The intellectual blinders that direct our attention to advances in some areas and not in others produce paradoxical results when we expect people and organizations to act in certain ways. We are surprised when they don't and perplexed as to why. Nowhere is this sense of paradox more pronounced than in the management of complex organizations. Since the end of World War II there have been phenomenal advances in the technical and conceptual bases for management practice. Foremost among these advances are developments in systems analysis, the application of advanced statistical techniques to production and administrative problems, more sophisticated accounting systems, breakthrough developments in microchip technology, and the introduction of the personal computer.

Given these developments, we should expect the performance of contemporary organizations to surpass anything in history in terms of quality, productivity, and efficiency. Paradoxically, however, this has not been the case. In the private sector the productivity of many key American industries has fallen behind their European and Far Eastern rivals.[1] Top-level managers are handsomely rewarded for ignoring long-term production considerations in favor of short-term profit taking.[2] There are indications of growing employee discontent, particularly among clerical and manufacturing workers.[3] Drug and alcohol abuse has become widespread in the work place. Large numbers of employees, blue and white collar alike, experience structural unemployment as their skills become obsolete and opportunities for finding new niches in the work force dwindle.

In the public sector there is growing suspiciousness on the part of the general public regarding the motivations and intentions of public institutions and public bureaucrats.[4] The ability of government to deliver services competently is questioned by both the general citizenry and professional analysts.[5] When a sample of citizens was asked what proportion of each tax dollar they believed the federal government wastes, the median response was 48 cents.[6] Both Presidents Carter and Reagan adopted an antibureaucracy posture and made criticism of public services and public servants an important part of their presidential campaigns. Dissatisfaction with the performance of the social services in particular has prompted renewed interest in "privatization," including the transfer of services to commercial sponsors.[7]

A number of explanations have been put forth to account for the discrepancy between promise and performance in the public and private sectors. These explanations include the idea of a general "malaise" which has affected the American spirit; inability to compete with innovative Japanese management and production styles; an overly regulated economy; an unregulated economy; sapping of initiative and resources by the welfare state; corrupt, venal, or indifferent public servants; unbridled self-interest among business executives, professionals, and other educated elites; and resignation in the face of the incredibly large and complicated "megastructures" which are today's public and private bureaucracies.

The purpose of this book is to look at another explanation of why organizations — particularly social service organizations — perform the way they do, and to suggest ways for improving that performance. A central argument of the book is that a major change in contemporary life has been a shift in the location of many political struggles from the public to the organizational sphere, with a resulting increase in the politicization of organizational life. A central function for any political system is the *allocation of values*.[8] One of the distinctive features of modern societies is that answers to the classic political question of "who gets what, when, and how" are increasingly made by bureaucrats — both public and private — who are not elected by or held accountable to a constituency, at least not in the usual sense of those words. While many people confine the meaning of politics to electoral politics, this is an overly limited definition that does not reflect current realities. Elections are a critical part of politics, but they do not account for the entire political process. To argue that they do, Rohr observed,

> would suggest that when values are allocated authoritatively, or when the common good is pursued by the state outside the electoral process, the activity in question is simply not political. This would be a very impoverished concept of politics.[9]

Most of the things that people value and want — jobs, physical and emotional well-being, social status and prestige, recreation, spiritual solace — are determined more and more by the operation of bureaucratic organizations, and not by membership in political or community associations. Ours is an organizational society and is becoming more so as the scope and influence of bureaucratic organizations expand. Nearly 20 percent of the total nonagricultural employed labor force works for local, state, or federal government. Another 30 percent is employed by business enterprises with more than 500 people on the payroll, and more than 12 million Americans work in firms that employ over 10,000 people. These latter figures do not include employees of organizations such as social agencies, universities, and hospitals that, while they can't be called businesses, are often run like them.[10] Even professionals — long considered the antithesis of "organization man" — are affected, with nearly 75 percent of all professionals working as salaried employees.[11] There is a growing realization, Ewing observed,

> that our actual freedom, as opposed to the conventionally interpreted constitutional freedom, is determined not alone by the power of political officials, judges, and policemen, but also, and perhaps more importantly, by the power of employers.[12]

In addition to being mechanisms for getting things done, organizations are repositories of practically all the valued commodities of modern life. Our growing awareness of this role has led to a greater concern with how organizations actually go about deciding how these commodities are distributed. No longer are people willing to accept the notion that organizational leaders make decisions solely on the basis of the best use of resources for achieving organizational goals. People are less inclined to accept organizational actions without probing to find out who gains and who loses and how these decisions are made.

Concentrations of wealth and power in economic organizations are taken for granted in a capitalist society. However, an important development in the United States since the 1930s has been the emergence of government — particularly the federal government — as a major source of wealth and power. Moreover, each expansion in the power of government, as Lowi pointed out, "has been accompanied by demands for equally significant expansion of representation" on the part of the people that government serves and employs.[13] Along with increased demands for representation, there has been a change in the nature of representation. No longer confined to formal political institutions and processes, representation nowadays means access to the internal organizational processes which determine the outcomes that have profound consequences for people's well-being. At the same time that participation in electoral politics has declined in the United States (fewer than half of those eligible to vote went to the polls in the 1988 presidential election), the number of organized interest groups has grown. Increasingly, the opportunity to influence policymaking is acquired not by access to politicians through the ballot box, but by access to the bureaucrats and professionals — both high and low — who not only implement policies but actually make them.

The rise of what Lowi called "interest group liberalism" has meant that the environment of public and private organizations has become dense with organized interests seeking to promote their claims. This development has prompted a number of scholars to examine the ways in which interest group demands affect organizational practices and to suggest ways in which administrators might better handle them. A political perspective on organizational behavior has emerged, and it is this perspective that forms the conceptual background for this book.

There are three distinct intellectual orientations to the study of social welfare. The oldest is the analysis of social welfare as an expression of *public policy*. From studies of the English Poor Laws to contemporary debates over Social Security, health insurance, and public assistance, policy analysts have viewed social welfare legislation as an opportunity to understand how societies set priorities and allocate scarce public resources. As the welfare system became institutionalized and its practitioners moved from volunteer to paid and then to professional status, the study of social welfare as *professional practice* emerged. Within social work, the study of practice — particularly clinical work with individuals and families — has become the dominant paradigm for thinking about social welfare in general. The third and newest approach takes the social service organization as its point of departure and treats social welfare as a form of *organizational behavior*. The newness of this approach reflects in part the youth of the disciplines of organization theory and administrative science upon which it is based. In addition, the dominance of the clinical paradigm has limited the receptivity of social work scholars to organizational and administrative models of analysis.

During the past three decades, however, there has been a significant increase in thinking about social welfare in organizational and administrative terms. This new direction has been due in large part to the unprecedented growth in the size, complexity, and importance of the welfare system since 1950. Furthermore, much of the research and theorizing about social service organizations converges around a point of view that emphasizes *political* processes in both the internal operations of these organizations and their relationships with their environments. The purpose of the present book is to apply a political framework to understanding the organization and administration of social service agencies. Although the focus will be on the social agency, many of the observations and analyses are applicable to other organizations, particularly those with similar structural features. As the American economy moves into a post-industrial phase characterized by a growing proportion of service industries, the problems facing social agencies are becoming the problems faced by other organizations that pursue ambiguous and contested goals, use poorly developed technologies, employ people with competing and strongly held notions of what the organization should be about, and must justify their activities to a skeptical but powerful audience. In many ways, the social agency may be the prototypical organization of the late twentieth century, in much the same way that the manufacturing organization was in the early part of the century.

This book has three goals: to develop a framework for applying political concepts to the operations of social service organizations; to describe how political processes operate in the administration of these organizations; and to suggest ways in which administrators and service providers can increase their effectiveness through a better understanding of organizational politics and the use of political procedures and skills in their work.

A theoretical framework for examining organizational politics and organizational politicians is presented in Chapter Two and applied to social service organizations in Chapter Three. The next three chapters examine political processes in three aspects of agency administration: the management of money, the management of people, and program implementation. Ways in which administrators and service providers might profit from a political approach to their organizations and their work are presented in Chapters Seven and Eight. The ethical and professional issues raised by a political approach to social administration are discussed in the concluding chapter.

Because the study of organizational politics is still in an early stage of development, the theoretical discussions and empirical findings currently available are scattered among a number of disciplines and reflect a variety of organizational settings. The discussions that follow, therefore, draw on the works of researchers from most of the disciplines of the social and behavior sciences, as well as on the findings of scholars and practitioners in applied fields such as social work, public administration, and business administration. The goal throughout, however, is to use this information to show how social agencies currently operate and how those operations can be made more effective.

NOTES

1. Robert B. Reich, *The Next American Frontier* (New York: Penguin Books, 1983).
2. Seymour Melman, *Profits without Production* (New York: Knopf, 1984).
3. M. R. Cooper et al., "Changing Employee Values: Deepening Discontent?" *Harvard Business Review*, 57, no. 1 (January-February 1979), 117–25.
4. Robert B. Denhardt, "Toward a Critical Theory of Public Organization," *Public Administration Review*, 41, no. 6 (November-December 1981), 628–35; Terrence R. Mitchell and William G. Scott, "Leadership Failures, the Distrusting Public, and Prospects of the Administrative State," *Public Administration Review*, 47, no. 6 (November-December 1987), 445–52.
5. James L. Sundquist, "The Crisis of Competence in Government," in *Setting National Priorities: Agenda for the 1980s* (Washington, D.C.: The Brookings Institution, 1980); Everett C. Ladd, "The Reagan Phenomenon and Public Attitudes toward Government," in *The Reagan Presidency and the Governing of America*, ed. Lester M. Salamon and Michael S. Lund (Washington, D.C.: The Urban Institute, 1984).
6. Steven Kelman, "The Grace Commission: How Much Waste in Government," *The Public Interest*, no. 78 (Winter 1985), 62–82.
7. Marc Bendick, "Privatizing the Delivery of Social Welfare Service," in *Working Paper No. 6: Privatization* (Washington, D.C.: National Conference on Social Welfare, 1985).
8. David Easton, *A Systems Analysis of Political Life* (New York: John Wiley and Sons, 1965).
9. John A. Rohr, *Ethics for Bureaucrats* (New York: Marcel Dekker, 1978), p. 28.
10. Rosabeth Moss Kanter, *Men and Women of the Corporation* (New York: Basic Books, 1977), p. 15.
11. Joseph A. Raelin, "An Examination of Deviant/Adaptive Behaviors in the Organizational Careers of Professionals," *Academy of Management Review*, 9, no. 3 (July 1984), 413–27.
12. David W. Ewing, *Freedom inside the Organization: Bringing Civil Liberties to the Workplace* (New York: E. P. Dutton, 1977), pp. 49–50.
13. Theodore J. Lowi, *The End of Liberalism: Ideology, Policy, and the Crisis of Public Authority*, (New York: W. W. Norton, 1969), p. 94.

2

The Evolution
of a Political Perspective
on Organizational Behavior

From its beginnings in Weber's studies of government and business organizations in turn-of-the-century Prussia, the field of organizational theory has grown to include a number of perspectives for looking at a range of organizations from neighborhood associations to multinational corporations.[1] While Weber's conception of the bureaucratic organization as the ideal type for rational action is still the leading point of view, there are currently as many other theoretical approaches as there are kinds of organizations. The purpose of this chapter is to trace the development of one of these perspectives — the political — and to locate it within the general field of organizational theory.

All organizational theories are concerned with purposive action. Organizations are assumed to be able to get things done more efficiently and effectively than individuals working on their own. Organizations are evaluated in terms of their abilities to achieve desired ends with a minimum of expense and a maximum of quality. As studies of purposive action, all organizational theories must pay close attention to organizational goals and goal-directed behavior. Changing views about organizational goals and how they are set provide a background for understanding why a political approach to organizational behavior emerged when it did.

CHANGING IDEAS ABOUT ORGANIZATIONAL GOALS

Much of contemporary organizational theory is predicated on a harmony of interest theme that assumes the unity of purpose of the organization as a whole and views the parts as they contribute to this unity.[2] This orientation emphasizes broad-based acceptance of organizational goals, task interdependence, and integration of functions, and views organizations as essentially cooperative systems, highlighting what Kenneth Boulding called organization's "friendly face."

The idea of the organization as a single-purpose, integrated system has its roots, Mintzberg suggested, in early economic theory which depicted the organization as consisting of *one actor/one goal*.[3] The organization was synonymous with the single entrepreneur whose only goal was to maximize profits. The near-autocratic power of the entrepreneur to determine organizational policy is exemplified in Henry Ford's famous dictum that the American people can have any color Ford they want "as long as it's black!" The one actor/one goal model was adapted to the noneconomic sector by replacing the entrepreneur with elected officials in the public sector and community elites in the private sector and by treating administrative organizations as neutral instruments for implementing their policies. This notion was apotheosized in Woodrow Wilson's classic paper on public administration in which he argued that the essence of scientific administration was the strict separation of goal setting (politics) from goal implementation (administration).[4] The early history of nongovernmental social agencies was characterized by the powerful role of business and community elites, acting through agency boards, in establishing policies and procedures to be carried out by paid staff.[5]

As the study of organizations progressed, weaknesses in the one actor/one goal model's assumptions were identified. The first tenet to be challenged was the idea that organizations have only one goal. Studies of business firms showed that the firms were often systems upon which multiple goals were imposed from the outside. The role of the chief executive, moreover, was evolving from the command and control style of the early entrepreneurs to that of "peak coordinator" with responsibility for establishing priorities among competing goals. This change in roles gave rise to a *single actor/multiple goals* model.[6]

Discussions of multiple goals within social service organizations began in earnest in the 1960s with the appearance of a number of studies in which the authors argued that the stated goal of services for clients was only one of several goals.[7] Other, unstated goals included the maintenance and enhancement of the agency; isolation and control of people deemed deviant or disruptive to the social order; defusion of resentment against the established social, economic, and political system; diversion of the dispossessed from taking political action; and provision of career opportunities for the growing number of human service professionals. Recently budget cutbacks in social welfare have meant that for most social agencies the number one goal has become cost reduction, regardless of the implications for program effectiveness.

Following hard on the heels of the idea of multiple organizational goals was the awareness that many organizations no longer conformed to the traditional notion of a hierarchy of control culminating in a powerful apex. As the work of organizations became technologically more sophisticated and the degree of task interdependence intensified, multiple centers of power emerged and the number of people involved in key organizational decisions increased. A *multiple actors/multiple goals* conception of the organization was first discussed in Cyert and March's theory of the business firm as a *coalition* of actors who bargained among themselves to set organizational goals.[8] This theory replaced one authority at the center of power with multiple authorities. Participants previously outside of the decision-making system, "negotiating individually with the peak coordinator for inducements for contributions, now became actors inside of it who bargained to determine outcomes and thereby to establish the organization's goals."[9]

The idea of multiple actors within social service organizations gained currency through studies of discretionary decision making by lower-level staff. In her research on state mental hospitals, Smith identified what she called the "front-line organization."[10] This type of organization deviates from the model of hierarchical control of lower-level employees because the locus of organizational initiative is with front-line units. Each unit's task is performed independently of other units, and direct supervision of unit activities is impractical. These characteristics enable line workers to exercise considerable power over individual clients and allows them to pursue practices different from official organizational policy. Although such arrangements are frequently justified on the grounds that they allow workers to be responsive to the special circumstances and needs of clients, they can also lead to pockets of arbitrary and unchecked power. (The abuses that can arise in a front-line organization were dramatically portrayed by Ken Kesey through the character of Nurse Ratchett in *One Flew over the Cuckoo's Nest*.)

Subsequent studies highlighted the extent to which line workers in a variety of human service organizations exercised an amount of discretion normally reserved to upper-level administrators in other kinds of organizations.[11] The issue of line-worker influence is further complicated by the fact that many of these workers have professional training and feel that they *should* have a lot to say about the content and goals of agency services. One of the hallmarks of a professional is the right to act autonomously, free from supervision except from colleagues, and then only on an advisory-consultative basis. To the extent that human service workers are successful in advancing their claims to professional status within their organizations, they are likely to become part of the organization's ruling coalition.

The last stage in Mintzberg's theory of organizational goal evolution is that of multiple actors with *no* goals.[12] Proponents of a *multiple actors/no goals* conception of organizations tend to come from social science disciplines where, free from the constraints of a managerial perspective, they have developed theories and pursued lines of inquiry independent of their relationship to or impact on management practice. Georgiou, for example, argued that organizations should not be viewed as distinct social units given meaning by their goals "but as arbitrary focuses of interest, marketplaces whose structures and processes are the outcomes of the complex accommodations made by actors exchanging a variety of incentives and pursuing a diversity of goals."[13] A major influence on the development of the idea of goal-less organizations was the work of Cohen and March in their conception of "organized anarchies."[14] Such organizations are characterized by problematic or unclear preferences, unclear technologies, and fluid participation of members in organizational activities. These properties give rise to a "garbage can" model of decision making in which problems, solutions, and participants move from one choice opportunity to another in such a way that

> the nature of the choice, the time it takes, and the problems it solves all depend on a relatively complicated intermeshing of elements. These include the mix of choices available at any one time, the mix of problems that have access to the organization, the mix of solutions looking for problems, and the outside demands on the decision makers.[15]

Proponents of a multiple actors/no goals approach to organizations do not argue that individual members or units do not have goals. Quite the contrary. It is the multiplicity of individual and unit goals that prevents the organization from settling on one overarching purpose to guide the work of the entire system. For a goal to fulfill the requirements for an *organizational* goal, it must refer, in specific and tangible terms, to a future state of affairs that the organization intends to bring about, and it must limit and direct the actions of organizational members so resources are concentrated on attaining the goal. When these conditions are not present, the organization does not have *a* goal, but *various* goals. It is at this point, moreover, that organizations can be profitably thought about in political terms.

The idea of goal-less organizations is particularly alien to social workers. Social work is infused with values — both those imposed by society and those coming out of the profession's philosophical positions. It is this very value ladenness, however, that produces the profusion of purposes characteristic of many social service organizations. All social services involve some conception of social health that social workers seek to help their clients attain. But, as Donnison pointed out, "there is no generally understood state of 'social health' toward which all people strive; our disagreements on this question form the subject matter of politics the world over."[16]

Disagreements over social service goals intensified with the increase in the number of social problems addressed by social welfare programs. The expansion in the scope of welfare activities has been accompanied by increased controversies over their purposes. As the social welfare system began dealing with problems arising from marital relationships, sexual practices, and child rearing, the amount of dissension surrounding these programs grew significantly. This situation is complicated further by the fact that many of today's social problems are solutions to yesterday's problems. The food stamp program contributed to better nutrition, which in turn lowered the age of fecundity and improved the ability to carry the fetus to birth, which in turn led to higher rates of illegitimacy. Deinstitutionalization of the mentally ill was a contributing factor to the rise in the number of homeless people. Social agencies, consequently, have become arenas where competing values and beliefs clash. When there is agreement about goals, it is usually an uneasy one, the result of one group's ability to gain hegemony over others, at least for the time being. Usually, the disagreements are resolved by agreeing to disagree, with different organizational and professional factions independently pursuing their own goals.

THE ASSAULT ON ORGANIZATIONAL RATIONALITY

One outgrowth of the above developments is the appearance of a point of view that treats rationality in organizations as either highly problematic or, in the view of some critics, nonexistent. Astley and Van de Ven posed a series of questions that contemporary organizational theories attempt to answer. Two are particularly relevant to the present discussion:

> Are organizations functionally rational, technically constrained systems, or are they socially constructed, subjectively meaningful embodiments of individual action?...Are organizations neutral technical instruments engineered to achieve a goal, or are they institutionalized manifestations of the vested interests and power structure of the wider society?[17]

The dominant paradigm in organizational theory has been that of instrumental rationality. The requirements for instrumental rationality — whether in individual, organizational, or societal action — are generally agreed to include:

- Specification of values and objectives prior to selecting means for reaching them.
- Identification of all alternative means for attaining the desired ends.
- Identification and evaluation of the consequences of each alternative.
- Selection of the best alternative through means-end analysis that identifies the most efficient means to the desired end.

In the rational model for organizational action, the organization is conceived of as an instrument,

> a rationally conceived means to the realization of expressly announced group goals. Its structures are understood as tools deliberately established for the efficient realization of these group purposes.[18]

Criticisms of the ability of modern organizations to behave rationally come from two intellectual orientations. The first has its bases in political science, political sociology, and public administration, and proceeds from a recognition of the proliferation of organizational goals and actors discussed above. The second comes from a variety of social scientists and philosophers and concerns the capacity of humankind in general for rational thought. Its criticism is of rationality itself — not just organizational rationality.

The first line of criticism stresses the extent to which organizations have become arenas in which competing interests vie for control of organizational resources and processes.[19] Following the multiple goals/multiple actors model, these authors argue that individual organizational members and groups rationally pursue their interests within an organizational context of diffuse authority and multiple centers of power. Rationality, however, cannot be imputed to the actions of the organization as a whole because of the absence of system-wide objectives toward which all factions strive. Nevertheless, coherence in the organization's activities can be brought about by what Lindblom called "epiphenomenal solutions." Competition over goal setting and the diffusion of power "sets in motion a political interaction among individuals and groups in which no person or group analyzes the problem, and arrives at a solution but in which a 'solution' nevertheless emerges from the interaction."[20] Organizational goals are best seen as an amalgam — often with major internal contradictions — of the preferences of the most powerful organizational actors and units, rather than a predetermined, unitary set of objectives.

The second critique of rationality in organizational and other forms of human endeavor comes from a number of authors generally associated with the symbolic interaction school of social psychology. These authors attempt to demonstrate, as Brown suggested, how

> social actors employ rationality retrospectively as a rhetoric to account for actions that, from a rationalistic point of view, were chaotic and stumbling when performed....[R]ationality emerges in interaction, and then is used retrospectively to legitimate what has already taken place or is being enacted.[21]

Organizations, according to Weick, are composed of building blocks made up of interactions between two or more people.[22] Since each person's behavior is contingent upon another's, the interactions are more appropriately termed "double interacts." The meaning of an activity produced through a double interact can only be established after the action has taken place, since its actual meaning is different from the individual intentions of the parties to the interaction. Meaning is constructed intersubjectively, after the action, through the process of "retrospective sense-making." People cannot know the meaning of their actions until after they have performed them; or, in Weick's words, "How can I know what I think until I see what I say?"[23] Thus rationality, "rather than being the guiding rule of organizational life, turns out to be an achievement — a symbolic product that is constructed through actions that in themselves are nonrational."[24]

Unlike the political criticism of organizational rationality, the social psychological critique denies the possibility of rationality at both organizational *and* individual levels. If carried to its logical conclusion, organizational behavior is reduced to an Alice-in-Wonderland creation such as the one envisioned in March's "unconventional soccer game":

> the field for the game is ground; there are several goals scattered haphazardly around the circular field; people can enter and leave the game whenever they want to; they can throw balls in whenever they want; they can say "that's my goal" whenever they want to, as many times as they want to, and for as many goals as they want to; the entire game takes place on a sloped field; and the game is played as if it makes sense.[25]

Of the two critiques of organizational rationality, the social psychological critique seems less pertinent to public sector organizations and to those private sector organizations like social agencies which are creatures of public policy. The reduction of reality to what two people can retrospectively agree has happened trivializes organizational purposes.[26] It fails to take into account the fact that public organizations are created to fulfill public purposes, to pursue the interests of the society as a whole, and are constrained to do so. These purposes, moreover, are determined — albeit quite broadly — by bodies external to the organization, bodies which also possess oversight power.

The political critique, on the other hand, explicitly deals with the issue of public purpose. Public organizations are viewed as rife with *disagreements* over purpose. The political critique maintains, therefore, that one of the basic concepts that should underlie public organizations is the need to structure them to "enable faction to counteract faction by providing political representation to a comprehensive variety of the organized political, economic, and social interests that are found in the society at large."[27] It is this perspective, moreover, which informs the present approach to organizational politics.

WHY POLITICS IS A DIRTY WORD

Any discussion of politics immediately runs up against the aversion that most Americans have toward things political. Politicians are seen as avaricious wolves wrapped in the sheep's clothing of public interest rhetoric. They are self-serving, power-hungry predators with loose morals (for those willing to concede that they have morals at all). Aphorisms like "no one's life, liberty, or property are safe while the legislature is in session" aptly characterize popular sentiments about politics and politicians. To refer to an action as political is to impute to it the basest of motives and consequences.

In fact, many politicians are venal, self-aggrandizing, and unscrupulous. But so are many investment bankers, orthodontists, lawyers, marital counselors, automobile mechanics, university deans, and evangelists. If anything, the incidence of wrongdoing among public officials is probably exaggerated compared to that among people in other walks of life. In the United States every public official "lives in the shadow of the courthouse" and under the watchful eyes of a vigorous and free press.[28] The likelihood of wrongdoings being uncovered and punished is much greater for those in public life than for others. The source of the opprobrium that is reserved for public officials lies in factors other than the extent to which their behaviors — real or imagined — conform to general stereotypes.

One reason for the popular antipathy toward politics has to do with the nature of political work itself. Politics, as noted earlier, is concerned with the allocation of values. It is one of two societal institutions for allocating the things that people want, the other being the economic marketplace. Politics, at the institutional level, is synonymous with government and public affairs. But this is not the politics that most people feel so negatively about; those feelings are reserved for individuals formally designated as politicians, namely, elected legislators and executives. While politicians play a key role in the conduct of government and public affairs, they are not the only people involved. Insight into negative attitudes toward politics and politicians can be gained from contrasting politicians and the work they do with other key actors and functions in the public arena.

Price suggested that the conduct of public affairs can be thought about in terms of scientific, professional, administrative, and political functions that can be located along a spectrum that has *truth* at one end and *power* at the other.[29] Pure science is concerned with knowledge and truth, and pure politics with power and action. The professions — particularly those whose knowledge is derived from the physical and biochemical sciences — are closer to the truth end of the spectrum, whereas administration is closer to the power end.

These different purposes shape the occupational cultures which characterize each area. The defining feature of basic science is the relentless search for truth, irrespective of practical applications or consequences. It is, as the physicist Percy Bridgman remarked, "nothing more than doing one's damnedest with one's mind, no holds barred." While the professions are closely tied to science, they differ in one major respect: they pursue a social purpose. Basic science, Price argued, "has become steadily more powerful as it freed itself from the constraints of values and purposes."[30] Although the professions are organized around bodies of knowledge derived from science, they use that knowledge in the service of their clients. It is knowledge for a socially useful purpose, in contrast to knowledge for knowledge's sake, that distinguishes the professional from the scientist.

The administrator, in this sense, is not a professional. Administrators, like professionals, aspire to the highest levels of competence in the performance of their duties and seek the best available knowledge for attaining their goals. But the purposes of administrative work are determined not by mandates from the general society but directives from immediate superiors — be they political or business executives — to whom administrators are accountable. Their knowledge is knowledge in the service of power.

Which brings us to the politician. The ultimate basis of political work is power. In a democratic society, power is transferred from the sovereign people to the institutions of government. This power is then exercised over those very people by the politicians who accede to public offices through elections and appointments. Elections are used as a way of deciding — rather than scientific analysis or administrative rules — because politics is the preferred method for making decisions in areas dominated by values rather than facts, by beliefs rather than knowledge. Politicians must act on the basis of what they *believe* to be true since they are required to act when knowledge is either absent or contested. Politicians, whether in legislative or executive chambers, corporate boardrooms, or social agencies,

> make their most important decisions on the basis of value judgments or hunch or compromise or power interests....[T]heir business is to deal with problems in which either the inadequacy of scientific and professional data, or the conflict of expert opinion, makes it necessary or possible to come to decisions that are based on judgment and must be sustained by persuasion or authority.[31]

What makes politics a dirty word is its intimate connection with power. Western societies consider science and the technologies derived from it as the ultimate source of truth. Science, moreover, is not only a method for investigating phenomena, be they physical, chemical, social, or psychic. It is the *defining* mode of thinking for modern times. Not only is science a part of modern consciousness and ideation, it shapes the very nature of that consciousness. Decisions made on other than scientific grounds are seen as less than good, somehow or another defective, and, at best, a temporary accommodation until science comes up with the *correct* answer. Correct answers are based on objective and universally verifiable facts that are subjected to calculations derived from scientific formulas. The fact that many decisions are made on the basis of power is seen as a throwback to the Stone Age, an unfortunate regression to brute force rather than logic and facts. Because positive science is seen as the only acceptable grounds for acting, Westerners tend to legitimize their activities by accounting for them in scientific terms or, as is more often the case, in scientific metaphors and imagery. Thus, power and the political processes based on it became the dirty little secret of modern times.

Negative attitudes toward power and political processes in the general life of society, where there are elaborate constitutional bases for their legitimacy and legal safeguards to limit their abuse, are magnified tenfold when these concepts are applied to organizational behavior. The modern organization is seen as the quintessence of rationality, as a "giant computer, with its input and output, its feedback loops, and its programs."[32] Administrators — the servomechanism that guides the organization/computer — are expected to function in a dispassionate, technically proficient, and politically and ideologically neutral fashion. They are, in Weber's famous epithet, *sine ira et studio*, without hatred or passion.[33]

These vastly different social evaluations of scientific and political work mean that administrators often engage in a kind of schizophrenic dialogue in order to justify their actions to the different publics to which they are accountable. Administrators have always had to make political, i.e., power-based, decisions. The need for administrators to act politically is more pressing now than ever before. While organizational life is increasingly political, administrators — whether in business, government, education, health, or social services — are a growing occupational group with the same aspirations to public esteem, status, and material rewards as any other occupation. To justify their claims to professional status, administrators must maintain a public image of the disinterested technician whose decisions, based on rational analysis and calculation, are the best ones for advancing the interests of the organization as a whole. No administrator regards himself or herself as a politician, Burns argued, or as acting politically, except on occasions when

> he is led into accounts of successful intrigue and maneuvering, when he bolsters his self-esteem and reputation by projecting the whole affair into the safe social context of a game or a joke....It is backstage, so to speak, that the imputations of empire-building, caucus log-rolling, squaring, and obstructionism occur.[34]

Students of organizational politics are in somewhat the same position as psychoanalysts who contend that their patients' stated reasons for their actions are not the real ones. Consciously and unconsciously, patients sanitize their motivations to make them conform to socially acceptable or desirable norms for action. Similarly, administrators want to present themselves in the most desirable light — that of the scientific manager carrying out the policies of duly constituted superiors. If carried to an extreme, this kind of analysis — both in psychiatry and organizational behavior — leads to an inverted solipsism in which reality becomes not what the actor in the situation says it is, but what the analyst says it is. There is no easy safeguard against this kind of excess. As with any theory, a political approach to organizations must be held to high standards of logic and empirical demonstration. Ultimately, of course, it is the reader's own healthy skepticism and demand for cogent reasoning and persuasive evidence that is the best defense against sophistic or self-serving arguments.

ELEMENTS OF A POLITICAL FRAMEWORK

Organizations can be seen from a number of vantage points. Many organizations are, in fact, rational instruments capable of high levels of efficiency and precision. Other organizations seem more like friendship groups or extended families where what occurs among employees is more important than anything that is produced. There are also organizations whose operations are so confused, disjointed, and chaotic that, compared to them, March's soccer game is a paragon of rationality. Finally, there are organizations in which politics are so rampant that they look and act like neighborhood ward associations.

Not only do organizations differ among themselves, but a single organization — seen at different points in time, from different vantage points, or in different arenas — can be all these things. Each perspective provides a frame for examining one or another of the elements that make modern organizations complex. The remainder of this book will concentrate on one perspective, the political, because of the insights it offers into how social agencies operate and how those operations might be improved. Concentrating on one topic, however, is like looking through a microscope; you see the object better by both enlarging it *and* by excluding everything else from view. You see more of one thing by seeing less, or nothing, of everything else. This perspective becomes dangerous if you forget that you're looking through a microscope and start to think that what you see is all there is to see. "When all you have is a hammer," the saying goes, "everything looks like a nail." Suffice it to say that although the present discussion stresses political processes within social agencies and will try to make a convincing case for their importance, these processes are not the only ones.

Politics is concerned with deciding about the distribution of scarce resources. A political perspective on organizational functioning can be defined as one in which political processes replace scientific, technical, professional, or interpersonal ones in organizational decision making. The political framework concentrates on five organizational features: scarce resources, conflicting goals, uncertain technologies, multiple centers of power, and irreverent attitudes toward authority.

Scarce Resources

A resource is anything an organization needs to accomplish its work. Resources are scarce, obviously, when there's not enough of them to go around. What is not so obvious, however, is what is meant by enough. An important insight into modern life was Durkheim's concept of anomie, or normlessness.[35] People left to their own devices, Durkheim argued, tend to have unlimited aspirations. This statement can be roughly taken to mean that the more you get, the more you want. Limits on human aspirations and wants, therefore, must come from external regulatory forces, be they social norms, religious proscriptions, or budgetary constraints.

Applied to organizational behavior, the concept of anomie suggests that organizational subunits can never have enough resources. Moreover, this human proclivity for wanting more is exacerbated in organizations like government and social agencies that pursue goals that are difficult to identify and measure. Lacking clear measures of their effectiveness, these organizations — and the people who evaluate and fund them — seek other, surrogate indicators of how well they're performing. One frequently used measure is whether the organization grows in size and increases the scope of its operations. Increased budgets, staff, and number of items on the organization's agenda become measures of organizational effectiveness. Consequently, limits to the amount of resources a member or unit can realistically claim must be set by external forces. A key management function is setting limits and deciding among competing claims on resources. What becomes critical, however, is the extent to which the limits set are perceived by organizational members as *legitimate*, that is, based on generally agreed upon shortages in the organization's total resource pool, or as *illegitimate*, shortages that are (or appear to be) contrived or in some way doctored in order to skew allocations from one unit to another.

Disagreements about the amount of resources available to societies as a whole and the legitimacy of government leaders' protestations of lack of money for specific programs fuel the flames of partisan politics the world over. How can a country like the United States, critics ask, with a one trillion dollar budget, be unable to afford more and better prenatal care, public education, housing, and the like? How can a country, the response goes, that plays a crucial role in maintaining the balance of power in a nuclear world spend less than it does on military preparedness? The fervor with which critics attack the status quo is directly related to the legitimacy that they accord to official pronouncements of how much money is available for what purposes.

A similar process occurs on a reduced scale within organizations. The issue is not whether resources are scarce or not — all organizations, like all societies, exist within a context of scarce resources — but how that scarcity is perceived by organizational members. If scarcities are viewed as illegitimately contrived, the organization becomes the scene of partisan battles. Resource scarcities will be seen as legitimate and accepted as limits to claims made by different units if the overall allocation of resources is seen as logically connected to the organization's goal structure. The nature of those goals and the degree to which they are accepted by organizational members, therefore, assume an important role.

Conflicting Goals

All organizations have the potential for goal conflicts because all organizations have multiple goals. Once the assumption of a simple, unitary goal structure was challenged, organizational analysts began to identify a number of goals that all organizations must pursue. Every organization, Perrow suggested, must

> (1) secure inputs in the form of capital sufficient to establish itself, operate, and expand as the need arises; (2) secure acceptance in the form of basic legitimization of activity; (3) marshall the necessary skills; and (4) coordinate the activities of its members, and the relations of the organization with other organizations and with clients or consumers.[36]

Since an organization's division of labor is structured around these tasks, different units generally will have only one of these tasks as their goal. Each unit, moreover, will strive to achieve its goal as efficiently and effectively as possible, with little regard to the activities of other units. If left to their own devices, units would very quickly conflict with each other.

Furthermore, if one of these tasks assumes central importance to organizational leaders (budget cuts, for example, put the task of securing new financial resources in the limelight), the unit charged with its accomplishment is in a position to sway, if not dominate, overall organizational policy. In such a situation, the more powerful unit will seek the highest organizational priorities for its goals and tasks. If the unit has enough power to dominate the others, its goals become *the* goals of the organization. The changing role of physicians in hospitals illustrates this point. Once very powerful in organizations in which they were not even employees, physicians are now finding that their influence is waning, while the role of administrators and corporate executives is rising. This change has been a response to the enormous rise in the cost of medical care and to the implementation of new corporate-based medical insurance arrangements. As a consequence, many hospital goals now reflect administrative and fiscal concerns at the expense of purely medical interests.

In addition to disputes between people doing different tasks, goal conflicts are generated by disagreements over the nature of the tasks themselves. People in the same unit will often disagree over the nature of the problem to be solved, the best ways of going about it, or both. Another source of goal conflict is the differences between individual and organizational goals. Individuals participate in organizations for a number of reasons (desire for status, income, socializing) which have to be reconciled with the organization's goal of producing a product or service.

What is important about goal conflicts to the political analyst is not their existence, since they are endemic to organizational life, but whether they are managed by rational or political strategies. Rational approaches to competing goals include ranking them in terms of their priorities (administrative triage) or sequencing them within a time frame (the front burner/back burner model). Both approaches, however, beg the question as far as conflict goes. If organizational members can agree on either a rank ordering or a sequence for addressing competing goals, the level of disagreement cannot be severe enough to be defined as goal conflict. Rather, it is a matter of disagreements over logistics and timing rather than substantive differences.

Political approaches, on the other hand, are invoked when the differences among individuals and units are so deeply and strongly held as to be irreconcilable. When rational calculations are no longer possible, goal priorities tend to be established on the basis of individual or unit strength. What is important is a unit's capacity to acquire sufficient power by demonstrating that its work and the goals it seeks to accomplish are central and critical to the organization's overall purpose.

Uncertain Technologies

Goals represent the ends of organizational action, and technologies are the means for accomplishing those ends. The nature of an organization's technologies is an extremely important factor that shapes its structures and processes. For something to be worthy of the name "technology," however, it has to meet certain criteria, foremost of which is the likelihood that it will produce the intended results. Technologies are more or less certain methods for solving problems. Problem-solving methods can be divided into heuristics and algorithms, depending upon their degree of certainty. A heuristic is an approach to a problem which *suggests* a solution but does not guarantee it. Thinking by analogy, for example, is a typical heuristic. A student beginning graduate school, for instance, might prepare for it by extrapolating from his or her undergraduate experience and assume that the new program will be like the old one. As with any analogy, this one will be helpful up to a point. The student will have to get the money for tuition, find a place to live, register for courses, and buy books. However, the analogy will eventually break down as new and unexpected elements in graduate school are encountered for which the student's undergraduate experience offered little or no preparation. An algorithm, on the other hand, is an approach to problem solving that *invariably* leads to the ends sought. For example, whenever and wherever two parts of hydrogen are combined with one part of oxygen, the outcome will be water, represented by the familiar algorithm H_2O.

High technology can be taken to mean technologies that have a high likelihood of producing their intended results. These technologies usually are based on algorithms derived from the physical and biochemical sciences. Technologies based on heuristics, on the other hand, are less likely to accomplish their purposes. These technologies — for example, how to select the most appropriate foster family for an emotionally disturbed child — suggest ways for proceeding but cannot guarantee a correct solution. Organizational technologies are uncertain when they are more heuristic than algorithmic, more art than science.

Organizations with underdeveloped, uncertain technologies must develop mechanisms for deciding which of several possible techniques for performing a particular task is the best. This problem is not likely to come up in situations where the technology is well developed because in those instances the technology speaks for itself. In high technology fields the proven effectiveness of a particular method (for example, the use of silicon rather than copper for microcomputer chips) does away with the need for discussion. Everyone agrees that a particular way is the best way to do something because it has been shown to most people's satisfaction to be the best way. In low technology fields, however, there is generally little or no agreement about the best way for doing something, and mechanisms must be found for settling the disputes that invariably arise.

Thompson and Tuden suggested that organizations with uncertain technologies must rely on *judgment* as a decision-making strategy. The quality of judgments would be improved when members operated according to rules which:

> (1) require fidelity to the group's preference hierarchy, (2) require all members to participate in each decision, (3) route pertinent information about causation to each member, (4) give each member equal influence over the final choice, and (5) designate as ultimate choice that alternative favored by the largest group of judges — the majority.[37]

Thompson and Tuden referred to this structure as a "collegium" because of the emphasis on equality of status for all members. But the term also describes a "legislative" organization that operates under a one person/one vote rule. The chief features of this approach to decision making are broad dissemination of information, efforts to convince others through discussion and debate, and putting the question to a vote. In short, the decision about which of several alternative means is the best one for accomplishing an organizational goal when the outcomes of all the proposed means are uncertain should be made through a political process.

Multiple Power Centers

When people think about organizations, the image that often comes to mind is a pyramid. In fact, one German corporation had its central office building constructed so each higher story had less floor space than the one below, until you got to the top floor, which consisted of only one office — Herr Direktor's. The pyramid graphically illustrates a central tenet of Weber's theory of bureaucracy — the hierarchical subordination of offices, with each office under the control of a higher one, culminating in an all-powerful chief executive at the apex. Although this description accurately portrays nineteenth-century economic organizations, the introduction of complex industrial and administrative processes in this century, accompanied by the growth of unionization and changing notions about the nature of authority and superordinate-subordinate relations, has done much to alter this picture. Unlike the factories and businesses of the last century whose owners possessed autocratic power to do as they pleased, modern organizations are likely to disburse power among departments and levels rather than concentrate power in a few people at the top.

Most discussions of organizational power begin with the distinction between *power* and *authority*. Power, Hall suggested, involves force or coercion, whereas authority is a form of power that does not imply force.

> Rather, it involves a "suspension of judgment" on the part of its recipients. Directives or orders are followed because it is believed that they ought to be followed. Compliance is voluntary. This requires a common value system among organizational members....[38]

Authority is based in shared values; the basis of power is the control of resources. Power emerges when one person controls resources that another wants, cannot get elsewhere, and cannot do without.[39] The latter individual is likely to comply with the former's wishes in exchange for those resources. The more important the resource is for one's work and the more difficult the resource is to attain, the greater will be the power of the person who controls the resource over the person who is dependent upon it.

Power also can be acquired, Astley and Sachdeva pointed out, when one is central to an organization's work flow. "To the extent that actors are located at tightly coupled interconnected nodes in the network, they gain power because their immersion in multiple interdependencies makes them functionally indispensable."[40] The technological advances of the past century have made the work of all organizations much more complicated than ever before. As work increases in complexity, the likelihood that any one manager will be able to control all aspects of a work process decreases. Accordingly, the power of individual workers — regardless of their hierarchical rank — increases with their ability to control something that, even though intrinsically minor (the ability to repair a piece of machinery used in production), is essential because of its location in the flow of work.[41] It's the modern day equivalent of "for want of a nail, the battle was lost."

When power is disbursed, the problem of compliance becomes critical. Managers in systems in which power is concentrated in one or a few locations can go about their business in a more rational and purposeful manner than those in systems with multiple centers of power. When power is concentrated, organizational leaders gain subordinates' compliance through their control of important resources like salaries, promotions, and perquisites. When power is dispersed, individuals or units that are low in the official hierarchy can influence organizational decisions by their threat to withhold critical skills, information, or other needed resources. Moreover, the method of compliance shifts from the asymmetrical relationship between a superior and a subordinate to the more balanced relationship between peers. In these kinds of relationships, one does not seek compliance but *agreement*. Obtaining agreement requires skills in the political processes of negotiation and bargaining.

Changing Attitudes toward Authority

Authority is *legitimized* power. Authority relationships are similar to power relationships in form (asymmetrical) and outcome (one person does what another person wants him or her to do). They differ, however, in one important way: the parties to an authority relationship accept that those giving orders *should* be doing so because of their unique qualities. In his original formulation of the concept, Weber presented three bases for legitimate authority: *rational-legal, charismatic,* and *traditional.*[42]

Rational-legal authority is one of the elements that distinguishes modern bureaucratic organizations from older associational forms such as tribes, clans, or guilds. It is based on the belief that people occupying supervisory and executive positions have a *right* to those positions because of superior knowledge and skills. In its ideal form, legal authority can be verified empirically by having candidates for bureaucratic office demonstrate their superior abilities through examinations. Charismatic authority, by contrast, is based on extraordinary personal characteristics that power holders have or are assumed to have by their followers. These qualities — for example, physical courage, unusual stamina and endurance, extraordinary devotion to a cause — may have no direct bearing on an organization's work. They create, however, a halo effect through which people attribute a variety of other talents to their possessors. Finally, traditional authority is based on a belief in the rightness of the established order. If someone is able to last over long periods of time — to stay the course — it is assumed that he or she must be doing something right.

Traditional authority has never been a strong feature of American life because of our cultural emphases on innovation, progress, and newness. While this attitude may be changing with the "graying" of America, veneration of traditional ways of doing things will probably never be a major feature of our society. Charismatic leaders have always been a part of American life, but they have not been able to acquire the extraordinary and widespread influence of the kind possessed by, for example, Mahatma Ghandi, Charles DeGaulle, or Fidel Castro. Bass suggested that charismatic organizational leaders need subordinates with highly dependent personalities. By contrast, "subordinates who pride themselves on their own rationality, skepticism, independence, and concern for rules of law and precedent are less likely to be influenced by a charismatic leader or the leader who tries to use emotional inspiration."[43] Support for this argument is found in the difficulties that American firms have had in introducing Japanese management techniques that rely heavily on traditional and charismatic authority to inspire worker effort. Receptivity to traditional and charismatic authority is deeply rooted in Japanese culture. Research indicates that American workers resist this management approach, in large part because of our culture's stress on individualism and personal freedom.[44]

But it is changes in attitudes toward rational or, more generally, bureaucratic authority that are central to the present discussion. Rational authority operates when employees comply with directives because they believe that the person issuing them is qualified to do so. There are indications that employees' willingness to recognize and accept rational authority is declining. Business executives complain of "the decline of the work ethic" and an "undisciplined labor force."[45] While middle- and upper-level managers continue to report high levels of job satisfaction, clerical and hourly workers increasingly express dissatisfaction, particularly with regard to unmet needs for equity, achievement, recognition, and job challenge.[46]

Shifting attitudes toward authority among public employees are indicated by the growth in "whistle-blowing." Employees are more willing than ever to disclose fraud, waste, abuses of power, and unethical behavior on the part of their superiors and others in high office. This willingness has been attributed to an erosion of faith in institutions that weakens unquestioning loyalty to them.[47] Another factor that promotes a contentious relationship between superiors and subordinates is the growth in the amount of information to which the average employee has access. Freedom of information and sunshine laws, quality circles and other participative management techniques, investigative journalism, and the growth of the electronic news media are among the factors producing a more informed citizenry and work force. As employees' knowledge of the inner workings of organizations increases, so does their skepticism about the official (that is, rational) reasons that organizational leaders give for their actions.

This last point is particularly relevant to a political perspective on organizational behavior. To think about organizations in political terms, one must have a certain irreverence toward established authority. One must be willing to entertain the notion that organizational structures, processes, rules, and regulations might be there because they promote certain interests, not because they reflect revealed scientific truth about the way things have to be. To see the image of an organization as "a thing made, as a symbolic artifact rather than as the fact is to reject it as a literal description of how the organization 'really is,' and to unmask it as a legitimating ideology."[48]

THE POLITICIZED ORGANIZATION

With the foregoing discussion as a framework, we can picture what the pure politicized organization might look like. Like all organizations, our hypothetical organization — we'll call it the Boss Tweed Memorial Service Center or, as it's known to employees and clients, Tweed Hall — operates in an environment of scarcity. There's never enough money, time, people, or facilities to do all the things that should be done. Unlike in some other organizations, however, the lack of resources is not gracefully accepted by organizational members as a fact of life, but is viewed with suspicion as an underhanded maneuver on the part of "them" (usually upper administration, but also people in other departments) to prevent "us" (the good guys) from getting all that "we" need and deserve.

As a multi-service center, Tweed Hall pursues a number of goals, each tied to the work of different departments (family counseling, support services for the elderly, case-finding and outreach to the homeless). The feeling of "us" and "them" is exacerbated by the fact that the agency administrators have never been able to come up with a ranking or priority ordering of the agency's goals that is acceptable to most members. As a result, there is a constant jockeying for influence among workers, department heads, and administrators as they try to promote their interests and goals ahead of others. This situation is further aggravated by the fact that while well over half of the service staff have professional training, there is tremendous disagreement among them as to the best way to pursue their particular goals. In addition to competition among the three departments, there are disagreements between workers with a behavioral orientation and the ego psychologists, both of whom are allied against the outreach workers who use community organization methods. The executive director has an MBA, and her response to staff squabbling is "a plague on both your houses." Her highest priority is to install a computer-based management information system that will automatically produce financial reports for the State Department of Social Services, which provides, through grants and purchase of service contracts, 54 percent of the operating budget.

Although the organizational chart resembles the Table of Organization and Equipment of a Tactical Bomber Wing of the United States Air Force, with clear lines of authority running from the executive director to department heads, to unit supervisors, and finally to line workers, most people in the organization have never seen it, let alone follow it. Most employees describe the agency as "balkanized," with power dispersed among department heads and, within departments, among unit supervisors. The executive director is one among equals rather than a commanding officer. Finally, all this takes place within a climate that is known in the agency as the "I'm from Missouri" attitude. The claims of upper-level administrators, supervisors, and senior service workers to special knowledge or skills that warrant the automatic compliance of their subordinates are generally met with a feisty "show me" response. At Tweed Hall, people don't obey; they agree. Moreover, if you can't get them to agree, they are likely to go their own way.

Of course this is a caricature. But as with any caricature, the elements that make it up are merely *exaggerations* of what actually exists. Many organizations, and most social agencies, have some, if not all, of the features of Tweed Hall. The factors that operate to politicize the internal operations of social agencies are the topic of the next chapter.

NOTES

1. Max Weber, *The Theory of Social and Economic Organization*, trans. A. M. Henderson and T. Parsons (New York: The Free Press, 1964).
2. Sherman Krupp, *Pattern in Organizational Analysis: A Critical Analysis* (New York: Holt, Rinehart and Winston, 1961).
3. Henry Mintzberg, *Power in and around Organizations* (Englewood Cliffs, N.J.: Prentice Hall, 1983), pp. 8–9.
4. Woodrow Wilson, "The Study of Administration," *Political Science Quarterly*, 2 (June 1887), 197–222.
5. Marvin E. Gettleman, "Charity and Social Classes in the United States: 1874–1900," *American Journal of Economics and Sociology*, 22 (April, July 1963), 313–29, 417–26.
6. Mintzberg, *Power in and around Organizations*, pp. 12–13.
7. Martin Rein, "The Social Service Crisis: The Dilemma — Success for the Agency or Service to the Needy?" *Trans-action*, 1 (May 1964), 3–8; Richard A. Cloward and Frances Fox Piven, "The Professional Bureaucracies: Benefit Systems as Influence Systems," in *Readings in Community Organization Practice*, ed. Ralph M. Kramer and Harry Specht (Englewood Cliffs, N.J.: Prentice Hall, 1969), pp. 359–72; Charles Perrow, "Demystifying Organizations," in *The Management of Human Services*, ed. Rosemary C. Sarri and Yeheskel Hasenfeld (New York: Columbia University Press, 1978), pp. 105–20.
8. Richard M. Cyert and James G. March, *The Behavioral Theory of the Firm* (Englewood Cliffs, N.J.: Prentice Hall, 1963).
9. Mintzberg, *Power in and around Organizations*, p. 16.
10. Dorothy E. Smith, "Front-Line Organization of the State Mental Hospital," *Administrative Science Quarterly*, 10 (1965), 381–99.
11. Joel F. Handler, *The Coercive Social Worker* (Chicago: Markham–Rand McNally College Publishing, 1973); Burton Gummer, "On Helping and Helplessness: The Structure of Discretion in the American Welfare System," *Social Service Review*, 53, no. 2 (June 1979), 214–28; Michael Lipsky, *Street-Level Bureaucracy: Dilemmas of the Individual in Public Services* (New York: Russell Sage Foundation, 1980).
12. Mintzberg, *Power in and around Organizations*, pp. 18–19.
13. Petro Georgiou, "The Goal Paradigm and Notes toward a Counter Paradigm," *Administrative Science Quarterly*, 18, no. 3 (September 1973), 291–310.
14. Michael D. Cohen and James G. March, *Leadership and Ambiguity*, 2nd ed. (Boston: Harvard Business School Press, 1986).
15. Ibid., p. 86.
16. David D. Donnison, "Observations on University Training for Social Workers in Great Britain and North America," *Social Service Review*, 29, no. 4 (December 1955), 341–50.

17. W. Graham Astley and Andrew H. Van de Ven, "Current Perspectives and Debates in Organization Theory," *Administrative Science Quarterly*, 28, no. 2 (June 1983), 245–73.

18. Alvin W. Gouldner, "Organizational Analysis," in *Sociology Today*, ed. Robert K. Merton, Leonard Bloom, and Leonard S. Cottrell (New York: Basic Books, 1959), p. 404.

19. Tom Burns, "Micro-Politics: Mechanisms of Institutional Change," *Administration Science Quarterly*, 6, no. 3 (September 1961), 257–81; Jeffrey Pfeffer, "The Micropolitics of Organizations," in *Environments and Organizations*, ed. Marshall W. Meyers (San Francisco: Jossey-Bass, 1978), pp. 29–50; Douglas Yates, Jr., *The Politics of Management: Exploring the Inner Workings of Public and Private Organizations* (San Francisco: Jossey-Bass, 1985).

20. Charles E. Lindblom, "The Sociology of Planning: Thought and Social Interaction," in *Economic Planning, East and West*, ed. Morris Bornstein (Cambridge, Mass.: Bollinger, 1975), p. 33.

21. Richard Harvey Brown, "Bureaucracy as Praxis: Toward a Political Phenomenology of Formal Organizations," *Administrative Science Quarterly*, 23, no. 3 (September 1978), 369.

22. Karl E. Weick, *The Social Psychology of Organizing*, 2nd ed. (Reading, Mass.: Addison-Wesley, 1979).

23. Ibid., p. 5.

24. Brown, "Bureaucracy as Praxis," 370.

25. Quoted in Karl E. Weick, "Educational Organizations as Loosely Coupled Systems," *Administrative Science Quarterly*, 21, no. 1 (March 1976), p. 1.

26. Larry M. Lane, "Karl Weick's Organizing: The Problem of Purpose and the Search for Excellence," *Administration & Society*, 18, no. 1 (May 1986), 111–35.

27. David H. Rosenbloom, "Public Administrative Theory and the Separation of Powers," *Public Administration Review*, 43, no. 3 (May-June 1983), 219

28. York Wilbern, "Types and Levels of Public Morality," *Public Administration Review*, 44, no. 2 (March-April 1984), 103.

29. Don K. Price, *The Scientific Estate* (Cambridge, Mass · The Belknap Press of Harvard University Press, 1965).

30. Ibid., p. 19.

31. Ibid., p. 134.

32. Brown, "Bureaucracy as Praxis," 375.

33. Weber, *The Theory of Social and Economic Organization*, p. 340.

34. Burns, "Micro-Politics," 259–60.

35. Emile Durkheim, *Suicide: A Study in Sociology*, trans. John A. Spaulding and George Simpson, ed. George Simpson (New York: The Free Press, 1966), pp. 246–54.

36. Charles Perrow, "The Analysis of Goals in Complex Organizations," *American Sociological Review*, 26, no. 6 (December 1961), 856.

37. James D. Thompson and Arthur Tuden, "Strategies, Structures, and Processes of Organizational Decision," in *Comparative Studies in Administration*, ed. James D. Thompson et al. (Pittsburgh: University of Pittsburgh Press, 1959), pp. 199–200.

38. Richard H. Hall, *Organizations: Structure and Process*, 3rd ed. (Englewood Cliffs, N.J.: Prentice Hall, 1982), p. 133.

39. Richard M. Emerson, "Power-Dependence Relations," *American Sociological Review*, 27, no. 1 (February 1962), 31–40.

40. W. Graham Astley and Paramjit S. Sachdeva, "Structural Sources of Interorganizational Power: A Theoretical Synthesis," *Academy of Management Review*, 9, no. 1 (January 1984), 107.

41. Michael Crozier, *The Bureaucratic Phenomenon* (Chicago: University of Chicago Press, 1964); Daniel J. Brass, "Being in the Right Place: A Structural Analysis of

Individual Influence in an Organization," *Administrative Science Quarterly*, 29, no. 4 (December 1984), 518–39.

42. Weber, *The Theory of Social and Economic Organization*.
43. Bernard M. Bass, "Leadership: Good, Better, Best," *Organizational Dynamics*, 13, no. 3 (Winter 1985), 39.
44. James R. Lincoln, Mitsuyo Hamada, and Jon Olson, "Cultural Orientations and Individual Reactions to Organizations: A Study of Employees of Japanese-Owned Firms," *Administrative Science Quarterly*, 26, no. 1 (March 1981), 93–115.
45. Howard R. Smith, "Who's in Control Here?" *Management Review*, 69, no. 2 (February 1980), 43–49.
46. M. R. Cooper et al., "Changing Employee Values: Deepening Discontent?" *Harvard Business Review*, 57, no. 1 (January-February 1979), 117–25.
47. James S. Bowman, "Whistle Blowing: Literature and Resource Materials," *Public Administration Review*, 43, no. 3 (May-June 1983), 271–76; Terrence R. Mitchell and William G. Scott, "Leadership Failures, the Distrusting Public, and Prospects of the Administrative State," *Public Administration Review*, 47, no. 6 (November-December 1987), 445–52.
48. Brown, "Bureaucracy as Praxis," 375.

3

The Social Service Organization as a Political Arena

The past quarter century has been a particularly significant period in the history of American social welfare. Whereas the 1930s witnessed the birth of the modern welfare state, the 1960s and 1970s were certainly the growing years. In 1950 public expenditures for all social welfare programs (income maintenance, welfare and other services, education, and health) amounted to $23.4 billion. By 1980 this figure had risen twenty-fold to $492.2 billion, or 18.7 percent of the GNP.[1] Moreover, nearly two-thirds of this amount ($314 billion) were spent on social programs alone. Since 1980 there have been aggressive efforts to reduce social welfare expenditures. These efforts have succeeded mainly in slowing the rate of growth, although some smaller programs have been eliminated. Reductions in spending have not been across the board; programs with strong political constituencies (Medicaid, food stamps, Social Security) have fared better than others.

Although the federal government played a leading role in the creation and initial growth of the welfare state, the current context is one of declining federal influence and the growing importance of the states. The policy known as the New Federalism introduced during the first Nixon administration has been followed, more or less closely, by subsequent administrations. Through revenue sharing and decentralized program administration, the policy has "consciously set out to force political decisions and the struggles that accompany them down to the state and local level."[2] The federal role was greatest during the period when social spending seemed on a permanent upward curve. The declining rate of growth for social spending in the 1980s, however, accompanied by increasing demands for services, prompted one state official to refer to the transfer of fiscal and administrative control to the states as "an idea whose time has passed." A major consequence of the New Federalism, Schramm suggested, is the privatization of conflicts over which goals, interests, and groups social programs should serve.

> In a time of increasing scarcity of public resources for social services, the privatization of conflict produced by social services block grants is enhancing the ability of established local interests to prod state elected officials to protect the status quo in social service provision.[3]

Not only have the size and administration of the welfare system changed, so has its character. The American welfare system came into operation only after people had exhausted other possibilities. The American system — unlike its European counterparts — historically has been for the very poor only. Starting with the Social Security Amendments of 1967, however, a series of policy changes uncoupled a number of social services from economic dependency, making them available to the general population. As the clientele has changed, so have the problems. Increasingly, social services are directed toward quality of life issues — problems that arise when the struggle for food, clothing, and shelter has abated and people address the subtler forms of personal and familial discontent.

The past two decades have also been a time of change for the social work profession, the largest occupational group within the welfare system. Primary among these changes has been the continuing professionalization of social work and a resulting shift in where social workers prefer to work. Since the mid-1960s, there has been a significant migration of professional social workers from public welfare (with the exception of child welfare services) to mental health (particularly community mental health) and private practice. Paradoxically, social workers are leaving public social services at a time when the demand for qualified administrators is increasing. Social workers who have remained in these systems are a minority — some would say an oppressed minority — and those seeking to enter them for the first time have to compete with professionals from other fields, notably public and business administration.

The foregoing developments are major contributors to the politicization of social agencies, both in their internal operations and their external relationships. The purpose of this chapter is to show how these developments have transformed many social agencies into political arenas. The discussion will show how the elements of the political framework presented in the previous chapter — scarce resources, conflicting goals, uncertain technologies, diffuse power, and resistance to bureaucratic authority — operate within social service organizations.

TIGHT MONEY

Money is tight when there's not enough of it. But people can be tight *with* money, regardless of how much is available, when they choose to ration and control its flow. Both meanings are critical to the politics of resource scarcity in the social services. The 1980 election of Ronald Reagan brought to Washington the first unequivocally and aggressively conservative administration since the New Deal. One of its major domestic goals was to reverse the direction of social policy by seeking drastic reductions in federal spending for social programs. Although the administration was able to accomplish some of what it set out to do, the impact has been uneven. In their review of the impact of the Reagan budget cuts on voluntary social agencies, Demone and Gibelman noted that 57 percent of the agencies surveyed reported reductions in governmental funding from 1981 to 1982, 35 percent reported no change, and 8 percent reported increased support.[4] Reports of decreases in funding from 1981 to 1982 ranged from

> a high of 72 percent of the legal service agencies to a low of 45 percent of the institutional and residential care agencies. Among social service agencies, 62 percent of the agencies reported a reduction in governmental funding between 1981 and 1983, 28 percent claimed no change, and 10 percent reported an increase. For health and mental health agencies, 57 percent and 59 percent, respectively, suffered decreases in funding, whereas 9 and 15 percent, respectively, reported increases.[5]

Decisions about the allocation of social service funds have benefited some, harmed many, and left the rest no worse or better off. There is an assumption, moreover, that these decisions were made according to what Potuchek called a "merit model." According to this model, "a funding organization should evaluate an application for funds by first assessing the *need* for the services proposed in that application and then evaluating the *effectiveness* of the proposed program for meeting those needs."[6] In other words, the decisions are rational. It is, however, extremely difficult to decide rationally about matters pertaining to the social services because the information needed to make the necessary calculations is rarely available. Goals must be stated in measurable terms; alternative means must be spelled out; the probability of an alternative actually attaining the goal must be calculable, along with its cost; and the decision maker must be able to rank order the criteria (cost, quality, quantity, scope, timeliness) to be used in making the final decision. Lack of such information means that decisions are usually made under conditions of extreme uncertainty.

Not only are decisions about social service funding often based on thin and inconclusive information, they are also marked by a high degree of dissension and controversy around program purposes. It is certainly no coincidence that one of the programs hardest hit by the Reagan budget cuts was legal services, since these agencies seek to redress clients' grievances against other social service organizations. Similarly, the difficulties that nontraditional services like shelters for battered women, counseling for AIDS victims, or sex education for preteenagers have in obtaining funding is not due to a lack of information about extent of need or potential effectiveness, but to substantive disagreements over what these programs are trying to accomplish. Conversely, programs that fare well are often ones that address safe social problems, enjoy broad public support, and have powerful constituencies among their providers and recipients (for example, services for the elderly).

When the conditions for rational decision making are not present, funders must use other devices for allocating scarce resources. One such device is to decide on the basis of the characteristics of the providers rather than on the merits of the program. Faced with uncertainty, people frequently turn to social similarity or social identification as a basis for acting. If there is no way of knowing how good a proposed service might be, you can at least make a judgment about the organization and the people behind the program. What is the organization's reputation and track record? What are the social and professional backgrounds of administrators and staff? Where have they worked before? With what success? Under conditions of uncertainty, "it is the merit of the applicant organization, not the merit of the proposed service that is evaluated."[7] Hence, a premium is placed on the ability to project a credible image by managing how information about an organization and its activities is transmitted to the general community. This, of course, is an important political skill.

If one accepts the idea that politics "describe social situations in which the dominant or primary relations are those between superior and subordinate," then funding relationships are inherently political.[8] Funding relationships are asymmetrical in terms of the balance of power since funders control resources needed by applicants. Recipient agencies will try to redress the power relationship through tactics such as building a unique niche in a service system, networking and coalition building with other organizations and community constituencies, and identifying and acquiring multiple sources of funds.

The power inherent in funding relationships points to the second way in which resource allocation contributes to politicization of the social services. Funders may choose to be tight with money when they use it to influence, if not directly control, the content and form of the programs they sponsor. Commenting on the discrepancy between expanding social welfare resources during the 1970s and an accompanying rhetoric of scarcity which demanded more rigorous accountability and management, Gruber suggested that the rhetoric may have been a "good whip for a particular viewpoint."[9] The nature of this particular viewpoint is suggested in Reich's discussion of the two cultures that shape public policy. Americans, he argued, tend to divide the dimensions of our national life into two broad realms. The first is the realm of government and politics. The second is the realm of business and economics. Our concerns about social justice are restricted to the first realm; our concerns about prosperity, to the second.[10]

The roughly 30-year period from the New Deal through the Great Society was clearly one in which the governmental culture was in the ascendancy. This period represented the greatest expansion in social spending in the country's history and witnessed a dramatic increase in the overall scope and importance of government, particularly the role of the president and the executive branch. By contrast, the period from the early 1970s to the present has been one in which the influence of the business community has achieved its highest level in this century.

During the ascendancy of the governmental culture, social policy was viewed as a positive device for promoting the well-being of all citizens. The emphasis was on innovative programs and the use of government funds to uncover and remediate previously neglected areas of social and economic malfunctioning. By contrast, the growing importance of the business culture has shifted the emphasis to businesslike management practices and fiscal probity. Persons who currently control the financial resources of service organizations, Martin suggested, "are likely to be more concerned with 'business-related' values and goals — such as growth, productivity, efficiency, and rationality — than with goals reflecting concern for a high quality of service provision or demonstrated service effectiveness."[11]

The transition from the governmental to the business culture was signaled by the policy debate over cash and services which began in the late 1960s. Cash is a rubric for concrete, tangible services (financial assistance and food stamps) that directly meet consumer needs. Services refer to nonmaterial assistance (counseling and psychotherapy) which seek to help people deal with social and economic problems by improving their ability to function as individuals. Cash strategists include economists and management-minded bureaucrats, whereas service strategists often are members of the service professions (social workers, psychiatrists, educators, rehabilitation counselors). The growing influence of the cash strategists reflects disillusionment with the ability of counseling services to solve problems and impatience with their amorphous, unmeasurable, and difficult-to-manage features and with their dependence on elaborate systems of service coordination and integration (which almost never work). The cash strategists prefer, instead,

> to operate through manipulated prices and markets rather than through substantive regulations, through delivering cash rather than services, through communicating by means of smaller rather than larger units of social organization, through seeking clearances from fewer rather than more levels of consultation and review.[12]

Not only do funders tend to hold conservative fiscal and managerial points of view; their social philosophies are often to the right of service providers. In particular, many funders are unsympathetic to the revolution in personal and family life-styles that began in the 1960s and continues to influence many of the programs offered by contemporary social agencies. In a study of the relationship between agencies providing services to women and their funding organizations, for example, Potuchek found that a crucial aspect of maintaining an image of professionalism is to avoid appearing too radical. For the women's organizations in her study, this often involved an attempt

> not to appear "too feminist," to make it clear that they were not "man hating." Having men involved with the organization was one way to avoid this danger: "One of the questions that I've gotten in talking to people from foundations [reported one manager], almost in an 'I've got you' sort of way, [is] 'Do you have any men in your organization?'...They're sometimes a little startled when I say, 'Yes.'"[13]

The politics of tight money involve people competing for scarce resources, coupled with competing social and political philosophies about how the resources, once acquired, should be used. These competing philosophies, moreover, reflect the current struggle over defining the character of the welfare state, to which we now turn.

FROM SOCIAL WELFARE TO HUMAN SERVICES

Social welfare has been defined as a collective intervention "to meet certain needs of the individual and/or to serve the wider interests of society...."[14] All welfare systems have built-in goal conflicts owing to the potential discrepancies between individual and societal needs. Social welfare performs a number of functions of which only one — providing assistance to people in need — coincides with the goals of individual recipients. Welfare programs are also expected to contribute to the economic and social functioning of society as a whole.

In a market economy it is assumed that people will provide for themselves by participating in the market through work or other profitable activity. It is realized, however, that for a variety of reasons some people will be unable to adjust to this system and will become marginal to it. Since the adoption of the Elizabethan Poor Laws, a primary purpose of the English and American welfare systems has been to provide for people unable to function in the economic marketplace, but in a manner that does not interfere with the market's operation. Social assistance must be provided in ways that do not undermine the motivations of those who are participating, or seek to participate, in the market. Welfare has contributed to this end primarily through the Poor Law Reform principle that the recipient of public aid was to be "less eligible" for the social and economic condition of the poorest paid worker. This provision was accomplished by setting a ceiling to public aid below the minimum wage provided in the marketplace and degrading the general character of the public aid recipient.

Welfare programs are also a mechanism for socializing people into acceptable patterns of behavior and sanctioning those who fail to comply. From the settlement houses of the beginning of this century to contemporary programs for parent effectiveness training, social services have provided role models for those deemed out of step with majoritarian approaches to personal and family functioning. When counseling and other therapeutic approaches fail, the social services are also used as mechanisms of social control in programs like child protective services and involuntary institutionalization of the mentally ill and delinquent. Admittedly, the socializing and sanctioning functions are not as vigorously pursued as they once were, primarily because of shifting attitudes about what constitutes acceptable social behavior. However, when consensus does emerge, the social services are one of the first institutions turned to for controlling deviant or wayward individuals.

Since conflicting goals are a defining characteristic of all welfare systems, the critical issue is whether these conflicts get on the public agenda or remain dormant. For a large part of our history, conflicts over welfare goals have been submerged. One reason is the invidious distinction between the haves and have-nots that has been a key element in the American welfare system. Instead of providing a system of common social services, Reich argued, our welfare programs

> were narrowly targeted to specific categories of unfortunates who were conspic-
> uously distinct from everyone else — the aged; the blind; single mothers; the
> medically indigent; the handicapped. Rather than emphasize the different needs
> that any citizen might experience over a life-time, America's welfare programs
> emphasized the differences of the needy.[15]

The roots of these attitudes lie in our national experiences and the culture formed by them. America's early history was of a country rich in natural resources, free of the harsh legacies of feudalism, with an open frontier that offered extraordinary opportunities for individual advancement. It is no wonder that those who failed to make it when opportunities seemed unlimited were treated with the harshness reserved for malingerers and incompetents. From the tracts of the Charities Organization Society to contemporary white papers proposing yet another scheme for cleaning up "the welfare mess," the American welfare system has evolved within a hostile, oppressive environment, characterized by the wistful hope that it would somehow just go away.

Within this climate, the notion of conflict between the interests of society and those of the beneficiaries of society's largess seemed unheard of. The latter, like Dickensian orphans and poor relations, were expected to be grateful for what they received. But times have changed. Starting in the 1930s and continuing through the present, the conflicts endemic to the welfare system have surfaced and are not likely to subside. Factors that have contributed to this situation include the growing importance of welfare benefits and services in the lives of ordinary people; the new style of confrontational politics; and the changing character of the welfare system as it evolves into a human service system.

The American welfare system has been referred to as the reluctant welfare state. Compared to other Western countries, the United States was slow in developing mechanisms for dealing with the problems that accompany urbanization and industrialization. Moreover, a primary factor behind the developments that have taken place has been the deepening discontent of the dispossessed, accompanied by their greater ability to advance their political claims to a greater share of the national wealth. Fear of political and social turmoil following the Great Depression of the 1930s prompted the enactment of the Social Security Act of 1935, the foundation of the modern welfare state. Even then, 20 other nations had had such schemes for almost a generation. The Great Society programs of the 1960s were primarily a reaction — and a disjointed and erratic one at that — to the awakening anger and demands of a frustrated and oppressed black minority. Similarly, current efforts to extend health insurance, provide adequate day care, revamp the benefit structures of public aid programs, and address the problems of the unemployed and never employed in an economy undergoing structural changes are primarily responses to the demands of better organized and more vocal groups rather than elements in a positive program to provide for the common welfare. In spite of its reluctance, however, the welfare system now plays an increasingly significant part in the general well-being of ever larger numbers of Americans. Reich's prediction of over 20 years ago that welfare benefits and services would become a form of "new property" has been largely borne out.[16] This new property, furthermore, has given the poor and near poor a stake in the system that they didn't have before and is an important dynamic in the growth of interest group politics.

The expansion of the welfare state has been accompanied by significant changes in the nature of politics, particularly at the local level. The maximum feasible participation clause of the Economic Opportunity Act of 1964 marked the beginning of the citizen participation revolution. Although opportunities for people to participate in and influence the decisions of government have waxed and waned over the quarter century since then, political processes are more open today than ever before. Statutory provisions for citizen advisory boards, freedom of information acts, televised legislative proceedings from the Congress to city councils, public hearings on proposed legislation and administrative regulations, and consumer protection agencies are some of the ways in which the inner workings of political and administrative processes have become more accessible to ordinary citizens.

There has also been a marked change in the conduct of politics. The 1960s were a time in which protest politics became a vehicle through which powerless groups like welfare recipients were able to exercise influence over powerful service bureaucracies. This form of political action, Lipsky suggested, is "oriented toward objection to one or more policies or conditions, characterized by showmanship or display of an unconventional nature, and undertaken to obtain rewards from political or economic systems while working within the systems."[17] The widespread adoption of this tactic is largely due to the heightened consciousnesses of the members of previously oppressed and excluded groups (minorities of color, gays and lesbians, women, the disabled, the poor), which has enabled them to organize and press their interests more vigorously, if not necessarily more successfully, than ever before. "Black is beautiful," "gay rights," and "women's liberation" are some of the rallying cries that have formed the bases for the political organization of previously atomized and unorganized groups of people. The success of gay rights activists to have homosexuality effectively eliminated as the basis for a diagnosis of mental illness is one example of the ability of a once powerless and stigmatized group to take on as stalwart an opponent as the American Psychiatric Association.

The newly found voice and power of the users of social services have not been the only factors in bringing the conflicts within the welfare system into the open. As the American welfare system has matured, the areas of life considered targets for intervention by service specialists have increased. Whether one views this development as empire building on the part of the burgeoning group of service professionals or the quest of ordinary people for the amenities of modern life, there is no denying the growth in the number of social service programs. Since the early 1960s, Gilbert suggested,

> a broad-scope service network has evolved that is concerned to a large extent with provisions that go beyond meeting the basic needs of the poor. These provisions are directed more at enhancing human development and the general quality of life than at reducing poverty....The changing purpose...is reflected in the host of...services...not associated with notions of personal deficiency or lack of character that in the past marked the main provisions of social casework to those dependent on public aid.[18]

In a society that still considers family allowances, national health service, and adequate public housing the slippery slope to socialism, the murkier and more contentious issues surrounding programs for promoting the quality of life have opened a Pandora's box of ethnic, class, racial, religious, and gender controversies which promise to dominate the domestic policy agenda for the rest of the century. Social services now seek to address issues that have traditionally been considered private matters (marital and family relationships, child rearing, sexual preferences and practices). Leaving aside for the moment the question of whether the helping professions have the technological wherewithal to deal with these problems, the design of services that will improve the general quality of life requires first making value judgments as to what constitutes a "higher quality" of living. Universal agreement is difficult to achieve on questions of this sort.[19]

The historic social and economic class distinctions of the welfare system, the growing importance of welfare benefits and services in the lives of more and more Americans, and the expansion of social service programs into new and controversial areas of personal and family life operate singly and in combination to politicize the field. No longer is there consensus about the purposes of social welfare, even a consensus imposed by a dominant social and economic elite. The American experience since the 1950s has been what Pfaff called one of "dismantled hierarchies." Although the United States has never been a country of fixed classes in the European sense, there has been a hierarchy of values in which a certain conventional system — of Protestant religious and British legal and social origin — dominated public life and education.

> Americans who did not accept this system of general beliefs at least paid it the tribute of hypocrisy. The United States was a puritan, entrepreneurial, unintellectual, middle-class nation, and those who did not belong to the white Protestant ascendancy but wanted to succeed made themselves as much like it as they could — Booker T. Washingtons of every race.[20]

The political and social turmoil of the past quarter century has followed inexorably on the heels of the demise of a ruling hierarchy of values — the decline of the WASP — and the enfranchisement and inclusion of more and more segments of American society into the body politic. Moreover, the social services, as the foremost institutional expression of society's social values, have been and will continue to be at the leading edge of these controversies.

SOLUTIONS IN SEARCH OF PROBLEMS

Although goal conflicts are an important ingredient in the politicization of organizational life, they do not have to lead in that direction. There are rational strategies for dealing with competing goals such as setting priorities and ordering the sequence in which different goals are addressed. The nature of an organization's technologies can also mitigate the consequences of disputes over goals. When organizational members agree about the correct way for providing a service, the technology assumes the status of a standard operating procedure. When standard operating procedures exist, organizational attention frequently shifts from the *purpose* that the service is to accomplish to the *process* for providing the service. Although this shift can lead to one of the most prevalent problems in bureaucratic organizations — goal displacement, or the substitution of means for ends and a preoccupation with conformity to rules and regulations — it is also an important mechanism for reaching consensus about a course of action.

Hospitals, for example, are organizations in which technologies often determine goals. There are frequently serious disagreements among staff and administration over the relative emphases given to community service, patient care, research, education, professional development, program innovation, and businesslike management. These disagreements often are resolved by the adoption of a major technological innovation (for example, open-heart surgery). The operational demands of the procedures — particularly capital-intensive and technologically advanced procedures — shape organizational priorities by setting criteria for who should receive treatment, what additional professional skills are needed, how patient care should be organized, and the like.

A similar process could be observed in social agencies during the 1950s and 1960s when one technology — psychoanalytically oriented casework — held sway over the field. Though lacking other than anecdotal and testimonial support for its claims to effectiveness, Freudian theory and practice played an important role in shaping the professional ideology and practice orientations of American social workers. The conditions necessary for using this technology, moreover, shaped agency policies regarding problems to be addressed and people to be served. In particular, the quest for clients with the characteristics believed necessary to benefit from psychotherapy — the young, attractive, verbal, intelligent, successful (YAVIS) individual — was pushing agencies, particularly those in the nonprofit sector who were not constrained by policy mandates to serve specified populations, into areas far afield of their original missions.

During the past few decades, however, the preeminence of psychoanalytic theory in social work has been successfully challenged. One authority identified 23 theoretical orientations that form the basis for an array of practice techniques from client-centered to transactional analysis.[21] The proliferation of methods and philosophies prompted Meyer to offer the following jeremiad:

> There exists a mélange of practice approaches, theories and models....[A] variety of social work purposes have been espoused...which might be called therapeutic, social control, preventive, rehabilitative, or adaptive. Schools of social work educate students in accordance with the idiosyncratic interests of their faculties; students learn one model of practice and not others; professional communities often prefer to train students for particular agency practices....Public and voluntary agencies are out of step with each other, to say nothing of their relationship to private practice.[22]

The American social work profession has never been highly unified. The profession began as a loose confederation of occupations and did not become a unified profession until the founding of the National Association of Social Workers nearly a century after social work appeared as a distinct occupational category. Like many other modern professions, it is less a corporate body than a loose confederation whose members pursue "different objectives in different manners held together under a common name at a particular period in history."[23] Even during the period of the Freudian hegemony, dissenting voices were often and loudly heard. The combination of a loosely coupled professional organization with the proliferation of competing practice theories and methods has exacerbated the centrifugal, internally divisive forces that have always plagued the profession. Competing definitions of clinical social work, Meyer suggested, now include practice as "psychotherapy, mental health work, private practice, work with individuals as opposed to communities, psychoanalytically based practice, work in clinics, MSW as opposed to BSW practice, or practice as opposed to policy analysis."[24] By adding administration and planning to this potpourri, we will have laid the foundation for a professional Tower of Babel.

Some of the most aggressive politicking that social workers engage in, consequently, is not with budget officers who make Scrooge look like a spendthrift or with social Neanderthals who want to replace juvenile courts with the scourge and the pillory, but with each other. With 23 theoretical schools to pick from, clinical social workers vie with each other over whose truth is *the truth*. Academic-based social workers argue with agency practitioners over the importance of empirical research in clinical practice. Community workers and social activists bemoan what they see as the growing social and political conservatism of a profession increasingly involved in fee-for-service private practice and corporate-based employee assistance programs. Social work administrators and planners, who have been losing out in the competition for jobs and influence with business-trained and quantitatively oriented managers, despair over the seeming inability of their staffs to tell them what they're doing, how long it will take, how much it will cost, and whether it's going to accomplish anything.

In addition to squabbles within the profession, there are challenges to social work's once dominant position in social welfare from a growing number of new service specialists. The social, or, as they are coming to be called outside social work, *human*, services are a growth industry. Americans more and more are concerned with their psychological well-being and are willing to go to considerable lengths to improve their ability to function as individuals, within relationships, and as parents. In their study of American society, Bellah and his colleagues suggested that psychotherapy has become one of the major forces defining late-twentieth-century American culture. Americans, it seems, are in need of cure.

> But cure of what? In the final analysis, it is cure of the lack of fit between the present organization of the self and the available organization of work, intimacy, and meaning. And this cure is to take the form of enhancing and empowering the self to be able to relate successfully to others in society, achieving a kind of satisfaction without being overwhelmed by their demands.[25]

Within the major social service systems, social workers must compete with alcoholism and drug counselors, activity therapists, child care workers, geriatric nurses, and occupational and vocational therapists for jobs and influence over policies and programs. A central focus for these inter-professional struggles is the administrative and legislative guidelines that establish educational and other qualifications for service workers, with each group lobbying to define themselves in and the others out. Knocking at the doors of the service bureaucracies are representatives of the growing number of self-help groups, for example, Alcoholics Anonymous, who challenge the very notion of a professional and bureaucratic monopoly over service systems. Many of the new service specialists, moreover, are former clients who argue that personal experience with problems like alcohol or drug abuse is essential for helping others deal with it. In the private marketplace, which more and more social workers are turning to for part- or full-time work, the number of therapies and therapists boggles the mind. Here, political struggles are over licensing and credentialing as competing groups seek to establish uncontested claims to a corner of the market (by demonstrating a unique competence to deal with a particular problem or client) and to qualify for third-party insurance payments.

Political struggles over domain within the social services reflect the changing nature of professions in modern societies. Traditional notions about professionalization, or how an occupation becomes a profession, stressed the *attributes* of professionalism. It was assumed that certain occupational characteristics made some kinds of work professional and others not. These characteristics included mastery of a body of abstract knowledge through prolonged education, systematic training in skills derived from that body of knowledge, an ideal of service, a code of ethics, a system of collegial review and regulation to ensure high levels of competence, and community sanction in the form of licensing or certification. Occupations aspiring to professional status were advised to acquire as many of these characteristics as possible. The more you had, the more professional you became. Current thinking, however, has moved away from the attributional approach and looks at professionalization as an *interaction process* between an aspiring occupation and society at large. The process begins, Popple suggested, with

> members of society experiencing a problem that involves a high degree of technicality....This creates a potential domain, or market for the services of an occupation. At this point, occupations will engage in power struggles for control of the domain. Professions that demonstrate a high degree of effectiveness in dealing with a problem...will be given nearly complete control of the domain; those that demonstrate questionable effectiveness...will be given less control.[26]

Social workers' claims to professional status and uncontested control of service provision have been hampered, in part, because the technologies they use have uncertain or unknown probabilities of success.

There was a time when this lack of certainty did not create the political problems that it does today. Up until the 1960s, social work and social services were virtually synonymous. Social work's claims to effectiveness were taken at face value since there were no competitors to challenge them. Now, however, it's more like a crap shoot, with many players wanting to get in on the action. From the point of view of the funders of services, you're better off playing in a crap game where the probabilities of making your point are known (between 1 in 6 and 1 in 36) than trying to pick winners among competing program proposals. The growing competition puts a premium on the skill with which service professionals advance their claims with funding organizations. Although these skills are not all political, the lack of unequivocal, objective information with which to evaluate the claims of different providers means that politics will play an important and often determining role.

POWER, POWER — WHO'S GOT THE POWER?

Politicization is more likely to occur in organizations with multiple power centers and a climate that encourages a skeptical attitude toward bureaucratic authority. Of all the elements in the political framework, the nature of power and power relationships in social agencies is most likely to *block* the emergence of organizational politics and mask political processes that do exist. Two factors that contribute to this are external pressures for artificially inflated levels of centralized control and the spread of an apolitical or antipolitical culture among professional social workers.

Mintzberg argued that organizational power configurations are primarily functions of the relationship between the *internal coalition* (employees who are key stakeholders in the organization) and the *external coalition* (funders, regulators, competitors, consumers). The external coalition can be "dominated" (one individual or organization, or a group acting together, holds the balance of power) or "passive" (no outsider seeks to exercise much power). When the external coalition is dominated, the internal coalition is encouraged to develop a highly bureaucratic structure, with power concentrated at the upper levels, in order to efficiently pursue goals imposed by the dominant influencer.[27]

The tight money climate surrounding social welfare (both in terms of the amount of resources available and efforts to control their use) has created a dominated environment which promotes centralized power structures within social agencies. Social welfare resources are increasingly concentrated in a few large government agencies at the federal and state levels. The prevailing point of view among these funders, moreover, is a managerial one that views social agencies, as Turem suggested, as

> economic units of activity with budgets to execute, paper clips to buy, revenues to raise, an external market to attract, and a labor force to maintain. The skills of efficient management are at this level not dissimilar to the management of comparable economic units of activity in other sectors.[28]

The funders' emphases, accordingly, are on productivity and efficiency. Like many organizations, social agencies are most productive when power is concentrated in the hands of a few and work is performed according to standardized procedures within a formal system of rules and regulations.

All organizations, however, are subject to what Caplow called the "double principle of limited possibilities."[29] There are only a few ways an organization can be structured, and, once provided with a structure, an organization can perform only a limited number of functions. Organizations designed for high-volume production are structurally unfit to pursue other goals. Production-oriented organizations, for example, have difficulty dealing with novel situations that require unconventional, innovative responses. They are designed, as Galbraith noted, to

> efficiently process the millionth loan, produce the millionth automobile, or serve the millionth client. An organization that is designed to do something well for the millionth time is not good at doing something for the first time.[30]

Ironically, many social agencies have modeled themselves after high-production business organizations when a turbulent and rapidly changing social environment has produced problems that require unconventional and innovative responses. Blended families, urban nomads, elder abuse, dating violence, aging out, and latchkey children are examples of social problems generated by the demographic and sociocultural changes within the United States. Solutions for these problems require organizations structured for innovative as opposed to routine work.

Centralized bureaucratic organizations also tend to be inhospitable places for conducting professional work. They are most appropriate for performing routine tasks based on standardized procedures that can be objectively monitored and controlled by a supervisor external to the work process. The service provider, on the other hand, operates in an environment made uncertain by the unpredictability of the problems presented and the tasks to be performed and must be able to respond flexibly. Bureaucratic controls, by contrast, prevent flexibility.

Social services, like many other service commodities, are distinctive in that they are consumed only during the process of production. They do not exist as a product separate from the process of providing them. Like diplomacy, the process *is* the product. This feature places considerable importance on the relationship between service provider and recipient. Bureaucratic structures, while they promote efficient production, have side effects that disrupt the emotional climate necessary for the development of sensitive interpersonal relationships. Consequently, centralization of power and authority in social agencies for the purposes of high productivity and efficiency creates, as Glisson and Martin pointed out, a difficult dilemma as

> a high degree of centralization leads to staff dissatisfaction…, a lower quality of client service…, and a diminished level of individual worker and organization-

level development....[T]o the extent that a centralized power structure stifles worker experimentation, innovation, and openness to change, the chances for discovery of new and better methods appear minimal.[31]

A second factor that suppresses political behavior in social agencies is the way professional social workers regard the organizations they work for and their proper roles within them. Although the factors that form the preconditions for a politicized organization (resource scarcity, conflicting goals, uncertain technologies) operate independently of the attitudes of organizational members, the likelihood that a particular organization will become political is very dependent on those attitudes. Since political behavior in organizations involves a willingness to acquire and use power, individual attitudes toward power assume a critical role. These attitudes reflect both general societal attitudes toward power and values introduced through professional education and socialization.

Power, as noted earlier, has become America's last dirty word. It is easier, Kanter suggested,

> to talk about money — and much easier to talk about sex — than it is to talk about power. People who have it deny it, people who want it do not want to appear to hunger for it, and the people who engage in its machinations do so secretly.[32]

The American antipathy toward power is rooted in an inclination to see power only as a destructive force. Power, however, may also be used constructively. Like physical power, it is the ability to get things done. The responsible expression of aggression is viewed by mental health professionals as an important ingredient of the mature, healthy personality. But because the exercise of power in a social context usually involves getting people to do things they don't want to do, it is seen as a threat to individual autonomy. As a result, Baum suggested, Americans often experience guilt in thinking of power as

> harmful aggression against others....It is difficult for us to consider ways in which power may be used to assist others or to strengthen ourselves without harming others....The aggressive impulses of power are conceived as a challenge by an individual against a multitude, likely resulting in the destruction of the lone individual. To any guilt about aggression is added anxiety about its anticipated end.[33]

This negative attitude toward power is magnified in the attitudes of many professional social workers owing to the demography of the profession and the values and beliefs transmitted through professional socialization. American social work has been a woman's profession since its beginning in the late nineteenth century. Recent trends suggest that the normally high proportion of women in social work is getting even higher. From 1972 to 1982 the female membership of the National Association of Social Workers increased from 59 to 73 percent.[34] The preponderance of women in social work has special significance for the present discussion because of indications that women's attitudes toward the use of power tend to be markedly different from men's.

Women often see the "acquisition of adult power as entailing the loss of feminine sensitivity and compassion."[35] McClelland reported that whereas men represent powerful activity as assertion and aggression, women portray acts of nurturance as acts of strength.[36] A minor growth industry has appeared in the past few years offering assertiveness training to women managers and would-be managers. Women are counseled to adopt male behavioral styles like directness, impersonality, and the willingness to act unilaterally. On the other hand, feminist writers urge women social workers to be true to their natures and pursue a feminist approach to practice that stresses power equalization, collaborative decision-making styles, and nonhierarchical organizations. Whether women are advised to be like men or like themselves, there is an implicit recognition that women and men approach the issue of power differently. Women are less likely to have a positive orientation to getting and using power when this quality is perceived as psychologically and ideologically alien.

Of course, these attitudes are not confined to women nor are they exhibited by all women. Power equalization and participatory management form an integral part of the human relations school of organizational behavior and the related field of organizational development. The human relations approach, moreover, has great appeal to social work managers. Its emphases on the motivation, involvement, and commitment of employees to organizational goals coincide with the professional philosophies of many social workers.

The preparation of managers within schools of social work is a relatively new undertaking and accounts for less than 20 percent of social work graduate students. Because of their newness and small size, administration programs occupy a precarious position within schools of social work and often function like departments within a host setting. The emphasis on human relations training in social work management programs is frequently as much a response to the tenuous status of these programs as it is a reflection of the philosophical orientations of their faculties. To be acceptable as a social work practice specialization, administration programs are constrained to employ models that are in tune with leading viewpoints within social work. This constraint has created opportunity costs in terms of the ability of social work administration programs to keep pace with the technological developments in management, as well as their receptivity to conflict-oriented political approaches to management practice.

There is a tension within administration programs between giving students the technical and political skills needed for management practice in today's service organizations — particularly public social service bureaucracies — and maintaining legitimacy as a social work practice specialty. There are indications, moreover, that this tension is increasing as social work moves in the direction of a primary emphasis on the provision of clinical mental health services. Employment trends show a marked preference on the part of social workers for mental health organizations and for-profit practice over public welfare. The direct practice curricula in schools of social work are overwhelmingly weighted in favor of psychotherapeutic theory and treatment. Organizational and administrative issues are presented as marginal concerns, and there is often the implicit or explicit assumption that fee-for-service private practice is the preferred form for professional practice.

The quest for professionalization has contributed to a climate within social work education and the field in general that, rather than being apolitical, is, to use Lasswell's more specific term, antipolitical, an attitude that arises when "participation in the power process is actively opposed on the grounds of its alleged incompatibility with other values."[37] Individuals socialized into this professional culture are likely to have a negative orientation toward issues of organizational power and politics and their appropriate role in professional practice. In this respect, at least, clinical social work training creates, as Sarri argued, a trained incapacity for future effectiveness in administrative work.[38]

To sum up, social service organizations operate under conditions of scarce resources in an environment in which there are no commonly accepted rules for how resources should be allocated. Consequently, resources usually go to those organizations most skilled at competing for funds. Social service organizations pursue a number of different goals, ranging from organizational maintenance to controlling socially unacceptable behavior. Priorities assigned to competing goals are more likely to reflect the interests of powerful factions within the organization or in its environment, rather than a rationally planned strategy. The technologies used by social agencies are often uncertain in their outcomes and are frequently the subject of debates among service professionals and the general public. These debates concern both the technologies' claimed effectiveness and their compatibility with general social norms of privacy, freedom from coercion, and parental control of children.

These characteristics suggest that social agencies can profitably be thought about within a political framework. The elements in the political framework not reflected in contemporary social agencies concern the distribution of power and organizational members' attitudes toward the exercise of power. It was suggested that these organizations tend to have artificially high levels of centralized control because of the pressure of funding agencies for high-volume production and economic efficiency. Also, the professional culture of social work operates to disparage the bureaucratic context of social work practice and does not prepare professional social workers to function effectively as organizational actors. These last features, moreover, tend to mask and obscure political processes that are present in social agencies rather than prevent their development. The ways in which organizational politics materialize in the operations of social agencies are the subject of the next three chapters.

NOTES

1. A. K. Bixby, "Social Welfare Expenditures, Fiscal Year 1980," *Social Security Bulletin*, 46 (1983), 9–17.
2. C. E. Barfield, *Rethinking Federalism* (Washington, D.C.: American Enterprise Institute, 1981).
3. Sanford F. Schramm, "Politics, Professionalism, and the Changing Federalism," *Social Service Review*, 55, no. 1 (March 1981), 90.
4. Harold W. Demone, Jr., and Margaret Gibelman, "Reaganomics: Its Impact on the Voluntary Not-for-Profit Sector," *Social Work*, 29, no. 5 (September-October 1984), 421–27.
5. Ibid., 422.
6. Jean L. Potuchek, "The Context of Social Service Funding: The Funding Relationship," *Social Service Review*, 60, no. 3 (September 1986), 421–22 (emphases in original).
7. Ibid., 425.
8. Gordon Tullock, *The Politics of Bureaucracy* (Washington, D.C.: Public Affairs Press, 1965), p. 11.
9. Murray L. Gruber, "A Three-Factor Model of Administrative Effectiveness," *Administration in Social Work*, 10, no. 3 (Fall 1986), 13.
10. Robert B. Reich, *The Next American Frontier* (New York: Penguin Books, 1983), p. 4.
11. Patricia Yancey Martin, "Multiple Constituencies, Dominant Societal Values, and the Human Service Administrator: Implications for Service Delivery," *Administration in Social Work*, 4, no. 2 (Summer 1980), 19.
12. Francine Rabinovitz, Jeffrey Pressman, and Martin Rein, "Guidelines: A Plethora of Forms, Authors, and Functions," *Policy Sciences*, 7, no. 4 (December 1976), 415.
13. Potuchek, "The Context of Social Service Funding," 432.
14. Richard M. Titmuss, "The Social Division of Welfare: Some Reflections on the Search for Equity," in Richard M. Titmuss, *Essays on 'The Welfare State'* (New Haven: Yale University Press, 1959), pp. 34–55.
15. Reich, *The Next American Frontier*, p. 113.
16. Charles A. Reich, "The New Property," *Yale Law Journal*, 73 (April 1964), 732–87.
17. Michael Lipsky, "Protest as a Political Resource," *American Political Science Review*, 62, no. 4 (December 1968), 1145.
18. Neil Gilbert, *Capitalism and the Welfare State: Dilemmas of Social Benevolence* (New Haven: Yale University Press, 1983), p. 65.
19. Ibid., p. 155.
20. William Pfaff, "Aristocracies," *The New Yorker*, January 14, 1980, p. 70.
21. Francis J. Turner, "Theory in Social Work Practice," in *Social Work Treatment: Interlocking Theoretical Approaches*, ed. Francis J. Turner, 3rd ed. (New York: The Free Press, 1986), p. 15.
22. Carol H. Meyer, "What Directions for Direct Practice?" *Social Work*, 24, no. 4 (July 1979), 268.
23. Rue Bucher and Anselm Strauss, "Professions in Process," *American Journal of Sociology*, 66, no. 3 (November 1960), 325.
24. Meyer, "What Directions for Direct Practice?" 268.
25. Robert N. Bellah et al., *Habits of the Heart: Individualism and Commitment in American Life* (New York: Perennial Library, Harper and Row, 1986), p. 47.
26. Philip R. Popple, "The Social Work Profession: A Reconceptualization," *Social Service Review*, 59, no. 4 (December 1985), 569–70.
27. Henry Mintzberg, "Power and Organization Life Cycle," *Academy of Management Review*, 9, no. 2 (April 1984), 208–10.
28. Jerry S. Turem, "Social Work Administration and Modern Management Technology," *Administration in Social Work*, 10, no. 3 (Fall 1986), 23.

29. Theodore Caplow, *Principles of Organization* (New York: Harcourt, Brace and World, 1964), p. 8.
30. Jay R. Galbraith, "Designing the Innovating Organization," *Organizational Dynamics*, 10, no. 3 (Winter 1982), 5–6.
31. Charles A. Glisson and Patricia Yancey Martin, "Productivity and Efficiency in Human Service Organizations as Related to Structure, Size, and Age," *Academy of Management Journal*, 23, no. 1 (March 1980), 34–35.
32. Rosabeth Moss Kanter, "Power Failure in Management Circuits," *Harvard Business Review*, 57, no. 4 (July-August 1979), 65.
33. Howell S. Baum, "Autonomy, Shame, and Doubt: Power in the Bureaucratic Lives of Planners," *Administration & Society*, 15, no. 2 (August 1983), 149–50.
34. June Gary Hopps and Elaine B. Pinderhughes, "Profession of Social Work: Contemporary Characteristics," in *Encyclopedia of Social Work*, volume 2, ed. Anne Minahan et al., 18th ed. (Silver Spring, Md.: National Association of Social Workers), p. 357.
35. Carol Gilligan, *In a Different Voice: Psychological Theory and Women's Development* (Cambridge, Mass.: Harvard University Press, 1982), p. 97.
36. David C. McClelland, *Power: The Inner Experience* (New York: Irvington, 1975).
37. Harold Lasswell, *Power and Personality* (New York: Viking, 1962), p. 151.
38. Rosemary C. Sarri, "Effective Social Work Intervention in Administrative and Planning Roles: Implications for Education," in Council on Social Work Education, *Facing the Challenge: Plenary Session Papers* (New York: Council on Social Work Education, 1973).

4
The Politics of Money

Resources are the things that organizations need to accomplish their purposes. The resources needed by social agencies include skilled personnel, physical facilities, clients, and community sanction. This list becomes more specific when we identify the resources needed to provide a given service. An agency serving parents with handicapped children at home will need *certain* skilled personnel (home aides, special education teachers, nurses, building contractors) and *particular* facilities and equipment (a place for respite care, specially equipped vans). Of all the resources that social service organizations need, money is the most important. While the amount is important, the advantage of money — regardless of the amount — is its liquidity, or the ease with which it can be exchanged for other resources. Money may not be able to buy love, but it can buy just about everything else. An agency administrator will no doubt be grateful if the local chamber of commerce donates a van, but he or she would be even more grateful if the chamber donated cash that could be used for whatever the agency needed at the time.

Money is not only important; it is scarce. Scarce funds are an inherent feature of the social services, although the degree of scarcity may be lessened or worsened by the actions of particular political administrations. Competition for resources among organizations and among units within organizations is a normal condition in the social services. Decisions about the allocation of money are thus both *critical* and *contested*. Money is allocated to and within social agencies through a budgetary process. The purpose of the present chapter is to examine how organizational politics affects that process. Specifically, we will look at the ways in which politics enters into the general budgetary process and at the political problems created when budgets are declining and decisions about budget reductions have to be made.

POLITICS AND THE BUDGETARY PROCESS

A budget is a document containing words and figures that propose expenditures for certain items and purposes. "The words describe items of expenditure (salaries, equipment, travel) or purposes (preventing war, improving mental health, providing low-income housing), and the figures are attached to each item or purpose."[1] From the perspective of organizations as rational instruments for goal attainment, budgets assume paramount importance. The essence of rational organizational behavior is efficiency in the achievement of goals. Organizations strive to accomplish their purposes with the least expenditure of resources possible. From the rational perspective, an agency that serves 100 clients with a budget of $100,000 is better than one serving 80 clients with the same budget. For most organizations, budgets are the only regularly produced documents that present goals and the means for attaining them in specific, quantified terms. Budgets often serve as blueprints for an organization's operations, describing what it plans to do and how it plans to do it. Of course, the degree of specificity varies with the type of budget used. Many organizations use line-item budgets in which an entire program such as maintaining a shelter for homeless adults will be listed as one item in the budget. By contrast, more elaborate budget devices like the program, planning, budgeting system (PPBS) or zero-based budgeting (ZBB) require that goals and objectives be spelled out; all goal-related activities be specified with direct and indirect costs estimated on a multi-year basis; and alternative means for attaining goals identified and their potential effectiveness assessed. Although these systems are not widely used today, they represent for many budget experts the ideal methods for rationally allocating organizational resources.

If these systems enable administrators to efficiently allocate resources, the question arises of why they are not used more extensively. One reason given is that they make excessive demands on an organization's ability to collect and analyze data. Although it is true that many social service organizations lack the abilities to perform the analytical tasks listed above, this situation has been changing. Advances in computer technologies have produced inexpensive, easy-to-use personal computers with software programs directly suited to the informational and analytical requirements of program budgeting systems. In addition, social work schools now place greater emphasis on providing students with management tools like cost accounting and computer-based management information systems.

From a political perspective, however, the answer to why rigorous budgeting procedures are resisted in social agencies lies not in their lack of analytical skills and reliable information (although this may exist) but in the nature of these organizations and their goals. Most social agencies, as previously noted, have conflicting goals, uncertain technologies, and multiple stakeholders with competing interests in the organization's affairs. These factors, and not the lack of technical skills, are the primary reasons why social service organizations persist in muddling their way through budget decisions rather than basing them on comprehensive plans derived from a systematic consideration of organizational capabilities, alternatives, and future directions.

> If politics is regarded as conflict over whose preferences are to prevail in the determination of policy, then the budget records the outcomes of this struggle. If one asks who gets what the...organization has to give, then the answers for a moment in time are recorded in the budget.[2]

Regardless of whether organizations approach budgeting in a rational or political manner, budget decisions are usually incremental. Most budget decisions involve relatively small percentage changes (usually around 10 percent, rarely over 30 percent) in the previous year's allocations. In most cases there is an increase over the previous amount, although more and more social service organizations now have to decrease previous allocations, changing the process to decremental budgeting. But whether it goes up or down, the best predictor of this year's budget is last year's budget. The issue of rationality versus politics in the budgetary process centers around the questions of how a budget got to look the way it does in the first place and how we can account for the incremental (or decremental) changes from year to year.

Organizational Power and Budget Outcomes

An early study of the role of politics in organizational budgets was Pfeffer and Salancik's research on how a university allocated funds to its departments.[3] From a rational perspective, budget allocations should be based on the relative contributions that different units make to achieving organizational goals. Those making more important contributions should receive greater shares of funds and other resources than those whose work is judged less significant. The authors rejected this assumption and hypothesized that university budget decisions involved a political process based on one department's power relative to other departments and did not rely on rational criteria such as the number of students instructed.

This hypothesis was based on the idea that universities, like many other organizations, simultaneously pursue a number of conflicting goals.

Although teaching is usually listed as the primary purpose, this ranking is generally taken with a grain of salt by people within and outside universities. Other less publicized but equally important goals include maintaining high rates of faculty publications, achieving national and international recognition for the university's departments and schools, acquiring federal and corporate funding, and developing innovative programs that attract new students, particularly those not in the dwindling 18–24-year-old age category. There is considerable dissension within universities over how these goals should be ranked, and few are able to develop a list of priorities that is supported by a majority of faculty and administrators. As a result, a vital prerequisite for rational decision making — goal consensus — is missing. Pfeffer and Salancik argued that in the case of universities, political processes will move in to fill this void.

The authors constructed two competing models for predicting the distribution of funds and then compared the predictions to the actual allocation of funds. The "universalistic-bureaucratic" model proceeded from the rational assumption that units making a greater contribution to achieving organizational goals should receive proportionately more resources than those that contributed less. Since a university's major stated goal is to instruct its students, this model measured the relationship between a department's instructional work load and its annual budget appropriations. The "particularistic-political" model was based on the assumption that differences in budget allocations would result from the power of departments relative to each other rather than their share of the instructional work load. Departmental power was measured in two ways. The first involved each department head's assessment of the power of the other departments. The ratings were averaged to give an overall power rank for each department. The second measure of departmental power was the number of faculty members from each department serving on key university committees. The data supported the authors' hypothesis, with the single best predictor of a department's budget being its average representation on key university committees.

This research has been followed by a number of studies that confirmed the role that unit power (or its absence) plays in how budgetary and other critical decisions are made in a variety of organizations. The main determinants of a unit's power are its abilities to import scarce and important resources from the environment and perform functions central to the organization's mission. Jansson and Simmons identified how these processes operated in hospital social service departments.[4] They hypothesized that the power of social service departments would increase when they reduced or eliminated adverse conditions in the hospital's external relations in areas like public relations, marketing, and accreditation; made top officials and other units dependent on them for information, services, or resources; developed formal and informal linkages with high level officials; and had assertive leaders willing to exercise influence to advance the department's claims for increased resources and important functions. They measured power by a department's size in proportion to the total number of beds and by "role complexity," or the number of service functions a department performed. In a survey of 50 hospital social service departments, the authors found that the more powerful departments were more likely to pursue the strategies hypothesized as leading to greater unit power.

Units that perform essential functions, control important resources, and are part of influence networks will be more powerful than those that don't. And the more powerful an organizational unit, the greater its budget share. But if an organization concentrates its resources on units performing key functions, isn't that the epitome of bureaucratic rationality? Then why call it political? Can an organization be bureaucratic and political at the same time? In the case of university departments and hospital social service units, larger budget allocations can be attributed to rational considerations only if it can be shown that the contributions of these units to reaching organizational goals surpassed those of other units or departments with smaller allocations. Is social work more important to a hospital than physical therapy? Does the teaching of accounting contribute more to a university's mission than the teaching of history? These questions are unanswerable for a number of reasons: (1) these organizations pursue a number of goals, with different units and departments contributing to one or two, but not all, goals; (2) without a ranking of the relative importance of these goals (medical education versus patient care; teaching versus funded research) there is no way to assess the importance of a specific unit's contributions; (3) regardless of impact upon organizational goals, it is hard to compare the quantity and quality of activities as diverse as social work and physical therapy; and (4) even without comparing one unit to another, the complexity of organizational life makes it difficult, if not impossible, to trace the impact of any one unit's efforts on the organization's overall accomplishments.

Rather, the units and departments that received larger budget allocations did so because they acquired power through their control of resources (work assignments, information, committee memberships, community contacts) that were important to top administrators. They were then in a position to negotiate for a larger budget allocation because of their ability to withhold those resources. Hence, increases did not result from management's assessment that a unit's substantive work was intrinsically more important and necessary to the organization than the work of other units. If units lost their power, they would also lose their larger budgets, even though the quality and quantity of their work remained the same.

An organizational unit's ability to maximize its budget share through adroit political maneuvers was highlighted in Roos and Hall's study of a hospital extended care unit (ECU).[5] ECUs are often poorly financed, low-status operations used as dumping grounds for patients who no longer need acute medical care. The ECU in the present study, however, was created at a time of heightened concern over the treatment of elderly patients, prompted, no doubt, by the growing political power of senior citizens. The director of the ECU capitalized on the changing climate for services for the elderly by insisting that the unit's primary mission be *rehabilitation* of patients selected by the ECU, rather than providing routine nursing care to patients sent to the unit to free acute-care beds elsewhere in the hospital. By avoiding the dumping ground stigma and stressing the rehabilitation of older patients for their return home, the unit director was able to argue for increased funding for the ECU.

One of the reasons that the director was successful in getting higher levels of staffing compared with other departments in the hospital, and other hospitals in the city, was the absence of guidelines for staffing ratios in special situations like nursing for rehabilitation. Sixty percent of the hospital's social workers, for example, were assigned to the ECU. By stressing the unit's unique contribution and its impact on the hospital's important constituencies, the director was able to get a number of special dispensations for the unit. The ECU director set rehabilitative criteria for admission and controlled the selection of patients to the unit. This selection process sharply contrasted with the usual practice of having transfer decisions made by acute-care units. Because of selective admission policies, the ECU had an occupancy rate of 79 percent, which was below its funded occupancy rate of 85 percent, both of which were below the 90 percent occupancy rate of other hospital units.

These practices naturally incurred the opposition of other unit directors. The establishment of the ECU was seen by acute-care unit directors as a much needed resource for easing the pressure for bed space in their units. Their disappointment when the ECU did not play this role was exacerbated by their belief that the ECU — despite its preferential budget allocations — was not carrying its fair share of the hospital's work load. The ECU director relied primarily on public relations strategies to defend the unit's surplus resources and other special considerations. He emphasized the contribution that the unit made in maintaining credibility with the hospital's external funding agency, which was favorably disposed to the rehabilitation goals of the unit. The authors concluded that the success of this strategy in defending the ECU's domain within the hospital suggested

> the viability of an externally oriented strategy for public-sector organizations; defining an organization's mission in positive terms like "rehabilitation for returning home" greatly enhances chances of funding. In the public sector, marketing may be more important than production. Improving "flowthrough" by ten percent is less important than generating and maintaining a favorable image.[6]

The Politics of Familiarity

It seems like a sorry state of affairs when appearances count more than substance in making such major decisions as which hospital departments or which social agencies should receive more resources and which less. Our disillusionment may be reduced, however, when we look at the factors contributing to this situation. An important inherent characteristic of the social services (as well as such business services as advertising, marketing, and public relations) is the absence of a firm technological base. Many of the technologies that social services rely on are diffuse and indeterminate. We are not sure of the impact that factors other than the ones we have identified have had on service success or failure, and we cannot accurately predict what the outcomes of a service intervention will be. Funders frequently cannot make allocations on rational grounds since they are uncertain about what one program's potential effectiveness is compared to another. Even when agency administrators present evidence of past program successes, funders are unsure about what was due to program interventions and what was a result of independent factors such as changes in the economy, improvements in the client's life situation, help provided by relatives or friends, and a host of other unknowns.

When faced with uncertainty, people often cope by turning to the familiar, the tried and tested. This tendency is true whether dealing with budget decisions or encountering strangers on the street. If you've ever been lost in a foreign country whose language you didn't understand, you know the feeling of relief when you hear an American accent or even see somebody wearing American clothes. You'll feel this relief, moreover, even though the American is about to pick your pocket. Funders of social service proposals may often feel like tourists in a strange city who are trying to find their way through a maze of alleys and passageways without a reliable map to guide them. (The maps they do have are printed by local businesses, and, regardless of where you want to go, each map invariably leads you to the business of the person who printed it!) Instead of having to decipher street signs in strange languages, social service funders have to make sense of the opaque professional jargon ("homeostatic equilibrium," "enmeshed boundaries," "deviance amplification") in which grant proposals and budget justifications are often written. Although some funders might deal with these situations by awarding the grant to the first familiar name on the list, the way in which most budget decisions rely on familiarity between funders and recipients is subtler and more complicated.

The 1960s was a growth period for the American welfare state. Not since the passage of the Social Security Act in 1935 was as much money spent on social programs in as short a period of time. As with any large-scale social experiment, the Great Society programs initiated by the Johnson administration experienced a number of start-up problems, including lack of experienced personnel to evaluate the hundreds of proposals for federal social service grants coming from cities and towns all over the country. The "politics of familiarity" was at its most rampant then, giving rise to cavalier decision rules like "You hatch it, we'll match it!" But the "you" was not just any you, but someone known by the funder, often through the professional old-boy network, or someone on whose behalf a congressperson's or mayor's office had already made inquiries. Moreover, service providers were encouraged to innovate and experiment with new ways of helping the poor, the uneducated, the unskilled, and the alienated. Even if enough staff were available, there were no guidelines for evaluating the unconventional proposals being presented.

The close relationship among funders and providers was attacked by critics of the welfare state as blatant cronyism. Influence networks developed, made up of federal and state bureaucrats (many of whom had human service backgrounds), special-interest groups, and sympathetic legislators. Referring to these networks as "iron triangles," critics charged that these groups acted collusively to divert millions of federal dollars to dubious social schemes. Partisan attacks aside, an elaborate influence network did in fact develop among these groups in the post–World War II period. Stern called this "administrative politics," in which the key role was played by officials of the Department of Health, Education, and Welfare (now the Department of Health and Human Services). Working with special-interest groups such as labor and the elderly and with sympathetic congressional leaders, these administrators "used their intimate familiarity with the programs of HEW...to develop proposals that generally appeared inoffensive and incremental and to insulate these programs from the control of the president and his cabinet."[7] State and local officials at first resisted the encroachment of administrative politics on their control and influence. With the expansion of the social services in the 1960s, however,

> they decided if they could not beat the Feds at their game, they would join them. Through the creative use of the amendments of 1962 [to the Social Security Act],...state officials...exploited [loopholes]...to pay for a host of social services for both poor and middle-income groups.[8]

In his study of federal grants for education during this period, Murphy identified a similar community of interest among education officials at federal, state, and local levels of government.[9] Viewing themselves and each other as professional educators,

> they are inclined neither to act as policemen nor to embarrass their colleagues. Problems are solved by "working things out" quietly through bureaucratic channels....The emphasis is on maintaining "good working relationships" and on providing friendly assistance.[10]

Public policy, however, seems to be subject to the same law as physics; for every action, there is an equal and opposite reaction. By the early 1970s, criticism of social services mounted as conservative politicians and academic analysts argued that federal spending for social programs had become uncontrollable. In addition, the programs themselves were attacked as ill-conceived, poorly administered, lacking in competent personnel, and pursuing goals that were vague, confused, and often hostile to the preferences of a majority of the people in their host communities. Although almost entirely funded by federal dollars, both the Congress and the federal bureaucracy had relinquished control over program purposes and operations by drafting and enacting legislation that was vague in what it sought to accomplish and offered few or no guidelines to direct or limit the activities of local service providers.

The election of Richard Nixon in 1968 resulted in a number of administrative and policy initiatives aimed at breaking up the influence of the iron triangle. The Department of Health, Education, and Welfare was reorganized and regionalized in an attempt to reduce the influence of program professionals sympathetic to the social legislation of the 1960s. Their influence was significantly curtailed as their functions were taken over by newly appointed management specialists in tune with administration policy goals. The new appointees frequently came from business backgrounds and sought to introduce business-oriented management practices into program operations. In 1972, for example, Francis DeGeorge was named associate administrator for management in the Social and Rehabilitation Service, the main welfare program unit in HEW. He came to this position with a Master of Business Administration degree, a bachelor's degree in accounting, and work experience as a treasurer, vice-president, controller, and cost-accounting manager of several private firms, including divisions of Litton Industries.[11]

The main Nixon strategy for restructuring the welfare system — a strategy that has been pursued by administrations since then — was the New Federalism. Through the fiscal devices of revenue sharing and block grants, federal dollars were returned to the states for allocation among different programs. This approach was augmented under the Reagan administration with deregulation, which lessened the power of federal departments to impose conditions on the use of federal funds by states and other recipients. These ideas had support among conservatives and liberals who felt that the federal government's role in social programs had gone beyond what it was administratively capable. Advocates of decentralization argued that by returning fiscal and administrative control to the states, program decisions would be made closer to the point of service provision and thus be more responsive to client needs and more accountable to funders.

These developments have not eliminated the politics of familiarity but have changed the ways in which they are played. The most important change has been the shift in decision arenas from Washington to the 50 state capitals. Block grants and deregulation have increased the discretionary power of state officials in the allocation of social service funds. Not only has the location changed, but the administrative context for funding decisions has changed as well. There tends to be a marked difference in the administrative cultures of the federal and state governments. Derthick described this difference as a "clash between two Americas," each with its own distinctive arrangement of public institutions, hierarchy of values, and mode of conducting public business.[12] The federal culture is bureaucratic and rationalistic.

> It values symmetry in the ordering of public institutions; universalism as the guiding principle of public programs (the development of abstract rules that apply equally to people); efficiency in the conduct of public business; and professionalism in public personnel.[13]

The culture of state government, on the other hand, is traditional rather than rationalistic. It conducts public business in ways that vary from one locale to another,

> through institutions and processes that have developed largely through custom and habit and are nowhere highly systematic. It places little value on rules and abstract principles, and much on molding public action to suit particular persons and local circumstances. It places little or no value on professionalism in personnel, but much on identification with the local community.[14]

Much has happened in the past 20 years to alter this picture, particularly in the large industrial states. State governments are now more fully staffed, and the staff are better trained. The number of states with full-time legislators has increased, as has the number with four-year gubernatorial terms. While many states have moved toward more rational and professional administrative and political systems, the factors identified by Derthick still play a prominent role, particularly in the social service area. As Lorenz pointed out, the politics of social service funding still requires personal contacts at all levels and in a variety of places, but contacts are now used differently than in the past. Instead of assuring funding through the old-boy network,

> personal contacts will be instrumental in helping the grantsman prepare and put forward a well-prepared proposal by providing information on the funder's criteria for reviewing proposals, by identifying biases of the funding source…, and by identifying points to emphasize in the application.…[15]

In her study of social service funding, Potuchek found that a key factor in securing funds was the impression agencies made on funders. In particular, agencies tried to project an image of professionalism, stability, and accountability.

> Credibility is, at least in part, a matter of "image." The organization must maintain an image that will appeal to funders; it must appear to be the kind of organization that will be a good risk.…At the most basic level, organizations tried to avoid any action that would give them a "bad name."[16]

These studies emphasize the importance of creating the right impression, in contrast to the rational expectation that all administrators should have to do to secure funding is demonstrate substantive accomplishments in attaining their goals. Of course, if administrators can demonstrate organizational achievements to the satisfaction of funders, impressions and familiarity wouldn't matter. However, because of the underdeveloped nature of social service technologies, administrators are rarely able to demonstrate conclusively the effectiveness of their programs. The need for social administrators to create the impression of effectiveness, rather than its substance, illustrates Salancik's argument that the effectiveness of social services is often demonstrated by the degree to which they conform to "standard operating myths," with myth used in its literal sense of an unverifiable belief.

> Many social service organizations that survive and manage to maintain resources are like butterflies that flit from political flower to political flower. Procedures shift with the shifting arguments in academic and political circles, and there is a great deal of trying-out of different strategies for solving the same basic problem.[17]

An inner-city youth in trouble with the law in the 1960s, for example, would probably have been referred to a community action agency where he or she would be treated as a victim of "blocked opportunities" brought about by the community's failure to provide adequate schooling and jobs. The same teenager, with the same problem in the 1980s, would most likely be labeled a PINS (Person in Need of Supervision) and involuntarily confined in a residential facility operated in a prisonlike manner. Moreover, it's quite probable that the same social agency was responsible for both programs. The problem of mental illness was defined in the 1950s as a lack of modern and properly staffed mental hospitals. By the 1970s, the problem had changed to one of too much hospitalization, and deinstitutionalization became the rallying cry for program reform. By the 1980s, the growing problem of the homeless, many of whom were former mental patients, had prompted calls for reinstitutionalization.

The public's attention span tends to be short and erratic when it comes to social problems. The process by which some situations and not others are defined as problems and public funds expended on their solutions is a complicated one. This situation is compounded by volatility within the human service professions as new interventions are regularly proposed, briefly experimented with, and rejected, to be replaced by the next wave of cures. According to the American Psychiatric Association, for example, there are currently 460 types of psychotherapy in use.[18]

Social agencies must frequently, as Salancik argued, "behave like chameleons" in order to attract and reattract the interest of funders.[19] This conduct creates serious ethical and professional dilemmas for administrators and staff as agencies become captives of their funders and structure programs to satisfy budgetary requirements regardless of the impact on the quality of the service provided. It places a premium on an administrator's ability to negotiate a complicated network of organizational and interpersonal relationships, develop and present budget proposals in ways that will command the attention of harried and beleaguered funding agencies, and — at the same time — maintain ethical and professional integrity. No easy task! Moreover, this situation has intensified as public and private funds for social programs decline and competition among service providers increases.

THE POLITICS OF CUTBACK MANAGEMENT

With the election of Ronald Reagan in 1980, reductions in social spending became the number one domestic priority. Although the Reagan adminis- tration was more aggressive and vocal than its predecessors in seeking cuts in social welfare budgets, efforts to reduce expenditures go back to the early 1970s, when concern with uncontrollable social spending first sur- faced. The focus then was on open-ended federal funding for social service grants to the states. Federal legislation did not put a ceiling on the amount that could be spent for social services, thus obligating the federal govern- ment to match whatever state governments spent for a particular activity. In 1972 this loophole was closed, and social service grants were capped at $2.5 billion. This action was accompanied, as already noted, by reorgani- zation in the Department of Health, Education, and Welfare and by the replacement of program administrators with human service backgrounds or sympathies by individuals with business and fiscal management back- grounds.

At state and local levels, frustration over rising costs of social and other government services found expression in the taxpayers revolt. The first shot was fired in California in 1978, when a large majority of voters endorsed Proposition 13, which cut local property taxes by 60 percent. The second volley came in 1979 in the Gann Initiative, which limited increases in state and local spending. Although only a few other states and localities enacted similar legislation, Proposition 13 became a symbol of growing taxpayer restlessness over the rising costs of government services. Moreover, it alerted state and national politicians to the role that fiscal conservatism was to play in upcom- ing elections. And an accurate message it was. In 1985, Congress passed the Balanced Budget and Emergency Deficit Reduction Act — Public Law 99-117 (the Gramm-Rudman-Hollings Act) — which mandated major reductions in the federal deficit and a balanced budget by 1991.

Since the mid-1970s social administrators have worked in a context of budgetary reductions and tight fiscal monitoring. Although program funds have been reduced, the number of people seeking help from social agencies has not, particularly as the economy continues to go through a structural transformation as profound as the move from farm to factory at the beginning of the century. Fund reduction has given rise to what Levine called "cutback management."[20] For the first time in recent history, agency administrators must routinely decide how to reduce spending rather than how to use the annual increases that had been a regular feature of agency budgets since the end of World War II.

At first glance, reducing spending seems a straightforward task. A number of simple, easy-to-implement strategies are available, such as across-the-board cuts (all units receive the same percentage cut), hiring freezes, and normal attrition through retirements and resignations. Moreover, these strategies have an intrinsic appeal to administrators and staff because they can be justified on commonsense grounds that can be readily comprehended (if not graciously accepted) by those affected. In addition, they bolster staff morale by treating all units alike and protecting the jobs of current employees. None of these strategies, however, meets the requirements for administrative rationality in terms of probable impact on organizational efficiency and effectiveness. They can have negative consequences for the current and future operations of an organization, which, while not immediately apparent, are nonetheless damaging.

All organizations are subject to what Levine called "the paradox of irreducible wholes."[21] Organizations, he argued, cannot be cut back by merely reversing the sequence of activities by which their parts were originally assembled as, for instance, in the strategy of last hired, first fired. Organizations are organic social wholes in which

> critical masses of expertise, political support, facilities and equipment, and resources are assembled. Taking a living thing like an organization apart is no easy matter; a cut may reverberate throughout a whole organization in a way no one could predict by just analyzing its growth and pattern of development.[22]

For example, an administrator can make a 10 percent budget cut by reducing each unit's allocation by 10 percent. It would be reasonable to expect that this cut will reduce overall productivity by a like amount. This approach assumes that all units contribute equally to the achievement of organizational goals. There is, however, considerable variation in the contributions that different units make. The productive capacity of a unit may be reduced because it is a long-established one that has become more concerned with self-maintenance than with goal attainment; changes in the unit's environment may have occurred which made present methods and procedures obsolete; or the unit's personnel may not be as competent as personnel in other units. Thus, Unit A might be responsible for a third of total productivity, while Unit B contributes practically nothing. If both units are cut by 10 percent, the effect on organizational performance will be greater than the 10 percent by which the units were cut. Conversely, if Unit A were "held harmless" (that is, received no budget cut) and Unit B received a 20 percent cut, overall productivity might remain the same while costs were reduced. The crux of the matter is in knowing what the relative contributions of different units are to total organizational achievements. Unfortunately, this kind of knowledge is difficult to come by in social agencies. It has been said that half of every dollar spent on advertising is wasted, but *no one knows which half*! A similar problem exists in trying to find out the contribution that different agency activities make to current accomplishments and what contributions they can be expected to make in the future.

While this information is difficult to come by, it is not impossible. Several studies have shown how some human service administrators deal with cutback management in a rational and effective manner.[23] All highlight the central role that *strategic planning* plays in the design and implementation of a rational cutback strategy. Strategic planning is customarily carried out at the highest administrative level and begins with a determination of major organizational objectives. It then specifies

> the types of service to be provided, type and number of personnel necessary to provide those services, capital expenditures, and costs associated with each of those activities. Strategic plans tend to be long-range and are stated mainly in broad terms to provide coordination of various elements composing the organization.[24]

To engage in strategic planning certain organizational conditions must be present. Levine and his colleagues identified these conditions as centralized managerial authority, continuity of top management, rapid and accurate feedback, budgetary flexibility, and incentives for conserving resources.[25] The degree to which these elements are present in social agencies plays a determining role in how rational cutback management will be.

Centralized Authority.   Strategic planning is top-down planning with key decisions made by upper-level administrators. Managers must have the formal authority to set objectives, adjust budgets, change services, trim or eliminate departments, terminate employees, and change relationships with clients. As noted earlier, there are indications that social agencies are moving in the direction of more centralization because of its demonstrated relationship with high productivity and efficiency. Centralized authority, however, goes against the ideological grain of most social workers. It violates widely held professional values of collegiality, power sharing, and broad-based participation in decision making.[26] Ideological considerations aside, there is evidence that centralized authority systems have negative effects on staff morale and commitment to organizational goals.[27] Such effects are particularly damaging in social agencies where staff must establish close working relationships with clients who are under great stress and are faced with difficult and demanding problems. Administrative practices which alienate staff by excluding them from critical agency decisions can lead to a lower quality of service as workers become more disgruntled and dispirited. Whether consideration of these negative effects will deter the trend toward centralization remains to be seen. It also remains to be seen whether centralization that is accomplished over staff resistance can successfully do the things called for by strategic planning. In particular, it is unlikely that goals and objectives unilaterally set by top administrators will be adhered to by staff without the use of expensive and intrusive management control systems.

Continuity of Top Management. Strategic planning is long-range planning, and continuity of leadership is essential if plans are to be consistently implemented over time. Unfortunately, little is known about the average tenure of social welfare administrators in either the public or private sectors. There are, however, data about administrators in other settings, plus considerable research on turnover in general, that offer clues to the stability of administrative positions in social agencies. In a study of turnover among university department heads, Salancik and his colleagues found that high turnover was a result of inability to cope with interdependencies among department members during periods of resource scarcity.[28] The critical factor was the extent of shared beliefs among department members about what to teach, whom to hire, whom to promote, and whom to graduate. Departments whose faculties disagreed about these issues had a significantly higher turnover of department heads during periods of fiscal stress than departments with high levels of agreement. Social work staff are also given to disagreements over agency goals, how to provide services, and who should provide them. The above findings suggest that the positions of administrators in agencies with little consensus over key policy issues will be more precarious during times of cutback than those with high levels of agreement.

For administrators in the public sector, a significant factor in turnover is the extent to which they support the policies of the political executives for whom they work. A study of federal bureaucrats' reactions to the election of Ronald Reagan, for example, showed a significant increase in the number of employees who intended to resign their positions.[29] On the other hand, public sector jobs are often highly desirable because of greater career opportunities, higher pay, and job security. Factors that influence turnover of social workers in both the public and private sectors are the extent of their satisfaction with their political or board sovereigns, investment in their jobs, opportunities for alternative employment, and the costs entailed in changing jobs. During periods of fiscal austerity, moreover, these factors will operate in contradictory ways. Conservative policies and cutbacks in resources make the administrator's job less satisfying and thus heighten the probability of resignation. On the other hand, the employment market will be tighter because of cutbacks, making the costs of leaving high. The two factors operating together can be expected to have a negative effect on an administrator's willingness to engage in something as proactive and future-oriented as strategic planning. Rather, as Bozeman and Slusher hypothesized, there will be few rewards available for those administrators who attempt to actively engage their environments. Administrators will be preoccupied with playing an internal zero-sum game to protect their own subgroup's goals....[30]

Rapid and Accurate Feedback. Strategic planning makes heavy demands on an agency's capacity to generate up-to-date, reliable information about its operations. Information is needed, Austin suggested, on the nature of the agency's mission; characteristics of the client population; characteristics of the service market and competing agencies; the impact of societal, governmental, economic, and technological factors; and internal management and operating strategies.[31] Although agency managers have made progress in improving the quality and quantity of the information upon which decisions are made, many agencies still lack modern management information systems. Furthermore, as they try to fill this gap, they often come up against what Levine called "the management science paradox."[32] The development of management information systems and the capability to analyze the information they produce is both capital and labor intensive and requires considerable agency resources. Such systems should be initiated when agencies have surplus resources in addition to what's needed for their service programs. However, when resource surpluses do exist, administrators are more likely to invest them in expanded program activities than in management information systems. When budgetary cutbacks occur and the need for strategic planning arises, administrators find themselves both without an information system in place and without the surplus resources needed to develop one.

Budgetary Flexibility. Funding relationships are potentially power relationships, since funders control resources that agencies need and for which there are often no alternative sources. Funders are thus in a position to compel recipients to change their policies and procedures by attaching conditions to the use of funds. For example, the treatment approach of one substance abuse agency used the idea of a therapeutic drug abuse community with a staff composed of individuals whose expertise was derived from their personal experiences with drugs. However, this staff found it difficult to operate under the accountability requirements attached to the agency's funds, and they were gradually replaced by professional social workers, thus changing the original treatment model.[33] As noted in the discussion on tight money, one factor that motivates funders to exercise their power is whether agency programs and philosophies agree with funders' policy concerns. If there is no agreement, funders can demand compliance through their control of the purse strings. This latter situation increasingly characterizes social welfare funding relationships. As funders impose more conditions on the use of funds — particularly in the areas of program efficiency and cost accounting — administrators have less discretion to use funds in the flexible fashion called for in strategic planning.

Incentives for Conserving Resources. The final precondition for the rational conduct of cutback management through strategic planning is the existence of rewards for administrators to save rather than spend, to cut back on operations rather than expand them. Incentives to use resources in the most efficient manner possible are built into most business organizations since their net income or profit is a product's price less what it costs to produce it. The more efficient the production process, the greater the net earnings. Social service and public sector organizations differ from business firms in the way they are paid. The latter receive income from the sale of products, whereas the former are paid out of budget allocations. For many analysts this is *the* difference between public and private organizations. A firm's dependence on market performance creates a close relationship between what it produces and how much it earns. Organizations paid through budgets, on the other hand, receive income from revenue sources that are not tied to what they are doing. This arrangement loosens the connection between how much these organizations earn and what they produce. The connection is further attenuated when what is produced cannot be easily defined or measured, as is the case with most social services. The major implication of this for the present discussion is that "results" in the budget-based institution means a larger budget. "Performance," as Drucker argued, "is the ability to maintain or to increase one's budget."[34]

For the social administrator, bigger is better. Whether public or private, an important determinant of agency status and prestige is size. Similarly, administrators' reputations are shaped by their ability to acquire new resources and expand operations. Rather than viewing declining resources as a constraint requiring a rational and systematic approach to reducing agency operations, many administrators will view it as a challenge to their abilities to capture new resources and preserve existing ones. People who invest their professional energies and reputations in creating and developing programs are unlikely to accept cutbacks without a fight. In a study of 43 agency executives' response to cutbacks, Pawlak and his colleagues found that virtually all viewed cutbacks as a political process.[35] While almost one-fourth of the executives interviewed felt powerless to affect their funding situation, a substantial number saw cutbacks as an opportunity to develop innovative influence strategies with funders in order to protect their fiscal situation.

The likelihood that agency administrators will employ rational strategies like strategic planning to deal with declining resources is dependent on the willingness of individual administrators to accept cutbacks without a fight and on the existence of organizational features that enable them to use those strategies if they are so inclined. The foregoing discussion suggests that neither of these conditions is likely to be met in most social agencies. If anything, the degree of politicization is likely to increase as competition for resources intensifies.

NOTES

1. Aaron Wildavsky, *The Politics of the Budgetary Process*, 3rd ed. (Boston: Little, Brown, 1979), p. 1.
2. Aaron Wildavsky, "Budgeting as a Political Process," in *The International Encyclopedia of the Social Sciences*, vol. II, ed. David L. Sills (New York: Crowell, Collier and Macmillan, 1968), p. 193.
3. Jeffrey Pfeffer and Gerald R. Salancik, "Organizational Decision Making as a Political Process: The Case of a University Budget," *Administrative Science Quarterly*, 19, no. 2 (June 1974), 135–151.
4. Bruce S. Jansson and June Simmons, "Building Departmental or Unit Power within Human Service Organizations: Empirical Findings and Theory Building," *Administration in Social Work*, 8, no. 3 (Fall 1984), 41–56.
5. Leslie L. Roos, Jr., and Roger I. Hall, "Influence Diagrams and Organizational Power," *Administrative Science Quarterly*, 25, no. 1 (March 1980), 57–71.
6. Ibid., 65–66.
7. Mark J. Stern, "The Politics of American Social Welfare," in *Human Services at Risk*, ed. Felice D. Perlmutter (Lexington, Mass.: Lexington Books, 1984), p. 10.
8. Ibid.
9. Jerome T. Murphy, "The Educational Bureaucracies Implement Novel Policy: The Politics of Title I of ESEA, 1965–72," in *Policy and Politics in America: Six Case Studies*, ed. Allan P. Sindler (Boston: Little, Brown, 1973), pp. 160–98.
10. Ibid., p. 196.
11. Ronald Randall, "Presidential Power and Bureaucratic Intransigence: The Influence of the Nixon Administration on Welfare Policy," *American Political Science Review*, 73, no. 3 (September 1979), 802.
12. Martha Derthick, *The Influence of Federal Grants: Public Assistance in Massachusetts* (Cambridge, Mass.: Harvard University Press, 1970), p. 10.
13. Ibid.
14. Ibid., p. 11.
15. Patsy Hashey Lorenz, "The Politics of Fund Raising through Grantsmanship in the Human Services," *Public Administration Review*, 42, no. 3 (May-June 1982), 247.
16. Jean L. Potuchek, "The Context of Social Service Funding: The Funding Relationship," *Social Service Review*, 60, no. 3 (September 1986), 432.
17. Gerald R. Salancik, "The Effectiveness of Ineffective Social Service Systems," in *Organization and the Human Services: Cross-Disciplinary Reflections*, ed. Herman D. Stein (Philadelphia: Temple University Press, 1981), p. 146.
18. Daniel Goleman, "Psychiatry: First Guide to Therapy Is Fiercely Opposed," *The New York Times*, September 23, 1986, p. C1.
19. Salancik, "The Effectiveness of Ineffective Social Services," p. 149.
20. Charles H. Levine, "Organizational Decline and Cutback Management," *Public Administration Review*, 38, no. 4 (July-August 1978), 316–25.
21. Charles H. Levine, "More on Cutback Management: Hard Questions for Hard Times," *Public Administration Review*, 39, no. 2 (March-April 1979), 179–83.
22. Ibid., 180.
23. Charles H. Levine, Irene S. Rubin, and George G. Wolohojian, *The Politics of Retrenchment: How Local Governments Manage Fiscal Stress* (Beverly Hills: Sage Publications, 1981); Larry Hirschhorn et al., *Cutting Back: Retrenchment and Redevelopment in Human and Community Services* (San Francisco: Jossey-Bass, 1983); Michael J. Austin, "Managing Cutbacks in the 1980s," *Social Work*, 29, no. 5 (September-October 1984), 428–34.

24. Richard T. Crow and Charles A. Odewahn, *Management for the Human Services* (Englewood Cliffs, N.J.: Prentice Hall, 1987), pp. 7–8.
25. Levine, Rubin, and Wolohojian, *The Politics of Retrenchment*, pp. 210–13.
26. Michael Fabricant, "The Industrialization of Social Work Practice," *Social Work*, 30, no. 5 (September-October 1985), 389–95.
27. William G. Ouchi and Jerry B. Johnson, "Types of Organizational Control and Their Relationship to Emotional Well Being," *Administrative Science Quarterly*, 23, no. 2 (June 1978), 293–317; Marcia J. Bombyk and Roslyn H. Chernesky, "Conventional Cutback Leadership and the Quality of the Workplace: Is Beta Better?" *Administration in Social Work*, 9, no. 3 (Fall 1985), 47–56.
28. Gerald R. Salancik, Barry M. Staw, and Louis R. Pondy, "Administrative Turnover as a Response to Unmanaged Organizational Interdependence," *Academy of Management Journal*, 23, no. 3 (September 1980), 422–37.
29. David Lowery and Caryl E. Rusbult, "Bureaucratic Responses to Antibureaucratic Administrations: Federal Employee Reaction to the Reagan Election," *Administration & Society*, 18, no. 1 (May 1986), 45–75.
30. Barry Bozeman and E. Allen Slusher, "Scarcity and Environmental Stress in Public Organizations: A Conjectural Essay," *Administration & Society*, 11, no. 3 (November 1979), 348.
31. Austin, "Managing Cutbacks," 430.
32. Levine, "More on Cutback Management."
33. William E. Berg and Roosevelt Wright, "Program Funding as an Organizational Dilemma: Goal Displacement in Social Work Programs," *Administration in Social Work*, 4, no. 4 (Winter 1980), 37.
34. Peter Drucker, "On Managing the Public Service Institution," *The Public Interest*, no. 33 (Fall 1973), 50.
35. Edward S. Pawlak, Charles Jester, and Richard L. Fink, "The Politics of Cutback Management," *Administration in Social Work*, 7, no. 2 (Summer 1983), 1–10.

5

The Politics of People

People tend to think about organizations in abstract terms because many of the terms we have for describing organizations are abstract. Phrases such as goal structure, reward system, and division of labor encourage us to think about organizations as if they were things themselves, independent of the people who make them up. But organizations are collections of people, and to understand why organizations act the way they do, one needs to know the ways in which people are brought into organizations and how they fare from then on. For social agencies this knowledge is crucial because people constitute their technical core. In manufacturing firms, machine technologies play an important role — often, many fear, more important than the people who operate them — and concepts such as sociotechnical system are used to portray these organizations as complex composites of people and machines.[1] By contrast, a social agency's primary technology is the skills, attitudes, and beliefs of its personnel. While social agencies are making more use of machine technologies, particularly computers, it is still the attributes of the people involved in the provision of social services — managers, workers, clients, external stakeholders — that play the determining role in shaping an agency's character and defining its goals.

The purpose of this chapter is to apply a political perspective to personnel practices within social service organizations. Specifically, we will look at the role of politics in the selection of new employees, particularly at upper management levels; the ways in which individual performance is appraised and evaluated; and the treatment of women and minority employees.

THE POLITICS OF SELECTION

The significance of a decision is determined by the ease with which it can be reversed or revised, and how far into the future its effects will last. Personnel decisions, once made, are difficult to unmake, and have long-term consequences. In a university, for instance, the decision to grant tenure is almost impossible to reverse and has consequences that can last for several decades. Although social agencies don't have a formal tenure system, they have something close to it in the form of civil service and union protection. In addition to having legal safeguards, moreover, agency personnel quickly learn the informal strategies for protecting their jobs. The amount of job security is less for positions at or near the top of the organizational hierarchy. Top management positions in both the public and private sector are exempt from civil service or union protection, and incumbents serve at the pleasure of their employers, be they political executives or boards of directors.

The rational approach to personnel selection takes the existence of jobs with different skill requirements as given, and presumes that people have a set of skills that "although potentially changeable over time with training, are fixed at one moment in time, and proceeds from the premise that the task of selection is to match the individuals with the most appropriate or highest level of necessary skills to the jobs...in question."[2] The rational approach is limited, however, in its ability to explain how most jobs are actually filled. In particular, the rational model neglects the fact that job requirements and selection standards reflect organization-wide interests as well as job-level characteristics. The choice of selection standards will result from the interplay of organizational interests and technical work requirements.

The rational model, with its emphasis on the intellectual tasks of finding a correct match between person and position, is most appropriate when only a few members of the organization are involved in the decision (which keeps the number of organizational interests at stake to a minimum) and when the decision is relatively simple in terms of the number of organizational values, beliefs, and procedures affected. The political model, on the other hand, with its emphasis on resolving conflicts over interests and goals, is most appropriate when several organizational members and the interests they represent are involved and when there is disagreement over the values that should be used to guide the decision.

One factor that determines how much politics will enter into selection decisions is the *hierarchical level* of the position involved. Parsons suggested that organizations can be thought of as having three hierarchical levels: institutional, managerial, and technical.[3] The institutional level is concerned with the organization's external relationships with its constituencies and seeks to ensure that the organization receives support in the form of resources and sanction and that its products or services have a market or clientele. The managerial level is responsible for internal administration, and its function is to coordinate the elements of the production process. The technical level is concerned with the actual production of goods or services and seeks to maintain a high level of product or service quality. In a social agency these hierarchical levels translate, respectively, into the positions of executive director, program or unit manager, and line worker.

In general, the higher the level of the position to be filled, the greater the role politics will play in the selection process. People in institutional or executive-level positions are able to shape the values, processes, and goals of the entire organization. Because of the range of the impact of these positions, the interests of every member of the organization are affected. Consequently, when executive positions must be filled, the number of actors in the selection process expands to include all those who, through their own power, the importance of their positions, or the organizational culture regarding participation, have access to those who make the selection decision.

In addition to being a focal point for value and interest conflicts among organizational members, the selection of upper-level personnel is further complicated by the absence of generally agreed upon educational and professional qualifications for these jobs. In fact, the determination of qualifications for the position will be one of the most intensely political phases of the selection process. Each group within the organization will do its best to see that its concerns find their way into the criteria for screening candidates and making a final choice. Those wishing to maintain the status quo will want someone who supports current agency policies and programs, whereas dissident members will be looking for an executive disposed to change. The clinicians will want someone with direct service experience; fiscal people will be looking for someone with legislative and community contacts; the personnel director will stress someone skilled in labor-management negotiations; the office manager will want someone who can computerize the accounting and clerical procedures.

Generally, political activities decrease in the selection of personnel for positions at the managerial and technical levels. The factors that promote politicization — the activation of organizational actors, interests, and values — lessen in intensity. In many instances, however, these factors come into play even when selecting personnel for line positions. Lacking determinate and effective technologies, social agencies develop ideological systems which guide and justify the behavior of their direct service workers.[4] Because of the value-laden nature of social service work, appointments at the lowest hierarchical level can be as politicized as those at the highest. The controversies that surround efforts of gay men to gain or retain employment in social agencies exemplify the conflicts that can be engendered by routine personnel actions.[5]

A second factor associated with the politicization of selection decisions is the existence of *organizational slack*.[6] Slack is the difference between an organization's resources and the demands made on them. When there is a great amount of slack, selection decisions can appear rational because conflicts in organizational interests and values remain dormant. The existence of slack, or surplus resources, allows managers to buy off potential conflicts over personnel decisions. Thus, one agency director in a city experiencing racial tensions was able to deal with the conflicting demands of white and black community groups by appointing co-directors — one white, one black — for each of the agency's major departments. This solution took place, however, at a time (the early 1970s) when social agencies had considerable slack owing to the munificence of federal grants. Reductions in federal social spending during the 1980s has meant that agency administrators have to make more controversial "either/or" personnel decisions, rather than the "both/and" decisions that were possible under the more generous Great Society funding of the 1960s and 1970s. Lacking the budgetary surpluses that allow them to paper over (with that nice green paper bearing the words "Federal Reserve Note") latent organizational conflicts, social work administrators must manage the political problems that arise when organizational factions compete for a decreasing pool of dollars.

A third factor in the politicization of selection decisions is the *amount of time* it takes to make the final choice.[7] The longer a decision remains unresolved, the greater the potential range of issues that are defined as relevant. Similarly, the longer a decision is open, the greater the number of organizational members who become involved in the process. As the number of issues and actors increases, the original decision situation becomes both more complicated and more conflictual. There is, moreover, added incentives for people to organize politically because of what Olsen called the "cumulation effect."

> As people with interests contrary to your own activate themselves, one will be in danger of coming into a relatively deprived situation. Organization tends to call forth organization. If people organize on one side of an issue, their opponents will organize on the other.[8]

The impact of time on the decision process calls attention to the role that deadlines can play in reducing politicization. Agency members interested in keeping potential political issues in a personnel decision to a minimum are advised to push for firm and reasonably short deadlines for the selection process. On the other hand, those who want to see a number of issues and people brought into the fray will seek to make the search process as open ended and extensive as possible.

One of the earliest studies of the politics of selection is Zald's analysis of the choice of a new general secretary (executive director) for the YMCA of Metropolitan Chicago.[9] The author identifies the *mechanism of selection* for choosing among candidates as the key political dynamic in this situation. At the time that the general secretary announced his decision to retire, the organization was deliberating over how much it wanted to change its traditional goal of character development for a relatively well-adjusted middle-class clientele and serve poorer people with a number of social and economic problems. The issue was precipitated by the changing demography of the communities served by the agency as middle-class whites moved to the suburbs and were replaced by lower-class whites and nonwhites. In addition, there were opportunities for program development as a result of new sources of finance available through the federal government's War on Poverty.

The outgoing general secretary, Mr. McClow, had begun a series of innovative efforts aimed at reaching the new groups moving into the area and wanted the agency to continue in that direction. The agency's chief program officer, Mr. Leaf, was McClow's choice for successor. Leaf strongly identified with social welfare and liberal points of view and was viewed as a progressive within the agency. However, the person considered most likely to succeed McClow was Mr. Maddy, the agency's chief business officer. Maddy was generally seen as a defender of the status quo regarding program policy. Although never formally made second-in-command, Maddy thought of himself, and was perceived by others, as McClow's successor. In addition, he had a long association with the more powerful and conservative members of the Board of Directors. Leaf's connection to the board, on the other hand, was limited to a few younger and less influential board members who had been brought on because of their interest in the agency's new programs. Leaf, moreover, did not consider himself a serious candidate for the executive position, whereas Maddy assumed the role of heir apparent.

Although he was not scheduled to retire for over a year, McClow requested that the board nominate a second-in-command with the explicit expectation that that person succeed him upon his retirement. The rationale McClow gave to the board president was that this designation would give his successor a training period for the chief executive's job. In fact, McClow made this proposal when he learned that Leaf had been interviewed for a chief executive's position in another city. McClow wanted a decision made before Leaf took the other job. In addition to structuring the timing of the selection process, McClow requested that an enlarged executive committee of the board meet with the candidates and then make its recommendations to the full board. The procedure in the past had been for the chief executive to directly advise the small executive committee, who then decided. McClow explained this departure from past practices as a means of allowing both a full discussion of the directions the board wanted the organization to take and a full analysis of the candidates. What McClow did not mention, however, was that it would also expose his candidate, Leaf, to a wider range of board members, in addition to the inner circle of the executive committee who were expected to support Maddy.

Finally, the board president asked McClow to draw up a list of areas where the organization needed strengthening; the list was to serve as a basis of discussion. Each candidate was asked to present his views on the future of the agency; the competition it faced from other organizations in qualifying for and earning public support; and the agency's capacity for expanding its services in fields and needs vital to the city. These questions were loaded in favor of Leaf, who clearly emerged as the more far-sighted and forward-looking candidate. The longer the board discussed the issues raised by McClow's list of questions, the more sentiment moved toward Leaf. Leaf was, consequently, selected by the board as McClow's second-in-command and the next chief executive.

The strategic lesson that Zald drew from this case was that, given an initial balance of power against a particular candidate (Mr. Leaf), a social process must be found which disengages the forces supporting one candidate and transfers them to another. When a traditional inner circle is typically involved in major decisions (the board's executive committee), other powers must be mobilized, or a procedure found with which the inner circle agrees but which commits them to a line of action that they might originally have opposed. The decision to expand the size of the executive committee, thus diluting support for Maddy, and to interview the candidates along the lines suggested by McClow's questions concerning the future of the organization, was just such a procedure. These political strategies are especially important, Zald argued,

> when the people who have the most at stake in the succession process cannot directly affect the outcome....In a large-scale organization, the strategy must be to specify the terms of the discussion and who shall participate in the election in such a way as to maximize the opportunities of the normally weaker group.[10]

THE POLITICS OF PERFORMANCE APPRAISALS

The procedures used to evaluate workers' performances and the resulting evaluations are two of the most important considerations in the contemporary world of work. Under the older craft organization of work, the relationship between workers' efforts and outcomes was clear and direct. A craftsperson was responsible for making an entire product, and fluctuations in quantity and quality were directly attributable to the worker's energy and skill. When this system was replaced by the bureaucratic work organization, with its extensive division of labor and fragmentation of the production process, the relationship between individual effort and organizational outcomes became harder to see. One of the commonest complaints of today's worker is, How do I know if what I do makes any difference? This problem is even more pronounced when we go from manufacturing firms, where the outcome is a tangible product, to social agencies, with their intangible services. The bureaucratic structure of the work organization and the elusive nature of service products have made the question of how well social agency employees do their jobs a central management concern. From the employees' point of view, a corollary and equally important issue is the fairness and accuracy of the procedures managers use to assess their performance. As Jaques pointed out, the contemporary work contract is one in which

> the employee agrees to be accountable to the governing body for the quality of his work, and to recognize that if the governing body is not satisfied it is entitled to dispense with his services. The conditions under which this judgment of quality is made, and the safeguards for the employee, are among the most important questions of social justice in industrial societies.[11]

Social work, like engineering and nursing, is an organization-based profession in which the key to career advancement is how well an individual performs in his or her organizational assignment. This contrasts with other professions, such as science and law, where career advancement is determined more by one's standing in the eyes of professional colleagues, most of whom are not members of the employing organization, than by how well one does at a particular organizational assignment. In fact, for the medical profession the organizational connection is even weaker since many physicians are not even employees of the hospitals in which they spend so much of their working lives. But for professions like social work which are tightly linked to an organization, appraisal systems have considerable relevance since they are a key to the recognition and advancement that people seek in their work. Social workers thus have a strong interest in seeing that their efforts are portrayed in ways they think are fair and that they are duly rewarded for their accomplishments. These are the outcomes that a rational system of personnel evaluation seeks to produce. An effective appraisal system should be able to

> (1) describe the major tasks of the position, (2) identify the criteria needed to test the knowledge and skills required to complete those tasks, (3) identify the job relevant attributes of a worker's experience, values, and attitudes, and (4) specify the criteria for performance evaluations.[12]

There are, however, several obstacles to the realization of a rational and objective system of performance appraisals. And the more obstacles there are, the more politics enter into the appraisal process.

One obstacle, the underdeveloped nature of social work technology, has been shown to be an impediment to rationality in a number of areas of social work administration. Social work is a "low paradigm" field with little agreement within the profession about what is proper professional conduct. It contrasts with a "high paradigm" field, such as medicine, in which the members generally agree about correct medical and surgical procedures. A social agency might hire a social worker, for example, who graduated from a social work school where he or she was trained in practice techniques such as behavior modification or cognitive therapy. If this worker is supervised by someone who is an adherent of the ego psychology school of practice, the first performance appraisal session will be more of an arena for competing professional ideologies than an objective assessment of how well the worker is doing his or her job.

When people must make evaluations of another's performance but lack rational, objective tools for doing so, there is a strong likelihood that subjective factors will become the basis for their judgments. In particular, the degree of perceived physical and social similarity between supervisor and subordinate has important consequences for whether or not the subordinate receives a positive evaluation. Pulakos and Wexley showed that subordinates whom supervisors perceive as similar to them are more likely to receive positive evaluations than those perceived as dissimilar. Moreover, there were indications that when managers perceived subordinates as dissimilar, they were less likely to "exhibit behaviors that enhance their subordinate's feelings of worth and that facilitate the subordinate's ability to achieve work goals."[13] The political lesson to be drawn from this situation is known to anybody who's been in a social agency longer than six months: you may not be able to pick your relatives, but you should do your best to pick your bosses. Like defense attorneys who try to get their clients before a sympathetic judge, social workers know that having a like-minded supervisor is three-quarters of the way to a positive evaluation.

A rational approach to performance appraisal assumes a high degree of goal consensus between supervisor and subordinate. The outcomes that supervisors expect their workers to achieve should be the same as the purposes that guide the worker's activities. There is evidence, however, that social agency supervisors and workers are increasingly experiencing goal conflicts. As funds become scarcer and the fiscal controls that funders attach to existing funds increase, social work administrators are likely to become more responsive to the wishes, aims, and needs of external resource controllers than to those of their own staff and clients. When the concerns of upper-level managers become those of improving the agency's ability to function in a business-like manner, the emphasis in agency policy moves from service issues (adequacy, effectiveness, timeliness) to fiscal ones (cost effectiveness, rationalized reporting and monitoring systems). Supervisors are responsible for translating broad agency policies into specific tasks for line workers to perform and for developing criteria for evaluating worker performance in accomplishing those tasks. Supervisors have some latitude, however, in the manner in which they convey the desires of top managers to operating staff. As Bunker and Wijnberg suggested, supervisors

> may passively adopt prevailing patterns with respect to formal control of activities…[and] the distribution of rewards and punishments…[They] may actively and enthusiastically either enforce central control or foster independent, mutually adjustive behavior. They may become buffers and employee

advocates when they sense the larger organization presents features inimical to group performance and morale or they may augment sparse signals from other sources when they sense employee needs for goal clarity, lateral coordination, or process definition.[14]

Weatherley and his colleagues studied one large public social service organization whose policies stressed fiscal accountability and management control of program operations.[15] The agency's upper-level managers were drawn primarily from the business sector. Eighty percent of the supervisors said that they often had to implement procedures that were unrealistic or contrary to their professional values. Over 30 percent of these supervisors described themselves as advocates for staff, compared to 12.5 percent who saw themselves as advocates for management. On the other hand, "85 percent of the supervisors agreed that they were viewed by others, subordinate and superiors alike, as part of management."[16] Both supervisors and workers saw themselves as having little to say about agency policies and procedures. On a 10-point scale, with 1 signifying no involvement, the workers' average rating was 2.63, and the supervisors' average was, at 2.95, only slightly higher. The majority of supervisors saw their primary responsibility as monitoring staffs' compliance with agency policies, and the staff "saw themselves as beleaguered at the bottom of a large insensitive bureaucracy concerned more about accountability to taxpayers than services to clients."[17]

The alienation and disaffection of middle-level and line staff from agency policies and goals can give rise to what Perry and Barney called "performance lies."[18] There are, they suggested, at least two explanations for why people lie. The first, a moralistic one, assumes that "a man lies as little as he can when he lies as little as he can, not when he is given the smallest opportunity to lie."[19] An alternative view, what Perry and Barney called the structural theory of lying, is derived from the legal concept of entrapment. Entrapment involves inciting crimes that otherwise would not have been committed. Implicit in this is the assumption that

> circumstances can be created that make it very difficult for an individual or a group to refrain from committing a crime. When authorities create such conditions, those who commit crimes should not be held responsible. Applying the same logic to dishonesty in organizations suggests that situational circumstances may exist that make it very difficult to avoid telling performance lies or maintaining the lies that have been told by others.[20]

The authors offered the following explanation of how performance lies are generated within a hypothetical corporation. This company is run by financial executives who have no feel for the business's products or the ways in which they are produced. For them, the bottom line is all that counts. They manage the bottom line to produce a desired profit and then order division executives to produce their share — or else! With four hierarchical levels, performance expectations are set at Level IV by top management and then are communicated downward, contributing to the performance expectations of Level III and Level II managers. In evaluations of managers at all levels, actual performance is compared with expected performance. Lower-level evaluations contribute to higher-level evaluations. That is, when Level II managers give their subordinates high evaluations, they increase the likelihood that they themselves will be evaluated highly. And so on, up and down the line. Moreover,

> because lower-level evaluations contribute to higher-level evaluations, a performance lie benefits both the teller and the receiver — and in turn, the receiver's receiver....For this reason, managers at all levels have a clear self-interest in maintaining a performance lie.[21]

In all hierarchical organizations, lower-level managers have the power to administer performance policy, but not to make it. This situation frequently creates two groups — those with and those without the discretion to set organizational performance goals. A principal function of the performance lie is to set up a barrier that insulates the managers lacking the power to set performance expectations from the control of top management. The less powerful managers

> form a network of informal alliances that are held together by the benefits accruing from the lie and the potential negative consequences that would occur if the lie were discovered. We...call this network of informal alliances the *coalition to effect and preserve the organizational performance lie*.[22]

The organizational dynamics promoting performance lies were demonstrated in the authors' case study of a family service organization (FSO). The FSO had a highly centralized management system with five administrative levels between the executive director and line workers. Policy for the entire organization was set by the executive and the board of directors and executed by lower-level administrators. The authors studied the agency's home visiting policy: every member family was to be visited at home at least once a month; all home visits were to be made by two-person home visiting teams; and no more than five families were to be assigned to each home visiting team. From the outset these goals were unrealistic because they did not take into consideration long travel distances and the limited number of qualified home visitors. The discrepancy between the expected performances and the resources available to branch managers created incentives for telling performance lies. The branch in the case study used several lies to bolster performance reports.

> First, it increased the number of home visitors by splitting up the two-person teams; second, more than five families were assigned to each home visitor; and

third, letters sent to marginally involved member families were reported to the district manager as home visits.[23]

Additional incentives to tell performance lies were provided by the reporting system used to monitor home visits. Information concerning home visits was conveyed by the branch manager to the district manager through a single statistic — the percentage of families in the branch that were home-visited monthly. No questions were asked about the statistic's source or its validity.

> If the statistic communicated to the district manager was high, compared with that of other branches, the...branch manager was duly commended. However, if the statistic was comparably low, the...branch manager was criticized by the district manager in front of his peers at a monthly meeting. Moreover, each time the...branch manager reported an acceptable percentage of families home-visited, the district manager raised his performance expectations.[24]

Similar practices were found by Weatherley and his colleagues in their study of a public social service organization. As one child service worker put it:

> CPS workers do not accept the agency rules and norms as legitimate. Their compliance and conformity is to the extent required to avoid being fired. They have developed their own set of rules.[25]

One ingenious device that these workers developed was the "bootleg form." They used whiteout, rulers, and the photocopier to invent new forms which deviated from the forms prescribed by agency policy but which they saw as more suitable to their work. Workers were aware that the use of these unsanctioned forms undermined management control and stood in the way of uniform service delivery. Yet workers justified the unofficial forms "as more realistic and relevant to their immediate needs than those passed down from above which, from the workers' point of view, are not designed to facilitate the day-to-day management of work at the front line."[26]

The politics of performance appraisals has its roots in the difficulty managers have in evaluating the work of subordinates when the technology that underlies that work is both diffuse and contested by experts in the field. Also influential are the efforts of lower-level managers and line workers to have their professional and occupational interests reflected in the policies that direct their work. The first situation gives rise to a politics of impression management in which, lacking clear technical guidelines with which to evaluate worker performance, judgments are made subjectively on the basis of the degree of similarity of supervisor and subordinate. The second situation points to the existence of substantive conflicts of interests between upper-level administrators responsive to fiscal-minded funding bodies and line workers and their supervisors who resist what they see as unrealistic or illegitimate policies and program practices.

THE POLITICS OF GENDER AND RACE

The past decades have been a time of rising expectations for women and minorities in the United States. Beginning with the U.S. Supreme Court's 1954 decision prohibiting segregation in public schools, a number of laws have been passed which seek to end discrimination, whatever its basis. At first limited to *preventing* discrimination, whether at the voting polls, in schools, or in the work place, legislation has adopted a more active posture of *promoting* fair treatment through the policy of affirmative action. These laws were stimulated in large part by the liberation movements of the 1960s and 1970s, and the growth of grassroots and national organizations to combat racism and sexism. Although these organizations initially concentrated on civil and political rights, emphasis has shifted to economic concerns, and their primary focus today is access to jobs for women and minorities, and fair treatment in the work place.

Affirmative action policies and practices experienced a number of reversals in the 1980s because of the Reagan administration's opposition to governmental interference in the marketplace. Although there have been setbacks, the movement to promote fair treatment in the work place continues, despite the absence of vigorous federal support. Within social work, there has been a concerted effort — particularly by women — to open upper-level administrative positions to other than white males. Although women make up nearly three-fourths of the membership of the National Association of Social Workers (NASW), less than 18 percent list administration as their primary occupational role. Men, who make up 27 percent of the membership, are twice as likely as women to be in administrative positions, with 37 percent giving administration as their primary job.[27] Ironically, women are less likely to be social work administrators now than 30 years ago. A survey of social agencies showed that in 1976 only 16 percent were directed by women, compared to 44 percent in the 1950s; during this period men had replaced women in administrative positions at the rate of 2 percent a year.[28]

Racial and ethnic minorities make up 11.5 percent of the total NASW membership. Current statistics on the percentage of minority social workers in administrative positions are not available. Studies of minority employment in the federal government show that minorities in social service–oriented federal agencies occupy administrative positions at a rate equal to or greater than their proportion of the work force.[29] For black social workers, however, the situation is worsened by the fact that there are relatively fewer black social workers than other minorities, compared to their proportion of the general population. In 1982, 5.8 percent of the membership of NASW was black (down from 6.9 percent in 1972), representing less than half the percentage of blacks in the general population. When one considers the high percentage of racial and ethnic minorities who make up the clientele of social service organizations, the small number of black and other minority administrators becomes even more problematic.[30]

The problems facing women and minorities as social work administrators are both gross and subtle. The gross problems include basic issues such as the number of women and minorities in administrative positions and whether or not overt discrimination takes place in hiring practices. As affirmative action laws and practices have become institutionalized, blatantly discriminatory hiring practices have been reduced. Today, women and minorities represent a higher proportion of employees in fields traditionally dominated by white males than they did 15 years ago. For example, in 1972 women constituted 3.6 percent of craft workers and 9.1 percent of engineers; by 1981 those percentages had increased to 6.3 and 18.8, respectively. In 1972 blacks and other minorities constituted 4.3 percent of computer specialists and 3.4 percent of engineers; by 1981 these percentages had increased to 9.9 and 7.3, respectively.[31] Between 1977 and 1982 the proportion of minority managers in all fields rose from 3.6 percent to 5.2 percent. In 1982, 4.3 percent of all officials and managers were black (including 1.6 percent black females), and 20.4 percent were white females.[32] The number of female managers in public welfare is estimated at 40 percent, although most of them are in entry- and middle-level positions, with few women holding top-level positions.[33]

Yet, even as access to employment improves for nontraditional employees (that is, people who have not occupied high-status, high-paying positions in the past), new problems have emerged which are subtler and harder to detect. These problems include the ways in which women and minorities are evaluated and paid, the organizational climate within which they work, and their opportunities for career advancement. It is in these areas, moreover, that organizational politics play an important role.

Your Facts or Mine?

One of the more ironical findings to emerge from research on women and minorities in organizations is the tendency of these individuals to deny the existence of unfair employment practices *in reference to themselves.* While recognizing that women and minorities as a group are often treated unfairly in terms of salaries, promotions, and the like, individual women and minorities frequently report that they are fairly treated on the job. A cross-sectional study of the U.S. labor force, for example, showed that 95 percent of female workers were discriminated against in pay, but only 8 percent perceived any discrimination.[34] In a survey of the attitudes of a sample of employed men and women in a Boston suburb, Crosby asked, "In view of your training and abilities, is your present job as good as it ought to be?" Men and women did not differ from each other on any of the measures used. On a grievance scale ranging from 1 (very gratified) to 30 (very aggrieved), the men in the sample scored 9.43 (on average), and the women 8.94.[35]

The gap between the objective situation of women and minorities in the work place and their subjective experience of it can be explained, in part, by the social-psychological processes of identification with the oppressor and the need to reduce cognitive dissonance. The first phenomenon refers to the tendency of minority members to accommodate to majority opinions by internalizing the dominant group's negative image of themselves. Kanter referred to this tendency as "role entrapment," a process by which women employees accept the stereotypical images ("mother," "seductress," "pet") projected onto them by men.[36] With a devalued self-image, female and minority managers are apt to have lower expectations about their jobs than their co-workers and to evaluate their own positions as positive, even though they may be objectively worse off compared to their white male counterparts.

Reducing cognitive dissonance, Crosby argued, stems from people's need to believe in a just world.[37] For many people, the idea that they are paid less than others for the same work, or are systematically overlooked for promotions even though their qualifications are equal to or superior to those who are promoted, is an unacceptable one. Even though a female manager knows that women's pay, on average, is less than 60 percent of men's, or that the higher one goes in the organizational hierarchy, the fewer the number of females and nonwhites, a variety of psychological defenses are used to prevent applying that knowledge to one's own situation. People rationalize, justify, and systematically ignore certain facts in order to suppress awareness of a gap in their belief in a fair and equitable world and the actual circumstances of their own jobs.

Because of the role that these psychological processes play in retarding the progress of women and minorities in managerial careers, a great deal of emphasis has been placed on consciousness raising and support groups.[38] This strategy has begun to pay off as women and minorities show greater awareness of their disadvantaged occupational situations and have increased the stridency of their demands for fair treatment. But psychological defense mechanisms and false consciousness are not the only obstacles to understanding how well or poorly women and minorities fare in organizations. There are structural features of organizational life, particularly the ways in which information is gathered and disseminated, that can either promote greater awareness of the occupational situation of women and minorities or create bureaucratic smokescreens that make this knowledge difficult to come by. In short, there is a "politics of information" that can be used to help or harm nontraditional employees.

The data in Table 5-1 were developed by Crosby to portray personnel features of a hypothetical organization. In each of the ten departments male and female managers have been selected as representative cases. Does discrimination exist in this organization? Most employees tend to have bits and pieces of information about their organizations; very few, particularly those at lower levels, have access to the kind of comprehensive data presented in Table 5-1. They have information about other individuals, but not about all individuals as a group. A female manager in Department E, for example, will have information about her male counterpart and may know something about

TABLE 5-1. Managerial Characteristics (Hypothetical) By Gender.

FEMALE MANAGERS

Department	Level	Seniority	Education	Motivation	Salary ($)
A	14	25	BA	3	30,000
B	13	20	BA(+)	2	14,000
C	13	20	BA	3	30,000
D	13	20	BA	3	28,000
E	12	15	BA	2	24,000
F	12	15	Some College	1	20,000
G	10	5	Graduate Degree	1	20,000
H	10	2	Some College	1	17,000
I	9	5	BA	2	12,000
J	10	2	BA	3	11,000

Note: Levels 8–14 are middle management; seniority means years with the company. Education can be some high school, some college, bachelor's degree (BA), some graduate work (BA+), and graduate degree. Motivation ratings are 1 = adequate; 2 = good; 3 = excellent.

Source: Faye Crosby, "The Denial of Personal Discrimination," *American Behavioral Scientist*, 27, no. 3 (January/February 1984): 379, copyright 1984 by Sage Publications. Reprinted by permission of Sage Publications, Inc.

the characteristics of managers in Departments D and F. But that will probably be the extent of her knowledge. Even if one had all the information presented in the table, it would still be difficult to tell whether discrimination exists. Department J, for example, has the largest salary discrepancy, but education may be critical to the work of that department.

However, if these data are presented in an aggregated format, where one can compare *group averages* rather than *individual characteristics*, the existence of discrimination becomes apparent. The average job level is 11.6 for female managers and 11.8 for male managers. The females average 12.9 years with the company; the males, 12.5. Educational levels are equivalent. Using a scale where a high school education equals 1 point, some college equals 2, and so forth, the average female educational level is 3.1, and the average male level is 3.2. Average motivational ratings come to 2.3 and 2.0 for females and males, respectively. Males, however, earn an average of $25,800 per year, while females earn $20,900. "Many small differences do discrimination make!"[39]

By contrast, Stewart and Gudykunst found that after controlling for length of tenure, age, and years of education, the females in the organization they studied received more promotions than males.[40] This information, by itself, leads one to conclude that the organization not only did not discriminate against women, but gave them preferential treatment. However,

MALE MANAGERS					
Department	Level	Seniority	Education	Motivation	Salary ($)
A	13	25	Graduate Degree	2	35,000
B	9	20	High School	1	10,000
C	13	20	High School	3	30,000
D	13	20	BA(+)	2	30,000
E	13	20	BA	3	35,000
F	13	10	Graduate Degree	3	32,000
G	9	5	High School	1	16,000
H	11	2	Graduate Degree	2	28,000
I	10	2	Some College	1	13,000
J	14	1	Graduate Degree	2	29,000

when the number of promotions was correlated with an individual's level in the organizational hierarchy, there was no correlation (.03) for women and a positive one (.41) for men. Women received more promotions but did not advance as far in the hierarchy as their male counterparts, a phenomenon referred to as "pacification by promotion." When men were promoted, they advanced upward in the hierarchy; similar advancement did not occur for women. This same pattern was identified by Knapman for women in family service agencies. Fewer female social workers "were hired initially at the supervisory level, females were promoted at a slower rate than males, and there is a significant relationship between sex and position level."[41]

The way that information is presented in an organization shapes perceptions of whether or not employees are treated fairly. The upper-level managers of an organization, moreover, determine how information is disseminated. In Gunnar Myrdal's words, "unfortunate facts are usually more difficult to observe and ascertain, as so many of the persons in control have strong interests in hiding them." A first step for women and minorities seeking to change organizational practices that they perceive as discriminatory is to acquire information that allows them to *compare* their situation with that of others. This is no easy task, for "comparing one's situation with that of other women and men...breaks taboos."[42] Comparisons can, however, form an important data base. Administrators are not the only ones capable of accumulating comparative data. Women and minorities themselves should begin to look for gender, racial, and ethnic patterns in the distribution of requirements and rewards within their organizations.

Is More Better? The Politics of Numbers

Even though the percentage of women and minorities in managerial positions increased during the 1980s, their absolute numbers are still small. Most female managers, and practically all black and Hispanic managers, are likely to be one of a few others of their gender, race, or ethnicity — or the only one — in a managerial position in their unit. In the case of smaller agencies, there may be only one female or minority administrator in the entire organization. Beginning with the work of Kanter, there have been a number of inquiries into the effects of "tokenism" — being in a category of one or a few in an organization — on the well-being and careers of female and minority managers.[43]

Group composition plays an important role in shaping how the members perceive and interact with each other. Tokenism occurs in "skewed" groups, which Kanter defined as groups with a preponderance of one type or another, up to a ratio of about 85:15. The more numerous types

> control the group and its culture in enough ways to be labeled "dominants." The few of another type in a skewed group can appropriately be called "tokens," because they are often treated as representatives of their category, as symbols rather than individuals. If the absolute size of the skewed group is small, tokens can also be solitary individuals or "solos," the only one of their kind present.[44]

The skewed group characterizes the situation of female and minority managers in most social agencies. Although antidiscriminatory policies and practices have improved the representation of these groups in managerial positions, they are still likely to constitute a very small proportion of an agency's total management. This will be especially true when we move beyond first-line supervisors into unit and agency-wide management positions. Research on the impact of token status on managerial careers and the questions that have been subsequently raised have given rise to a "politics of numbers."

Kanter delineated the negative effects of token status on people's ability to function in their jobs and to progress in managerial careers. Tokenism, she argued, generates three processes that operate to the disadvantage of female and minority managers: *visibility, polarization,* and *assimilation.* Tokens have higher visibility because they stand out from the rest of the group. They consequently have a larger "awareness share" since, by making up a smaller numerical proportion of the group, "they potentially capture a *larger* share of the group members' awareness."[45] Polarization produces an exaggeration of differences between dominants and tokens, as well as a heightening of commonalities among dominants. Assimilation involves the use of stereotypes about a person's social type. Tokens find it difficult or impossible to individuate themselves and their special attributes as they are assimilated into the stereotypical roles expected by dominants. These processes interact to form a vicious circle of negative influences on the token manager.

> Visibility generates performance pressures, polarization generates group-boundary heightening, and assimilation generates role entrapment. All of the phenomena...are exaggerated ones: the token stands out vividly, group culture is dramatized, boundaries become highlighted, and token roles are larger-than-life caricatures.[46]

Kravetz and Austin's survey of women in middle-management positions in traditional and alternative social service agencies highlighted the performance pressure experienced by women administrators.[47] The women in their study reported that they had to do more than their male counterparts in order to get equal consideration. One women stated that it takes

> an extra something — a great deal of time and energy for women to get fair consideration for an administrative job. She has to do more than a man would; women's opinions and influence are less valued and they have to work harder....[48]

Similarly, Bush found that black and Chicano social work managers were expected to be more self-reliant and their behavior was "under constant scrutiny with less support than is needed or given to their Anglo-American counterpart."[49]

Ruble and his colleagues found that the tendency to use stereotypes when evaluating the work of female managers was greatest when definitions of quality were subjective or ambiguous.[50] This tendency is particularly relevant to social agencies, given the highly subjective and normative nature of much of the work of managers and direct service providers. When objective information was available, performance evaluations often failed to show bias or were biased in favor of females performing well in masculine activities. Favorable performance evaluations of women, however, did not necessarily lead to favorable evaluations of long-term potential or general ability. Male successes were attributed to stable personal attributes such as ability, whereas female successes were attributed to unstable causes such as effort or luck.

> [I]f males are expected to be competent, their successes are consistent with expectations and are therefore attributed to something stable about them....In contrast, if a woman is expected to do poorly on a masculine task, her success is attributed to a temporary cause, such as unusual effort, thereby maintaining a low expectation about her future performance.[51]

In a survey of public welfare managers' perceptions of whether women possessed the necessary skills, characteristics, and motivation required for management positions, Ezell and her colleagues found that positive attitudes toward women as managers were associated with a respondent's previous experience with female managers.[52] Specifically, respondents who had been supervised by a woman at some point in their career held more positive views of the managerial skills, abilities, and motivations of women as managers. Similarly, managers with social work educational backgrounds also had more positive responses toward women as managers. This perception can be attributed to their having had previous experiences with women in positions of authority as professors and school administrators. These findings, the authors concluded, suggest that "'early' exposure to women in positions of responsibility may lead to greater reduction in stereotypical attitudes regarding the ability of women to function in leadership positions."[53]

These studies show the importance of increasing the exposure of white males to female and minority administrators as a means of combating the negative effects of tokenism. Other organizational factors, however, operate to keep female and minority administrators from the dominant white male group and from mainstream administrative activities. In business organizations, for example, black managers are often channeled into what Jones called "The Relations": community relations, industrial relations, public relations, and personnel relations.

> The higher you go, the greater the acceptance of blacks for limited purposes, such as for all those programs that reach out to communities for various projects, the velvet ghetto jobs. And you become an expert on blacks. At my company, if an issue has anything to do with blacks, they come and ask me.[54]

Rich identified a similar process operating with black administrators in community mental health agencies.[55] Black managers often seek these jobs to make agency activities more relevant to black communities and to deal more appropriately with the stresses that make black community residents so vulnerable to mental illness. Once hired, however, the black administrator finds that his or her *real* job is to serve as "'fireman or lightning rod' to absorb flack from the black community demanding services."[56] In their survey of female social agency administrators, Kravetz and Austin found that women were regularly excluded from male-dominated informal networks.

> It was noted frequently that top male administrators went out socially together, for drinks, for lunch, for sporting activities, and that women in management were generally excluded: "It's hard to be 'one of the boys' when you're not 'one of the boys.'" All-male social events were seen as arenas where major decisions were made.[57]

In addition to overt actions to manipulate the assignments of female and minority managers and exclude them from male-dominated informal networks, there are subtle, structural features that operate to disadvantage non-traditional managers. One of the more important is the nature of career ladders within organizations. Career ladders, or occupational chains, refer to the number of hierarchical levels within an organization that are encompassed within one job title. Smith, for example, studied a state civil service system that had 21 job levels, with each level differing in salary, authority, and the degree of responsibility required by the employee.[58] Level 11 was the lowest managerial level, and the percentage of jobs in a chain at levels 11 to 21 indicated the advancement potential for that chain. A "high opportunity chain" was one in which more than 5 percent of the jobs were at or above level 11. Not surprisingly, job chains in the high opportunity categories

> were predominantly male, with men holding 72.4 percent of all jobs in that category; low opportunity chains were predominantly female, with men holding only 27.4 of those jobs. Two theoretically possible categories (high female, high opportunity and low male, low opportunity) were not found in the occupations selected for study.[59]

Of particular relevance to social work is the fact that the low opportunity chains included the only two social work titles in the study, clinical social worker and public welfare worker. The high opportunity chains included administrative analyst, management system analyst, and computer programmer.

This last finding points to one of the criticisms made of the tokenism argument. Several analysts contend that the reason female and minority managers are discriminated against is not because of their low numbers within organizations, but because of institutionalized attitudes of sexism and racism. Pfeffer and Davis-Blake, for example, argued that if proportions count, the higher the number of women or minorities in an occupational category, the better off they should be.[60] In their study of the salaries of female college administrators, however, they found that this was not true. They expected to find that, because of increased power, diminished stereotyping, and more favorable interaction patterns, increasing proportions of women would reduce wage discrimination against women. Instead, they found no evidence at any level that increases in the proportion of women positively affected the economic well-being of women in administrative structures. They concluded that

> there is a point at which work becomes defined as women's work....Increasing proportions of women lower salaries for both men and women; at the same time, a lower salary level leads to a higher proportion of women working in organizations....[61]

Another criticism of the tokenism theory is that the effects are not the same when men are token or solo members of a group. Crocker and McGraw conducted an experiment with undergraduates that sought to test the effects of tokenism when the token group members were male as well as female.[62] They found that solo-status females never perceived themselves to be group leaders, whereas solo-status males did so 30 percent of the time. Group members were more satisfied with the group composition when the group contained a solo male than when it contained a solo female. Males were perceived to be most masculine when they had solo status, whereas females were perceived to be least feminine when they had solo status. This study adds weight to the argument that it is women (and, by extension, minorities) *as* women who are discriminated against and that changes in the proportions of women in an organization will not change the situation.

In the views of most analysts, however, the evidence favors the tokenism argument.[63] The conclusion generally drawn by those concerned about women and minorities in social work administration (and administration in general) is that *numbers count.* Increasing the number of females and minorities in management positions is not the only avenue for creating more equitable practices in the work place. Other strategies include flex time, reevaluating career ladders in female-dominated occupations, and educating majority groups about the special needs of minority administrators and employees.[64] Most research, however, suggests that these other strategies, by themselves, will not work unless gender, racial, and ethnic heterogeneity in work groups is maximized.

Social science research aside, the opening up of more and better employment and advancement opportunities is a central goal of advocates for women and minority interests. The political strategies used by these groups to advance their interests involve activities within and outside social service organizations. Women's and minority's caucuses are becoming commonplace in social agencies. These informal groups or formally constituted employee associations provide information, career strategizing, job-related feedback, confirmation, emotional support, personal feedback, and friendship. In addition, the groups lobby on behalf of female and minority candidates for positions within the organization. Activities outside of the agency include the creation of special interest advocacy associations, such as the National Association of Black Social Workers, as well as university-based think tanks, such as the Center for Women in Government at the State University of New York at Albany. Through a combination of direct political lobbying, research on issues relevant to women and minorities, education, and training, these organizations seek to redress the grievances of female and minority employees. Their strategies include improving the number of female and minority individuals in upper-level positions, as well as addressing the structural causes of job inequities such as limited career ladders, pay inequities, and biased hiring and promotion criteria. Research and analysis are important to the effectiveness of these groups, but their ultimate success depends on their political skills in organizing and mobilizing their constituencies.

NOTES

1. F. E. Emery and E. L. Trist, "Socio-technical Systems," in *Management Science, Models and Techniques*, vol. 2, ed. C. W. Churchman and M. Verhulst (London: Pergamon, 1960), pp. 83–97.
2. Yinon Cohen and Jeffrey Pfeffer, "Organizational Hiring Standards," *Administrative Science Quarterly*, 31, no. 1 (March 1986), 1–2.

3. Talcott Parsons, *Structure and Process in Modern Societies* (Glencoe, Ill.: The Free Press, 1960).
4. Rosemary C. Sarri and Yeheskel Hasenfeld, "The Management of Human Services — A Challenging Opportunity," in *The Management of Human Services*, ed. Rosemary C. Sarri and Yeheskel Hasenfeld (New York: Columbia University Press, 1978), pp. 4–5.
5. Raymond Berger and James J. Kelley, "Do Social Work Agencies Discriminate against Homosexual Job Applicants?" *Social Work*, 26, no. 3 (May 1981), 193–98.
6. Johan P. Olsen, "Choice in Organized Anarchy," in *Ambiguity and Choice in Organizations*, ed. James G. March and Johan P. Olsen (Oslo: Universitetsforlaget, 1976), pp. 87–88.
7. Ibid., 86.
8. Ibid.
9. Mayer N. Zald, "Who Shall Rule? A Political Analysis of Succession in a Large Welfare Organization," *Pacific Sociological Review*, 8, no. 1 (Spring 1965), 52–60; Mayer N. Zald, *Organizational Change: The Political Economy of the YMCA* (Chicago: University of Chicago Press, 1970), pp. 178–90.
10. Zald, "Who Shall Rule?" 60.
11. Elliott Jaques, *A General Theory of Bureaucracy* (New York: Halsted Press, 1976), p. 55.
12. Peter J. Pecora and Michael J. Austin, "Declassification of Social Service Jobs: Issues and Strategies," *Social Work*, 28, no. 6 (November-December 1983), 425.
13. Elaine D. Pulakos and Kenneth N. Wexley, "The Relationship among Perceptual Similarity, Sex, and Performance Ratings in Manager-Subordinate Dyads," *Academy of Management Journal*, 26, no. 1 (March 1983), 137.
14. Douglas R. Bunker and Marion Wijnberg, "The Supervisor as Mediator of Organizational Climate in Public Social Service Organizations," *Administration in Social Work*, 9, no. 2 (Summer 1985), 62.
15. Richard Weatherley et al., "Accountability of Social Service Workers at the Front Line," *Social Service Review*, 54, no. 4 (December 1980), 556–71.
16. Ibid., 565.
17. Ibid., 568.
18. Lee T. Perry and Jay B. Barney, "Performance Lies Are Hazardous to Organizational Health," *Organizational Dynamics*, 9, no. 3 (Winter 1981), 68–80.
19. Ibid., 69.
20. Ibid.
21. Ibid., 70.
22. Ibid., 70–71 (emphases in original).
23. Ibid., 73.
24. Ibid., 76–77.
25. Weatherley et al., "Accountability," 568.
26. Ibid., 569.
27. David Fanshel, "Status Differentials: Men and Women in Social Work," *Social Work*, 21, no. 6 (November 1976), 448–54; "Membership Survey Shows Practice Shifts," *NASW News*, 28, no. 10 (November 1983), 6–7.
28. Toba Schwaber Kerson and Leslie B. Alexander, "Strategies for Success: Women in Social Service Administration," *Administration in Social Work*, 3, no. 3 (Fall 1979), 313–26.
29. Adam Herbert, "The Minority Administrator: Problems, Prospects, and Challenges," *Public Administration Review*, 34, no. 6 (November-December 1974), 556–74.
30. Felice Davidson Perlmutter and Leslie B. Alexander, "Exposing the Coercive Consensus: Racism and Sexism in Social Work," in *The Management of Human*

Services, ed. Rosemary C. Sarri and Yeheskel Hasenfeld (New York: Columbia University Press, 1978), pp. 207–31.

31. Jennifer Crocker, "Introduction — After Affirmative Action: Barriers to Occupational Advancement for Women and Minorities," *American Behavioral Scientist*, 27, no. 3 (January-February 1984), 285–86.

32. Edward W. Jones, Jr., "Black Managers: The Dream Deferred," *Harvard Business Review*, 64, no. 3 (May-June 1986), 84–93.

33. Office of Personnel Management, *EEO Statistical Report on Employment in State and Local Government* (Washington, D.C.: Office of Personnel Management, 1977).

34. Charles N. Weaver, "Sex Differences in the Determinants of Job Satisfaction," *Academy of Management Journal*, 21, no. 2 (June 1978), 265–74.

35. Faye Crosby, "The Denial of Personal Discrimination," *American Behavioral Scientist*, 27, no. 3 (January-February 1984), 372.

36. Rosabeth Moss Kanter, "Some Effects of Proportions on Group Life: Skewed Sex Ratios and Responses to Token Women," *American Journal of Sociology*, 82, no. 5 (March 1977), 965–90.

37. Crosby, "The Denial of Personal Discrimination."

38. Marie Weil, "Preparing Women for Administration: A Self-Directed Learning Model," *Administration in Social Work*, 7, nos. 3/4 (Fall-Winter 1983), 117–32; Kathy E. Kram and Lynn A. Isabella, "Mentoring Alternatives: The Role of Peer Relationships in Career Development," *Academy of Management Journal*, 28, no. 1 (March 1985), 110–32.

39. Crosby, "The Denial of Personal Discrimination," 378.

40. Lee P. Stewart and William B. Gudykunst, "Differential Factors Influencing the Hierarchical Level and Number of Promotions of Males and Females within an Organization," *Academy of Management Journal*, 25, no. 3 (September 1982), 586–97.

41. Shirley Kuehnle Knapman, "Sex Discrimination in Family Agencies," *Social Work*, 22, no. 6 (November 1977), 463.

42. Crosby, "The Denial of Personal Discrimination," 383.

43. Kanter, "Some Effects of Proportions"; Rosabeth Moss Kanter, *Men and Women of the Corporation* (New York: Basic Books, 1977).

44. Kanter, "Some Effects of Proportions," 966.

45. Ibid., 971 (emphases in original).

46. Ibid., 985.

47. Diane Kravetz and Carol B. Austin, "Women's Issues in Social Administration: The Views and Experiences of Women Administrators," *Administration in Social Work*, 8, no. 4 (Winter 1984), 25–38.

48. Ibid., 28.

49. James A. Bush, "The Minority Administrator: Implications for Social Work Education," *Journal of Education for Social Work*, 13, no. 1 (Winter 1977), 21.

50. Thomas L. Ruble, Renae Cohen, and Diane N. Ruble, "Sex Stereotypes: Occupational Barriers for Women," *American Behavioral Scientist*, 27, no. 3 (January-February 1984), 339–56.

51. Ibid., 350–51.

52. Hazel Ezell, Charles A. Odewahn, and J. Daniel Sherman, "Women Entering Management: Differences in Perceptions of Factors Influencing Integration," *Group & Organization Studies*, 7, no. 2 (June 1982), 243–53.

53. Ibid., 251.

54. Jones, "Black Managers," 89.

55. Wilber Rich, "Special Role and Role Expectations of Black Administrators of Neighborhood Mental Health Programs," *Community Mental Health Journal*, 11, no. 4 (Winter 1975), 394–401.

56. Ibid., 395.

57. Kravetz and Austin, "Women's Issues," 32.
58. Catherine Begnoche Smith, "Influence of Internal Opportunity Structure and Sex of Worker on Turnover Patterns," *Administrative Science Quarterly*, 24, no. 3 (September 1979), 362–81.
59. Ibid., 369.
60. Jeffrey Pfeffer and Alison Davis-Blake, "The Effect of the Proportion of Women on Salaries: The Case of College Administrators," *Administrative Science Quarterly*, 32, no. 1 (March 1987), 1–24.
61. Ibid., 21.
62. Jennifer Crocker and Kathleen M. McGraw, "What's Good for the Goose is Not Good for the Gander: Solo Status as an Obstacle to Occupational Achievement for Males and Females," *American Behavioral Scientist*, 27, no. 3 (January-February 1984), 357–69.
63. For a review of this research, see Patricia Yancey Martin, "Group Sex Composition in Work Organizations: A Structural- Normative Model," *Research in the Sociology of Organizations*, vol. 4 (Greenwich, Conn.: JAI Press, 1985), pp. 311–49.
64. Kerson and Alexander, "Strategies for Success"; David F. Arguello, "Minorities in Administration: A Review of Ethnicity's Influence in Management," *Administration in Social Work*, 8, no. 3 (Fall 1984), 17–28.

6

The Politics of Program Implementation

In the early summer of 1952, before the heat of the campaign, President Truman used to contemplate the problems of the General-become-President should Eisenhower win the forthcoming election. "He'll sit here," Truman would remark (tapping his desk for emphasis), "and he'll say, Do this! Do that! And nothing will happen. Poor Ike — it won't be a bit like the Army. He'll find it very frustrating."

Richard E. Neustadt
Presidential Power[1]

Harry Truman was one of the first chief executives to identify implementation — the translation of policy into practice — as an emerging problem in public administration. Interest in implementation has grown as analysts and practitioners have recognized that, more and more, policies are significantly changed as they are put into operation as programs. Traditionally, the policy-program process was seen as consisting of two stages: policies were established by organizational or political elites (chief executives, legislatures, boards of directors) and then carried out by middle- and lower-level personnel (managers, supervisors, service providers). This model assumed that the actions of program personnel would directly reflect policymakers' intentions.

During the 1970s, a number of studies appeared that challenged this idea.[2] Aimed primarily at federal programs, and particularly the spate of social programs initiated under the Great Society legislation of the late 1960s, these studies found that, more often than not, governmental policies were not carried out in the form that policymakers had intended and, in some instances, were not carried out at all. A number of theories were developed to explain these failures in the policy process; they differ in their views of the central causes of the breakdown. The theories can be grouped into three schools of thought: (1) failures in policy design, (2) failures in the management of inter- and intra-organizational linkages, and (3) the growth of administrative discretion among front-line workers. These perspectives roughly correspond to what Rein and Rabinovitz called the three "imperatives" that actors in the policy process must take into account:

> the legal imperative to do what is legally required; the rational-bureaucratic imperative to do what is rationally defensible; and the consensual imperative to do what can establish agreement among contending influential parties who have a stake in the outcome.[3]

Each imperative seeks to accomplish a different purpose, thus creating a system of potentially conflicting demands on policymakers, program administrators, and service providers. When the goals and interests of these and other actors (service users and representatives of the general public) conflict, the implementation process becomes politicized as different parties seek to advance their separate interests.

The purpose of the present chapter is to review the arguments of these schools of thought on policymaking and program implementation and show their implications for the practice of social administration. Specific attention will be paid to how these ideas and research findings increase our understanding of the context within which social administrators operate, and the roles they should assume.

WEAK POLICIES AND "THE END OF LIBERALISM"

One of the most influential contemporary books on American public policy is *The End of Liberalism* by Theodore Lowi.[4] Subtitled "The Crisis of Public Authority," the book attacked the growing practice of legislators to enact vague and amorphous public policies that were unclear or confused as to their purposes and provided little or no direction to administrators for how they should be carried out. In the social welfare field, Lowi's criticism was directed to two major pieces of social legislation of the 1960s — the Social Security Amendments of 1962 and the Economic Opportunity Act of 1964. The thrust of his criticism reflected the failure of these acts to conform to the legal imperative.

From a legal point of view, the test of a good policy is the clarity with which policymakers frame policy goals and the strategies for pursuing them. Nakamura and Smallwood pointed out that clarity means being *specific* about both *what* is to be achieved and *how*. Both the goals of a policy and the means to achieve those goals must be stated in terms that are precise enough so that implementers know what they are supposed to do. In addition, policy directives should involve a statement of the implementers' responsibilities that is specific enough so that their performance can be assessed and they can be held accountable for their actions.[5]

Factors that promote good legislation include the technical soundness with which a bill is drafted; the strength and prestige of a bill's sponsors; the extent to which disagreements are faced and clarified during legislative debate; and the level of support for the bill, both in the legislature and in the communities it will affect.[6]

For Lowi, a model of good social welfare legislation was the original Social Security Act of 1935. In addition to well-formulated goals, there were clear rules, standards, and definitions that facilitated administrative decision making by providing officials with guidelines that identified responsibilities and powers in relation to specific problems. By contrast, the social welfare legislation of the 1960s, and many of the laws passed since then, "represent vague expressions of general sentiment rather than clear and coherent statements of public policy."[7] They are expressions of what Lowi called "interest-group liberalism," the tenets of which are:

> (1) It is better not to state hard policy but only to start a process. (2) Everything is good to do. Make everything available and the bargaining process will provide the appropriate mix. (3) It is not desirable to distinguish too clearly between public and private agencies. Authority hampers the bargaining process. (4) The distinction between public and private is in general undesirable because it interferes with delegation of power…and you cannot have a real policy-making process without broad delegation of power.[8]

These last two points — the breakdown in the boundaries between public and private authorities and the broad delegation of powers to define program purposes — are leading contributors to the politicization of the implementation process. The growing reluctance of legislators to take unequivocal positions in their policy pronouncements has resulted in the extension of the policymaking process into administration. A policy is "the definition of public purpose by responsible authority."[9] In a democratic society, the responsible authorities are the elected representatives of the sovereign people. When elected officials abrogate their responsibility to define public purposes, however, that function passes to other actors in the policy system, namely, the administrators and line workers who carry out policy. Hence, the distinction has been blurred between the political act of making policy and the supposedly nonpolitical, technical work of administering it.

Much of the social legislation passed since the 1960s lacks the clarity, consensus, prestige, and expertise called for by the legal imperative. Bills are often phrased in language so general and abstract as to be nearly meaningless.

Key terms are left undefined — sometimes purposely — or defined in ambiguous terms that lend themselves to a number of interpretations. These shortcomings are the result of a lack of clarity and consensus about a bill's purpose and the failure to resolve disagreements that arose during the legislative process. There are technical and political reasons for these problems. Many legislators lack the specialized knowledge needed to make legislation technically sound. Even when expertise is available, legislators are often constrained by the difficulty of predicting what future contingencies to cover by laws. Legislators and their assistants, Davis suggested, have limited confidence in their capacity

> to dig very far into the specialized subject matter, and such a state of mind produces general and vague formulations of objectives, not specific and precise ones....[Also], developing policies with respect of difficult subject matter often can best be accomplished by considering one concrete problem at a time, as an agency may do: generalizing in advance is often beyond the capacity of the best of minds.[10]

Technical limitations arise when little is known factually about the policy area in question and conceptual understanding is at a beginning level. Advances in the field of artificial insemination and the spread of practices like surrogate mothering, for example, have created legal, ethical, and psychological problems that require policy responses. These issues, however, are so new and uncharted that we do not yet have adequate frameworks for thinking about what the nature of these problems is or what information is needed by the policymaker. Even in policy areas with a long history, such as substitute care for children, changing theories and practices among child welfare specialists often leave policymakers undecided as to the best course of action to take.

While lack of knowledge or changes in the body of knowledge pertaining to a policy question constrain policymakers' abilities to detail policy goals and objectives, the rapid rate of knowledge production and technological development means that these constraints are often time limited. More serious obstacles to good social policies are those that arise from political considerations. In a pluralistic society such as ours, the policy process must accommodate the competing interests of constituencies with a stake in a policy's outcomes. These interests often reflect deep-seated economic, social, and ideological divisions, and the limitations they impose on policymaking are far more intractable than those arising out of technical factors.

It may be technically possible to draft explicit, tightly organized legislation that sets clear goals and prescribes programming and implementation strategies, but political considerations usually prevent this from happening. Rein and Rabinovitz argued that well-crafted legislation, although legally and technically correct, also

> limits political maneuverability in the legislative arena and makes coalition building difficult....[F]ully resolving disagreements in the legislative process so

that clear statutory guidelines will follow is not possible most of the time. Controversial issues are often left open and ambiguous in order to avoid confrontations that could threaten support for and successful passage of a bill.[11]

The function of political rhetoric, Kenneth Burke observed, is "to sharpen up the pointless and blunt the too sharply pointed." In a similar vein, Congressman John Brademas spoke of the "calculated ambiguity of political utterance." These remarks highlight the fact that policy directives are often purposefully written in vague and ambiguous terms in order to protect the political coalitions needed to support a particular policy. There are a number of ways in which vague policy statements can help the coalition-building process. First and foremost, it is easier to get agreement on abstract statements of principles — such as "promoting economic and social independence" — than on more concrete statements that involve difficult trade-offs among values. Furthermore, Nakamura and Smallwood suggested,

> vagueness may be regarded by interest groups as a further opportunity to influence the shape of policy once it leaves the formal policy-making arena....Two kinds of vagueness can result from the need for policy makers to build coalitions. Coalitions can be built around vague goals that sound good to participants for a variety of reasons. And coalitions can be built by offering to address many diverse and even conflicting goals, each of which is attractive to particular actors.[12]

An example of calculated ambiguity in policy formation is found in Davis and Hagen's analysis of the Reagan administration's policy response to the issue of battered women.[13] Wife abuse was first recognized as a widespread social problem in the 1970s, primarily through the efforts of feminist scholars and activists, who argued that the causes of the problem are rooted in sexism and the powerlessness of women. Violence against women was seen as distinct from other forms of family violence, such as child abuse and sibling violence. Policies for dealing with the problem, therefore, should be specifically tailored to it. In particular, advocates argued for policies that would work toward correcting sex-role stereotyping, power imbalances between men and women, and limited economic opportunities for women. Programs should include job training, financial assistance, women's shelters, and psychological and legal counseling.

This definition of the problem, as well as the recommended strategies for addressing it, went against the ideological grain of the Reagan administration. They posed a threat to the traditional ideas of family relations and gender roles that formed the basis of the conservative approach to social policy. But the problem could not be ignored or swept under the carpet (which is probably what conservative policymakers would have preferred) because of greater awareness of its prevalence and the demands of increasingly powerful and influential feminist organizations. Instead, the administration dealt with the problem by a policy which muddled and obfuscated the issue of wife abuse.

Federal legislation directed at wife abuse was first introduced in 1978 during the Carter administration under the title of the Domestic Violence Prevention and Services Act. By the time the legislation was revamped by the Reagan administration, it had been retitled the Family Violence Prevention and Services Act and made part of the Child Abuse Prevention and Treatment Act Amendments of 1984. The focus of the legislation shifted from a specific emphasis on wife abuse to a general consideration of all family violence. The legislation employed a generic definition of family violence which detracted from the special circumstances of abused wives. This focus enabled the administration to circumvent the original policy initiative aimed specifically at battered women, which had recommended expanded social and economic opportunities for women through the elimination of pay inequalities and the provision of child care and job training. At the same time, the act had features such as strengthened law enforcement around family violence, and the provision of emergency shelters that were sufficient to enlist the support or, more likely, dampen the opposition, of feminist organizations. The feminists, no doubt, viewed the act as a foot in the door that could be expanded later along lines more amenable to their special interests.

Chambers offered another example of poor policy design in his analysis of the provisions for disability insurance under the Social Security Act.[14] The legal flaws in public policy on disablement grew out of legislative efforts to accommodate divisiveness among the competing interests.

> The American Medical Association (AMA) was concerned with protecting the interests of the private practice of medicine....The private insurance industry was concerned with protecting its own financial interests....On the other hand, disability programs gained increasing support as members of Congress perceived the wide popularity of social security programs among their constituencies, and the support of labor, who saw the advantages of a public disability program for workers.[15]

The resulting weaknesses in the design of disability policy provided few constraints on medical and administrative discretion and allowed administrators and physicians to interpret medical facts and policy intentions liberally. These weaknesses were exploited by both liberals and conservatives, as the former sought to expand coverage and benefits and the latter sought to limit coverage, particularly in the area of mental impairment.

The gist of the policy design school's argument is that problems in policy implementation arise because there isn't *a policy* to be implemented. Rather, there are *various policies* that emerge from the different interpretations that competing stakeholders give to poorly designed legislation that does not set goals in specific enough language or provide adequate guidelines for determining which program activities are acceptable and which go beyond legislative intentions. This situation motivates and empowers administrators to rely on "professional ideology, personal temperament, or organizational expedience in exercising informal discretion."[16] Political factors are injected into the entire policy process, from the initial conception of what a policy should be about, to the details of daily decisionmaking by administrative and line personnel. The prospects for correcting the shortcomings of poorly designed policies are dim. The factors that contribute to them — organized and militant interest groups seeking to promote single issues and legislators unwilling to take hard positions on substantive policy questions — are, if anything, on the rise.

IMPLEMENTATION ANALYSIS AND POLICY ARENAS

The traditional two-stage model of policy formation and implementation can be likened to a computer process in which instructions (policy directives) are inputted by a programmer (policymaker), who produces actions (operating programs) which conform to the original instructions in every detail. A different way to think about the process is to compare it to the old parlor game of "telephone." A word (policy directive) is whispered to the first person in a line of people (policy arena), who then whispers it to the next person in line. By the time the last person in line is given the word (the implemented program), it is usually quite different from the original. To understand how the word changed, one must examine each step in the process to see how the word was transmitted (audibility and enunciation) and the conditions that surrounded its transmission (the nature of the prior relationships between the two people, their psychological predispositions to hear certain words and not others, their vested interests in particular outcomes).

The telephone analogy is an example of the "implementation analysis" approach to policy implementation. Whereas the policy design school concentrates on a policy's substantive content, implementation analysts are concerned with how policy directives are transmitted from one hierarchical level to the next and from one organization to another. They are also interested in the characteristics and interests of the individual and organizational actors in the process.[17] Implementation analysis challenges the traditional assumption that policy decisions are one-time actions. In the classic conception of the policymaker as a rational actor, a policy decision is the action taken after the policymaker (1) specifies the goal to be accomplished; (2) identifies all alternative ways of reaching that goal; (3) evaluates the merits of each alternative in terms of its efficiency and other relevant criteria; and (4) *makes a decision*, that is, selects the best alternative.

Implementation analysts argue that this conception of policy decisions misrepresents what actually happens in policymaking. Ugalde, for example, suggested that a policy decision is actually a *series of decisions* — the total number of decisions made in the process of achieving a goal.[18] As depicted in

Figure 6-1, the series can be broken down into *input decisions, programming decisions,* and *implementation decisions.*

> Input decisions are high policy decisions which are not concerned with the possible alternatives which might be available in the attainment of a goal....Programming decisions can be made outside the public bureaucracy, in congress, legislatures, cabinets, special commissions....A formal decision...separates in time the phase of programming decisions from that of implementation decisions....It could...happen that during the implementation phase, the formal decision was modified — frequently without the consent or knowledge of the formal decisionmaker — and then implemented.[19]

The series of decision concepts reflects the importance that implementation analysts assign to the *inter-organizational* nature of policy decisions. Each stage of the decision series usually takes place within separate organizations. Input decisions are likely to originate with the political executive (president, governor, commissioner); programming decisions are made by specialists within the administrative bureaucracies; and implementation decisions are made by the operating agencies responsible for carrying out the policies. The traditional approach to policy development recognized that a number of organizations were involved in the process but assumed that they constituted an integrated policy system, or chain, held together by a combination of bureaucratic controls and overlapping interests. This assumption has been challenged, however, by studies which showed that various actors and agencies in a policy chain "have such widely differing stakes in the outcomes of policy and are motivated so differently that the results diverge sharply from the stated intentions of the policy declarers."[20]

Actors and Arenas

The recognition of the potential lack of integration among the organizations and people involved in policy development led implementation analysts to talk about policy *arenas*, rather than policy *systems.* Arenas, with their gladiatorial overtones, suggest settings in which people, while physically together, relate to each other in an adversarial manner. Rabinovitz and her colleagues defined a policy arena as "the web of individual and institutional interrelationships which would develop over time among congressmen, ad-

FIGURE 6-1. Series of Decision Model. (*Source:* Antonio Ugalde, "A Decision Model for the Study of Public Bureaucracies," *Policy Sciences,* 4, no. 1 (March 1973), 75–84. Reprinted by permission of Kluwer Academic Publishers.)

Input Decision	Beginning of Series		Formal Decision		End of Series
⟶	A	Programming decisions	B	Implementation decisions	C

ministrators, interest groups, 'academic experts,' and other interested parties."[21] Arenas differ from each other depending on the level of agreement among members about the substantive nature of the policy issues and on the extent to which they have developed satisfactory ways of working with each other. Arenas can be categorized in terms of whether issues are "clear *versus* ambiguous" and working relationships are "settled *versus* open." Arenas range from those in which working relationships are settled and issues are clear to ones in which customary ways of working together are still open and issues are ambiguous. The first type functions very much like the policy system envisioned in the traditional model of policy development, whereas the second lends itself to a more contentious and politicized approach.[22]

The major actors in a policy arena are policymakers, formal implementers, intermediaries, administrative lobbies, constituency and recipient groups, and the media.[23] *Policymakers* are the elected officials, legislators, and high-level administrative appointees legally authorized to assign priorities and commit resources. *Formal implementers* are the administrators and their staffs with the authority, responsibility, and resources to carry out policy directives. *Intermediaries* are individuals who are delegated responsibility by formal implementers to assist in carrying out policies. Their presence reflects both the federated nature of the American policy system with its division of power and responsibilities among federal, state, and local levels of government, as well as a growing tendency to mix public and private agencies in the provision of public services. In the social services especially, the typical model for service provision is for federal funds to be allocated to the states, who then contract with local public and private agencies for the actual delivery of services.

The growing number of *administrative lobbies* reflects the efforts of government agencies to make legislation more responsive to their organizational and program concerns. These efforts have taken on added importance and momentum in recent years because of the antigovernment stance underlying many of the Reagan administration's policy initiatives. All government agencies have legislative liaison and public information offices which perform what are essentially lobbying and public relations activities. In addition, professional associations like the American Public Welfare Association, whose members are federal, state, and local welfare administrators, engage in lobbying and litigation on behalf of their members' agencies and programs. Other stakeholders with an interest in policy outcomes attempt to influence the process through *constituency lobbies*. In social welfare these lobbies include service providers, client advocates, representatives of the general public, and, in a few instances, clients themselves. They are represented by organizations such as the National Association of Social Workers, the American Association for Protecting Children, the National Coalition on the Homeless, the American Association of Parents of Retarded Children, and the American Association of Retired People.

Last, but by no means least, are the *media*. America prides itself on a vigorous and independent press that exercises surveillance over public officials and employees. People know what they know about government primarily through what they read in newspapers, hear on radio, and see on television. The power of the media is increasing, moreover, due to the rise of investigative journalism, and the growing competition between and among print and electronic media. Journalists, editors, and network news executives are ever on the alert for controversial stories which might get the reporter a Pulitzer Prize or raise newspaper circulations or network ratings. Policies and programs, as well as the careers of politicians and public managers, can be made or unmade in the media. A sophisticated understanding of the media — how they work and how they should be approached — is essential for all staff involved in the policy-program process.[24]

Conflicting Cultures

The goals, interests, and operating styles of the various actors in a policy arena make up different occupational and professional cultures which guide their work. The culture of the policymaker, as previously noted, consists of two potentially conflicting imperatives: the legal imperative, which stresses well-crafted legislation, and the consensual imperative, which reflects the need to draft legislation that accommodates the different interests to which elected officials must respond. Of particular concern to social workers is the growing conflict between the cultures that surround formal implementers — public managers and their staffs — on the one hand, and intermediaries, service providers, and client advocates on the other.

Administrators are heavily influenced by the rational-bureaucratic imperative. A primary ingredient in the bureaucratic perspective is workability, or the degree to which a policy idea can be translated into an administratively feasible form. Administrative feasibility requires the ability to delegate tasks to different units within an organization and hold the units accountable for their performance. However, the ideas that can survive delegation, Trilling suggested,

> incline to be the ideas of a certain kind and of a certain simplicity; they give up something of their largeness and modulation and complexity in order to survive. The lively sense of contingency and possibility, and of those exceptions to the rule which may be the beginning of the end of the rule — this sense does not suit well with the impulse of organization.[25]

Administrators favor straightforward programs that can easily be managed and resist programs that rely on "continuing high levels of competence, or expeditious inter-organizational coordination, or on sophisticated methods for accommodating diversity and heterogeneity."[26]

The tenets of the bureaucratic imperative present particularly knotty problems when applied to policy development in the social services. Contemporary social problems are complicated matters requiring equally complicated responses. Community care for the mentally ill, treatment and prevention of child abuse and neglect, the rehabilitation of substance abusers and alcoholics — all these problems require the services of a number of specialized agencies acting in an intricately coordinated way. In addition, a growing and diverse number of human service professionals advance claims to having expert knowledge about the best ways to approach these problems.

Tensions arise when the bureaucratic imperative clashes with the kinds of programs that human service professionals and client advocates want. These conflicts have been exacerbated because of the growing practice of excluding human service professionals from the upper levels of the federal and state social service bureaucracies. There has been a steady decline in the number of professional social workers in higher level federal and state positions since the end of the first Nixon administration.[27] They have been replaced by people with general management skills, often with business backgrounds. The declining influence of social workers and those sympathetic to human service programs has altered the climate surrounding the development of social programs. From the 1930s to the 1970s, the middle- and upper-level administrators in charge of the federal social security and social welfare agencies were men and women who were zealous advocates for these programs.[28] They have been replaced, for the most part, by people who are either ideologically opposed to social programs, or lack any experience in human services, or both. The administrative issues that receive their attention are "surveillance of local agencies for compliance monitoring; a system for upward reporting of required statistics; and fiscal control procedures."[29]

In hearings on management practices in the Department of Health and Human Services, for example, a congressional committee found that program managers systematically ignored the advice of human service professionals who were brought in as expert consultants.[30] In commenting on the failure of administrators in the National Center on Child Abuse and Neglect (NCCAN) — a part of the Office of Human Development Services (OHDS), the agency responsible for most social service programs — to seek the advice of human service professionals in developing program guidelines, Thomas Birch of the National Child Abuse Coalition argued that

> by ignoring the field's contributions to the development of NCCAN's priorities, OHDS exacerbates the distance it has already created between the agency and the field it is meant to serve. In isolating NCCAN, OHDS leaves the development of program priorities to staff with no guarantee that the programs in fact suit the needs of the field. Consequently, the administration runs the risk of funding programs which may be irrelevant or redundant to advancing the field's knowledge. The Federal child abuse effort in fact may be set up to operate ineffectually because of the HDS policy to disregard public comments.[31]

In a study of the Department of Health and Human Service's use of quality control as an administrative device to reduce errors in public assistance payments (overpayments, payments to people ineligible for grants), it was found that this device was as likely to restrict services to eligible clients as it was to uncover mistaken payments.[32] A high degree of legitimacy attaches to the quality control system, despite indications of its restrictiveness, because of its association with the tenets of the bureaucratic imperative. As Brodkin and Lipsky pointed out, quality control

> mobilizes the symbols of "quality" and "improved administration";...is metaphorically associated with technical processes bearing scientific management overtones;...is apparently directed at a problem in the welfare system that at least superficially concerns policy officials who otherwise hold widely varying views of welfare reform; and...its positive contributions can be trumpeted, while its negative consequences are largely hidden from public scrutiny.[33]

Whetten pointed to the unique problems social administrators experienced when they were caught between the bureaucratic demands of funders and the pressures for quality programming coming from their staffs. In a study of administrators of manpower agencies, he found that local managers "are in a position to feel very keenly the conflict between the pressures, on the one hand, of quickly processing many clients by means of standard procedures and, on the other, spending considerable time meeting the unique needs of each individual client."[34] Senior administrative positions in these agencies are generally filled from within the agency by people who have been with the organization for a long time. They have thus had ample opportunity to work closely with the agency's clients and observe the frustrations of being disadvantaged. These administrators also are receptive to the social service professional's concern with service quality. Since these agencies are relatively small organizations,

> senior administrators are frequently in contact with counselors, social workers, and teachers who are involved in the day-to-day processing of clients. Consequently, promotion to agency head does not also bring isolation from those who would likely be the strongest advocates for personalizing the agency's services to meet the unique needs of clients.[35]

A major contribution of the implementation analysis school has been to highlight the fact that a number of actors, organizations, and interests affect the way policies are made and carried out. They challenged the traditional notion of *the* policymaker, sitting at the top of a hierarchically structured system, issuing policy pronouncements that were translated into directives assiduously adhered to by bureaucratic subordinates. In its place they offered a more politicized conception of policy arenas where political officials, planners, administrators, service providers, clients, and other stakeholders seek to maximize their own interests, often at the expense of each other. Rather than superordinates and subordinates bound together in an integrated system with a single overarching goal, policy arenas consist of a number of semi-indepen-dent bodies pursuing separate and often contradictory ends, negotiating with each other from varying positions of strength.

Traditional conceptions of a hierarchy of power and control had to be modified as evidence mounted of the influence on the policy process exercised by people at all organizational levels, as well as those outside the organiza-tions formally charged with the responsibility to develop and administer policies. New metaphors were sought to replace the traditional pyramidal notion of the hierarchical organization. Organizations and their decision-making processes are now frequently thought of in terms of "negotiated orders," "organized anarchies," and "loosely-coupled systems."[36] Politics assumes a central role, Rein and Rabinovitz argued, since implementation is viewed "as a continuation into another arena of the political process" which enables the "contending views held by different interest groups to be worked out at each stage on the policy-practice continuum."[37]

WORKER DISCRETION AND PROGRAM IMPLEMENTATION

The "worker discretion" approach focuses on the point in the policy process at which services are actually provided. This approach makes the front-line worker the central actor in the implementation process. It looks at the extent to which workers are required to handle cases in ways predetermined by administrative regulations and policy directives, or are free to decide matters for themselves.

Organizational discretion refers to an individual's freedom "to make a choice among possible courses of action or inaction."[38] Discretion is not an "either/or" thing that one has or doesn't have, but is a matter of degree, depending on how binding administrative directives are on an employee's actions. Administrative directives can be almost always binding; always considered and usually binding; usually considered but seldom binding; occasionally considered but never binding; and almost never considered.[39] The first two categories describe nondiscretionary positions, the last two describe discretionary positions, and the middle category is a zone between policy and discretion. Discretionary positions have important implications for program implementation since people in these positions can, if they so choose, deviate from prescribed agency policies. People in high discretionary posi-tions can act without consulting organizational superiors or written regula-tions. People in low discretionary positions, by contrast, can rarely, if ever, take actions that have not been approved by their superiors or that are not in compliance with written policies and procedures.

Organizations need people in discretionary positions to deal with situ-ations that are unpredictable, that require immediate responses to rapidly shifting circumstances, or that demand innovative solutions. Administrative theories generally assume that discretion does and should increase as one moves up the organizational hierarchy. Because individuals in discretionary positions are expected to exercise independent judgment, these positions are usually reserved for those who have demonstrated their commitment to organizational goals and expert knowledge of organizational procedures. Accordingly, discretionary jobs are usually arranged "sequentially in career patterns so that those requiring larger amounts of discretion are filled after individuals have shown capacity to handle smaller amounts."[40]

There are two conditions under which organizations are likely to deviate from this general administrative principle: what Friedson called *autonomy by default* and *organized autonomy*.[41] Autonomy by default arises when

> an occupation is left wholly to its own devices because there is not strong public concern with its work, because it works independently of any functional division of labor, and because its work is such (in complexity, specialization or observability) as to preclude easy evaluation and control by others.[42]

Organized autonomy, on the other hand, is based on the demand of certain employees to be exempted from organizational rules and regulations on the basis of their expertise and skill. This claim is the basis for the special status often granted to professional employees in organizations. The claims of professions like medicine and law to special knowledge and expertise are widely accepted by the larger society and have been institutionalized in the form of licensing, certification, and other legal protections. Consequently, their demands for organizational autonomy and discretion in conducting their work are generally acceded to, however reluctantly, by administrators. For professions like social work and teaching, however, whose claims to expert knowledge and skills are disputed and who do not command the same institutional status in society, demands for organizational autonomy will be resisted.

While social workers' demands for organized autonomy within social agencies are often not realized, there is considerable autonomy by default arising from the front-line nature of most social agencies. As previously discussed, front-line organizations are ones in which activities are initiated in front-line units that operate independently of one another and whose work cannot be supervised directly by organizational superiors. This results in a reversal of the distribution of discretionary positions usually found in hierarchical organizations. In social agencies and other front-line organizations, line workers have considerable discretion to act on their own judgment. Social service activities typically begin when an individual contacts or is referred to an agency. The worker who receives the request has considerable discretion to decide if a service should be offered. If service is initiated, it takes place in the privacy of the worker's office or in the client's home. Reports on the course of a worker's contact with the client originate with the worker, who thus controls the amount and kind of information that go up the organizational hierarchy.

Another factor contributing to worker discretion is the underdeveloped technologies used in social work practice. Paradoxically, while this factor contributes to the worker's autonomy by default, it is one of the main reasons why social workers' claims to organized autonomy based on their professional expertise are denied. Professionals in technically advanced fields are constrained by the technical standards established within the field. When procedures achieve a high level of technical development and reliability and are widely endorsed by the field, practitioners are as obliged to follow them as if there were actual supervisors standing over their shoulders, monitoring their actions. Thus, physicians practicing in the privacy of their examination rooms, with no organizational superior to whom they are accountable, are supervised by the standard operating procedures set forth by the medical profession.

In the social services, by contrast, the level of technical development for most service interventions is not at the point where the technology prescribes what the worker should do in a given situation or sets limits on what the worker cannot do. Much of what a social worker does, Schorr argued, is determined "by the counselor's or the profession's judgment of what is good."[43] Definitions of what is good, moreover, are policy choices. As a result, social service practice is pervaded with policy choices.

> The practitioner may make his choices for reasons of social control; of turf, prestige, or other professional self-interest; of calculated judgment about the client's interest; or without any reason, simply out of habit....If much of practice involves value rather than technical formulations, practitioners are in a position to decide policy to the extent that they operate autonomously.[44]

When a worker's interpretation of appropriate actions to take with clients changes the substance of official agency policies, the worker becomes, in Shnit's words, "a miniature legislator."[45] In a study of how public welfare workers defined their roles, for example, Rosenberg found that while all workers in her sample subscribed to the same general role definition (to resocialize clients with the goal of establishing financial independence), there were clear differences in worker orientations at the operational level.[46] One group stressed the legitimate rights of clients to services, viewed clients as nondeviant in terms of chronic dependence, and adopted a narrow definition of their caseworker roles with respect to legitimate interventions in the client's life. The second group was more concerned with the community's interests than with the rights of clients and assumed a broader interventionist role in order to rehabilitate and control clients defined as deviant. A third group fell between these two. Workers in this group "moderately honored" the legitimacy of client rights but also saw the caseworker in an interventionist role to help the "immature client accommodate communal expectations relative to family and economic functions."[47]

The worker discretion school has shown the role that line workers play in altering the content of social policies by implementing them in ways that conform to their own preferences, their clients' wishes, and/or the values of the local community. This poses the larger question of the degree to which social service programs should be oriented vertically toward their policy and fiscal sponsors, or laterally toward the clients and communities they serve. The former conception of social services assumes a bureaucratic framework in which publicly enacted policies and laws are implemented in a form that adheres closely to the intent of the lawmakers. The latter approach proceeds from a mutual adjustment framework in which political processes are used to accommodate the special interests of service providers, community groups, and service consumers.

MANAGING THE POLITICS OF IMPLEMENTATION

The political and organizational issues surrounding the development and implementation of social policies point to the need for social administrators to think of their jobs in broad, rather than narrow terms. In order to manage the implementation process effectively, a social administrator should be a *policy advocate*, a *negotiator of organizational linkages*, and a *manager of worker discretion*. These roles roughly correspond to theoretical and empirical studies of the administrative styles of social agency managers.[48]

Policy Advocate

The existence of weak policies, the aggressive lobbying of organized interest groups, the increasing controversy surrounding social service goals, and the growing complexity of social programs all mean that administrators have a role to play in shaping the policies they will eventually be responsible for carrying out. This is true not only for social administrators, but reflects a general trend in public policymaking and administration. In a study of bureaucrats and politicians in the United States and Western Europe, it was found that the traditional distinction between policymaking and policy implementation has blurred.[49] The authors suggested that the last quarter of this century is witnessing "the virtual disappearance of the...distinction between the roles of politician and bureaucrat," and that future administrative practice may take the form of a "pure hybrid" between politics and administration that reflects a politicization of the bureaucracy and a bureaucratization of politics.[50]

The first step in any policy process is to see that the issues one is concerned with are placed on the public agenda. This task is not as easy as it might first appear. The capacity to determine which items go on, and which are excluded from, the policymaker's agenda is an important and much-sought-after source of power. As Schattschneider argued,

> there are billions of potential conflicts in any modern society, but *only a few become significant....The definition of the alternatives is the supreme instrument of power....*The definition of the alternatives is the choice of conflict, and the choice of conflicts allocates power.[51]

The exercise of power in policy arenas often takes a negative form since power can be exercised by *preventing* certain issues from reaching the attention of policymakers. As a result, "some issues are organized into politics while others are organized out."[52] If advocates are unable to negotiate the obstacles in the way of their getting the attentive interest of decision makers, their concerns will never see the light of day. An important advocacy function that administrators perform is to help get their policy issues on the agenda. Administrators, along with other program advocates, form the basis of what Heclo called "issue networks," which seek to "provoke and guide" certain issues onto the policymaker's agenda.[53] Not only must advocates see that their concerns reach the attention of policymakers, but the issues must be framed in ways that reflect their own programmatic, organizational, and ideological interests.

The controversial nature of most social policy questions attracts a number of competing stakeholders, each seeking to influence how social problems are defined and addressed. In her analysis of policy proposals for day care, for example, Boles identified a number of competing interest groups, each with its own conception of the goals for day care. Child welfare and child development specialists supported day care "which compensates for a home environment lacking in educational and economic resources by providing a setting which stimulates and develops the child's cognitive and sensory abilities."[54] Women's rights groups argued that mothers outside the labor force needed day care services so they could be relieved of the daily routine of child care and attend to their own personal development. This position was also seen as a strategy for abolishing rigid sex roles within the family and establishing the care of children as a responsibility for the entire society. For women in the labor force — whether because of economic necessity or for self-fulfillment only — "quality day care facilitates female career advancement without sacrificing child welfare."[55] For advocates of welfare reform through "workfare," day care services were an important policy tool for compelling mothers receiving AFDC assistance to accept job training or full-time jobs as a condition of welfare.

Social administrators seeking to influence the policies that shape their programs must engage in a variety of advocacy tactics, for example, public information campaigns, lobbying, preparing and giving legislative testimony, and providing leadership to interest networks and coalitions. The purposes of these activities are to ensure that the issues of concern to a particular agency are addressed by policymakers and that they are presented

in a form that reflects the organizational, professional, and ideological interests of the agency, its staff, and its clients.

Negotiating Organizational Linkages

Inter-organizational relationships have been a central concern of social administrators throughout the history of organized social welfare. The
American social work profession has its roots in the Charities Organization
Societies of the late nineteenth century. The initial purpose of this early
organization was to create an efficient system of linkages among social
agencies. While inter-organizational matters have always been an important part of the administrator's job, concern with external relationships has
heightened over the past several years as a result of increased competition
for scarce public dollars and the introduction of new mechanisms for
allocating those dollars.

The decentralization of the resource allocation process through the New
Federalism has been a major force in the politicization of the social agency's
environment. As decisions about the distribution of federal dollars increasingly are made at state and local levels, the influence previously wielded by
the more program-oriented federal bureaucrats has given way to a diffuse
system of control involving not only professional bureaucrats but state and
local politicians, community elites, and a number of organized interest groups
as well. The organizational environment of the social agency has become
denser and more complicated; social administrators have had to develop the
technical and political skills needed to get the information and formulate the
negotiating strategies upon which the survival of programs and agencies are
increasingly dependent.

While many administrators continue to go it alone, and pursue individual strategies for positioning their agencies with bureaucratic and political
influentials, others are turning to collective strategies through coalitions.
Whether a particular administrator pursues an individual or a collective
strategy will depend on a number of factors. Adrian and Press developed a
cost-benefit model for analyzing the advantages and disadvantages to coalition joining in general.[56] The factors in their model include information costs
involved in gathering information about potential strategies; responsibility
costs involved in allowing a person or group to have policy decisions attributed to them; division of payoff costs involved in distributing payoffs among
members of a winning coalition; dissonance costs incurred during periods of
disagreement; opportunity costs involved in transferring staff from agency
work to coalition work; and persuasion costs involved in recruiting reluctant
members.

Not only must administrators decide whether to join coalitions, they
must also decide how committed they and their agencies will be to the

coalition. Coalitions can occur with varying degrees of intensity and commitment on the part of their members. Schlesinger and Oshry suggested that joint efforts range from a minimum level of integration in which members do nothing more than share information, to a maximum level in which the group forms a power bloc capable of developing negotiating positions.[57] From the administrator's perspective, the advantages of entering into coalitions strong enough to act as a power bloc must be weighed against the costs, both in terms of agency resources and autonomy, that must be incurred.

Managing Worker Discretion

How can administrators ensure that the activities of front-line workers conform to agency policies and procedures? The strategies most often pursued concentrate on either increased *bureaucratization* or increased *professionalization*.[58] The first attempts to secure worker compliance with agency policies through administrative centralization. It uses mechanisms like management-based performance systems which emphasize task specification and performance evaluations based on objective measurements. The professionalization strategy is based on the assumption that competent and accountable worker performance can only be achieved through professional training. Workers with such training are both more skilled and better socialized to professional norms of practice.

The strategy that administrators are likely to choose depends on their overall orientation to how service delivery systems should be structured, the context within which their organizations operate, and the nature of the services offered. An essential ingredient of professional practice is the professional's freedom to make discretionary judgments on the basis of his or her appreciation of the situation. Administrators with a positive attitude toward professionalism seek to foster worker discretion by delegating to line professionals considerable autonomy in decision making. By contrast, bureaucratic structures seek to reduce worker discretion as much as possible; decisions are made according to a set of universally applicable rules and regulations. The administrator using this strategy wants to limit worker discretion so decisions are made according to predetermined criteria which apply to all workers and clients.

A positive attitude toward professionalism grows out of a view of professionals that emphasizes their skills and commitment to service rather than their desire to enhance their occupational or organizational status. The service perspective highlights the professional's commitment to aiding those in need, whereas the status enhancement orientation sees professionalism as a means to "protect and enhance professional prerogatives and status."[59] The case for bureaucracy is made by those who see bureaucratic organizations as the best mechanism for providing services on a large scale in a manner that is efficient, fair, and reliable. Critics of the bureaucratic experience, on the other hand, see depersonalized, rationalized, and complex bureaucratic structures as inimical to the provision of human services. By and large, we can expect administrators with social service backgrounds to be more receptive to the professional strategy; administrators with backgrounds in general administration or business are likely to be more attracted to the bureaucratic strategy.

The political and organizational context within which an agency exists also influences how administrators respond to worker discretion. As noted earlier, an important feature of an organization's environment is whether power is concentrated or dispersed among external stakeholders. Mintzberg labeled the environment *dominant, divided,* or *passive,* depending on whether one, a few, or no external bodies have concentrated power.[60] A dominated external coalition encourages the rise of bureaucratic structures within the organization; a divided external coalition encourages the rise of politicized structures; and passive environments are associated with a variety of internal structures, including personalized, ideologic, professional, and bureaucratic. The trend in social welfare has been toward dominated environments as resources are concentrated in one or a few powerful public agencies. This tendency is complicated further by reductions in funds for social welfare programs, resulting in more extensive management control systems that enable funders to ration available resources and monitor their use. Under these conditions, social administrators, even those who prefer the professional approach to organizing service systems, are constrained to structure their agencies and programs along bureaucratic lines

> because external control is consolidated most effectively through the use of performance standards and other formalized controls, the internal coalition emerges as bureaucratic, pursuing the operational goals that the dominant influencer imposes on it. Within the organization...a high level of internal expertise [is not] compatible with such control.[61]

When administrators are rewarded for curtailing worker discretion through bureaucratic controls, there will be increased role tensions and conflicts for those administrators with professional social service backgrounds.

The third factor that influences how administrators deal with worker discretion is the nature of the services offered and the extent to which community acceptance is important for a program's success. In general, there are two ways in which organizations develop.[62] In the first, technological innovations (for example, the silicon chip) foster the development of rational bureaucratic structures to coordinate technical work efficiently. In the second, social processes emerge (such as changing attitudes toward the causes and treatment of spouse abuse) that define certain rules and programs and recognize the organizations that incorporate these programs and conform to these rules as rational and legitimate. Social agencies develop along these latter lines and, consequently, are tightly linked to community values, attitudes, and beliefs.

Administrators interested in having their programs gain acceptance in the local community are constrained to allow workers more discretion in order to adapt general policy and program goals and methods to a community's unique needs, values, and customary practices. Programs that require the active support and acceptance of local communities include support services for deinstitutionalized psychiatric patients and outreach and preventive programs in areas like child abuse and neglect that need the cooperation of community residents for early detection and reporting. Administrators are also more susceptible to local influences when they seek money and other resources from local businesses, philanthropies, and individuals. This kind of fund raising is on the rise, moreover, as administrators seek to diversify their funding sources to make up for cutbacks in state and federal spending and to lessen the control of a dominant funding source.

NOTES

1. Richard E. Neustadt, *Presidential Power* (New York: John Wiley and Sons, 1960), p. 9 (emphases in original). Copyright © 1960 by John Wiley and Sons, Inc.
2. For a review of this literature, see Donald Van Meter and Carl Van Horn, "The Policy Implementation Process: A Conceptual Framework," *Administration & Society*, 6, no. 4 (February 1975), 445–88.
3. Martin Rein and Francine F. Rabinovitz, "Implementation: A Theoretical Perspective," in *American Politics and Public Policy*, ed. Walter Dean Burnham and Martha Wagner Weinberg (Cambridge, Mass.: The MIT Press, 1978), p. 308.
4. Theodore J. Lowi, *The End of Liberalism: Ideology, Policy, and the Crisis of Public Authority* (New York: W. W. Norton, 1969).
5. Robert T. Nakamura and Frank Smallwood, *The Politics of Policy Implementation* (New York: St. Martin's Press, 1980), p. 33 (emphases in original).
6. Rein and Rabinovitz, "Implementation," pp. 310–11.
7. Mark D. Jacobs, "The End of Liberalism in the Administration of Social Casework," *Administration & Society*, 18, no. 1 (May 1986), 17.
8. Lowi, *The End of Liberalism*, p. 238.
9. Don K. Price, "Purists and Politicians," *Science*, 163, no. 3862 (January 3, 1969), 29.
10. Kenneth Davis, *Discretionary Justice: A Preliminary Inquiry* (Baton Rouge: Louisiana University Press, 1969), p. 46.
11. Rein and Rabinovitz, "Implementation," p. 311.
12. Nakamura and Smallwood, *The Politics of Implementation*, p. 39.
13. Liane V. Davis and Jan L. Hagen, "Services for Battered Women: The Public Policy Response," *Social Service Review*, 62, no. 4 (December 1988), 649–67.
14. Donald E. Chambers, "Policy Weaknesses and Political Opportunities," *Social Service Review*, 59, no. 1 (March 1985), 1–17.
15. Ibid., 2–3.
16. Jacobs, "The End of Liberalism," 18.
17. Jeffrey Pressman and Aaron Wildavsky, *Implementation* (Berkeley: University of California Press, 1973); Eugene Bardach, *The Implementation Game* (Cambridge, Mass.: MIT Press, 1977); Michael Lipsky, "Standing the Study of Policy Implementation on Its Head," in *American Politics and Public Policy*, ed. Walter Dean Burnham and Martha Wagner Weinberg (Cambridge, Mass.: MIT Press, 1978), pp. 391–402; Nakamura and Smallwood, *The Politics of Implementation*.

18. Antonio Ugalde, "A Decision Model for the Study of Public Bureaucracies," *Policy Sciences*, 4, no. 1 (March 1973), 75–84.
19. Ibid., 77–78.
20. Lipsky, "Standing the Study of Policy Implementation on Its Head," p. 394.
21. Francine Rabinovitz, Jeffrey Pressman, and Martin Rein, "Guidelines: A Plethora of Forms, Authors, and Functions," *Policy Sciences*, 7, no. 4 (December 1976), 405.
22. Ibid., 404–06
23. Nakamura and Smallwood, *The Politics of Implementation*, pp. 31–32.
24. Gordon Chase and Elizabeth C. Reveal, *How to Manage in the Public Sector* (Reading, Mass.: Addison-Wesley, 1983), pp. 145–75.
25. Cited in Richard F. Elmore, "Organizational Models of Social Program Implementation," *Public Policy*, 26, no. 2 (Spring 1978), 185.
26. Rabinovitz, Pressman, and Rein, "Guidelines," p. 415.
27. Burton Gummer, "Is the Social Worker in Public Welfare an Endangered Species?" *Public Welfare*, 37, no. 4 (Fall 1979), 12–21; Ronald Randall, "Presidential Power and Bureaucratic Intransigence: The Influence of the Nixon Administration on Welfare Policy," *American Political Science Review*, 73, no. 3 (September 1979), 795–810; Sanford F. Schram, "Politics, Professionalism, and the Changing Federalism," *Social Service Review*, 55, no. 1 (March 1981), 78–92.
28. Martha Derthick, *Policymaking for Social Security* (Washington, D.C.: The Brookings Institution, 1979).
29. David A. Whetten, "Coping with Incompatible Expectations: Role Conflict among Directors of Manpower Agencies," *Administration in Social Work*, 1, no. 4 (Winter 1977), 379.
30. U.S. House of Representatives, Committee on Government Operations, *Mismanagement of the Office of Human Development Services*: Undermining Programs for Children, the Disabled, and the Elderly (Washington, D.C.: U.S. Government Printing Office, 1987).
31. Ibid., p. 17.
32. Evelyn Brodkin and Michael Lipsky, "Quality Control in AFDC as an Administrative Strategy," *Social Service Review*, 57, no. 1 (March 1983), 1–34.
33. Ibid., 30.
34. Whetten, "Coping with Incompatible Expectations," 380.
35. Ibid., 381.
36. Anselm Strauss et al., "The Hospital and Its Negotiated Order," in *The Hospital in Modern Society*, ed. Eliot Friedson (New York: The Free Press, 1963), pp. 147–169; Karl E. Weick, "Educational Organizations as Loosely Coupled Systems," *Administrative Science Quarterly*, 21, no. 1 (March 1976), 1–19; Michael D. Cohen and James G. March, *Leadership and Ambiguity*, 2nd ed. (Boston: Harvard Business School Press, 1986).
37. Rein and Rabinovitz, "Implementation," p. 400.
38. Davis, *Discretionary Justice*, p. 4.
39. Ibid., p. 106.
40. James D. Thompson, *Organizations in Action* (New York: McGraw-Hill, 1967), p. 118.
41. Eliot Friedson, "Dominant Professions, Bureaucracy, and Client Services," in *Organizations and Clients*, ed. William R. Rosengren and Mark Lefton (Columbus, Ohio: Charles E. Merrill, 1970), pp. 71–92.
42. Ibid., p. 76.
43. Alvin L. Schorr, "Professional Practice as Policy," *Social Service Review*, 59, no. 2 (June 1985), 181.
44. Ibid., 183, 191.

45. Dan Shnit, "Professional Discretion in Social Welfare Administration," *Administration in Social Work*, 2, no. 4 (Winter 1978), 447.
46. Janet Rosenberg, "Discovering Natural Types of Role Orientation: An Application of Cluster Analysis," *Social Service Review*, 52, no. 1 (March 1978), 85–106.
47. Ibid., 100.
48. Rino J. Patti, "Patterns of Management Activity in Social Welfare Agencies," *Administration in Social Work*, 1, no. 1 (Spring 1977), 5–18; William E. Berg, "Evolution of Leadership Style in Social Agencies: A Theoretical Analysis," *Social Casework*, 61, no. 1 (January 1980), 22–28.
49. Joel D. Aberbach, Robert D. Putnam, and Bert A. Rockman, *Bureaucrats and Politicians in Western Democracies* (Cambridge, Mass.: Harvard University Press, 1981).
50. Ibid., p. 16.
51. E. E. Schattschneider, *The Semisovereign People: A Realist's View of Democracy in America* (New York: Holt, Rinehart and Winston, 1960), pp. 66, 68 (emphases in original).
52. Ibid., p. 76.
53. Hugh Heclo, "Issue Networks and the Executive Establishment," in *The New American Political System*, ed. Anthony King (Washington, D.C.: American Enterprise Institute for Public Policy Research, 1978), p. 102.
54. Janet K. Boles, "The Politics of Child Care," *Social Service Review*, 54, no. 3 (September 1980), 350.
55. Ibid.
56. C. R. Adrian and C. Press, "Decision Costs in Coalition Formation," *American Political Science Review*, 62 (June 1968), 556–563.
57. Leonard A. Schlesinger and Barry Oshry, "Quality of Work Life and the Manager: Muddle in the Middle," *Organizational Dynamics*, 13, no. 1 (Summer 1984), 13.
58. John A. Yankey and Claudia J. Coulton, "Promoting Contributions to Organizational Goals: Alternative Models," *Administration in Social Work*, 3, no. 1 (Spring 1979), 45–55.
59. Neil Gilbert and Harry Specht, *Dimensions of Social Welfare Policy*, 2nd ed. (Englewood Cliffs, N.J.: Prentice Hall, 1986), p. 138.
60. Henry Mintzberg, "Power and Organization Life Cycle," *Academy of Management Review*, 9, no. 2 (April 1984), 207–24.
61. Ibid., 210.
62. John W. Meyer, W. Richard Scott, and Terrence E. Deal, "Institutional and Technical Sources of Organizational Structure: Explaining the Structure of Educational Organizations," in *Organization and the Human Services: Cross-Disciplinary Reflections*, ed. Herman D. Stein (Philadelphia: Temple University Press, 1981), pp. 151–79.

7

Managing Organizational Politics I: Power and Influence

The purpose of this and the next chapter is to suggest ways for managing organizational politics that will decrease the negative consequences of unresolved conflicts, and increase the overall effectiveness of an agency and its programs. Unless properly managed, political conflicts within organizations inevitably dissolve into factional disputes, mutual distrust, blaming behavior, and feelings of hopelessness and impotence. When successfully managed, these same conflicts and animosities can lead organizational members to a heightened appreciation of each other's goals, values, and interests and to a stronger sense of shared purpose.[1]

Organizational politics are based in the competing interests of actors within and outside the organization. Not all conflicts, though, give rise to political behavior. Many disagreements within organizations stem from misunderstandings, breakdowns in communication, poorly designed governance systems, or missing or inaccurate information. These differences can be resolved through improved communication and reporting channels, increased consultation and education, and the provision of timely and accurate information. Many other potential conflicts never surface because most employees are concerned with only a fraction of the issues that come up in an organization and ignore the rest — what Barnard called an individual's "zone of indifference."[2]

The conflicts that lead to political behavior, by contrast, are based in irreconcilable differences over important interests, such as an individual's position and prerogatives in the organization, and over deeply held values and beliefs regarding organizational goals and programs. There are, moreover, only three ways to resolve these conflicts productively. I say productively because there is a fourth way — stalemate — that, while often the course of action taken, represents a breakdown in an organization's ability to deal with conflict.[3] Conflicts are resolved when (1) bureaucratic authority is used to impose a resolution; (2) one of the parties to the conflict is able to acquire sufficient power to either force the other's compliance or to gain the other's cooperation in what is seen as a shared enterprise; or (3) the conflicts are reconciled through mutual adjustments brought about through negotiations and compromise. The bulk of organizational conflicts are handled bureaucratically. Conflicts among people at the same organizational rank are referred to their common superior at the next higher level for resolution. Disagreements between superiors and subordinates can ultimately be settled by the superior's invocation of his or her organizational authority.

Political behavior comes into play when bureaucratic mechanisms break down. The factors contributing to this breakdown in social agencies were detailed in Chapter Two. They include increased competition over declining resources, growing organizational interdependence and complexity, changing attitudes toward authority, and greater disagreement over the purposes of social service programs. Political strategies for addressing organizational conflicts involve (1) the acquisition and use of power and influence and (2) skillful negotiation. The present chapter looks at ways in which organizational members get and use power to further their goals, and Chapter Eight takes up issues involved in negotiations and bargaining.

THE POWER MOTIVE

Factors that influence individual attitudes toward the use of organizational power include personality traits, personal and professional values, the nature of one's organizational position, and contingencies that arise from the task at hand. These factors can be examined from the vantage point of Ripple's analytical scheme of "motivation, capacity, and opportunity" to assess the role each plays in promoting or retarding an individual's propensity to engage in the organizational power process.[4]

People's motivations to acquire and use power, whether within or outside organizations, vary from the pure political type to the antipolitical individual. Lasswell described the political type as an individual for whom

> the power opportunities of each situation are selected in preference to other opportunities. As such a person moves from infancy through maturity, he becomes progressively predisposed to respond to the power-shaping and

power-sharing possibilities of each situation in which he finds himself. If there is a political type in this sense, the basic characteristic will be the *accentuation of power in relation to other values within the personality when compared with other persons.*[5]

By contrast, the antipolitical type sees participation in the power process as incompatible with personal or professional values.

Motivated behavior is a function of the strength of various needs; people are motivated to do something to satisfy a particular need. Psychological studies of the power motive have found that people seek power to satisfy a need to have an impact on other people through influencing or controlling their behavior. McClelland suggested that this need may be shown "by strong action, such as assaults and aggression, by giving help, assistance or advice, by controlling another, by influencing, persuading someone, or trying to impress someone...."[6] There are a number of psychological measures that assess the strength of an individual's power motive. Figure 7-1 presents one such instrument that measures the strength of four motives (achievement, affiliation, autonomy, dominance) in shaping individual orientations to work. Although there has been little research on the

FIGURE 7-1. Manifest Needs Questionnaire (MNQ). (*Source:* Richard M. Steers and Daniel N. Braunstein, "A Behaviorally-Based Measure of Manifest Needs in Work Settings," *Journal of Vocational Behavior*, 9, no. 2 (October 1976), 251–66. Reprinted by permission of Academic Press.)

Achievement Items
    I do my best work when my job assignments are fairly difficult.
    I try very hard to improve on my past performance at work.
    I take moderate risks and stick my neck out to get ahead at work.
    I try to perform better than my co-workers.

Affiliation Items
    When I have a choice, I try to work in a group instead of by myself.
    I pay a good deal of attention to the feelings of others at work.
    I find myself talking to those around me about non-work-related matters.

Autonomy Items
    In my work assignments, I try to be my own boss.
    I go my own way at work, regardless of the opinions of others.
    I disregard rules and regulations that hamper my personal freedom.
    I try my best to work alone on a job.

Dominance Items
    I seek an active role in the leadership of a group.
    I find myself organizing and directing the activities of others.
    I strive to gain more control over the events around me at work.
    I strive to be "in command" when I am working in a group.

power motives of social workers, the studies that have been done suggest that social workers, particularly those in direct service provision, have low power motivation. A study of how business and social work students perceived their use of power, for example, found that social work students concentrating in administration had self-perceptions of power that were more like those of business students than of social work students concentrating in interpersonal intervention.[7] Another study found that students majoring in casework were less assertive than those majoring in group work or administration.[8] A study of social workers who had moved from clinical to management positions found that the major problems they encountered centered around the assumption and exercise of authority with subordinates and dealing with the political aspects of administration.[9] These findings assume added significance since the majority of social workers in administrative positions began their careers as clinicians.

If these findings actually tap into an aversion among social workers toward the use of power, the question arises of what can be done to correct this problem. Unless they can overcome this obstacle, social workers — whether clinicians or administrators — will find themselves excluded from the political life of their organizations and seriously limited in their ability to influence policies and practices. There are three possible strategies for addressing this issue. The first is to challenge the position that social workers are, in fact, averse to using power in their work. The second is to legitimize the use of power in social work practice. The third is to develop interventions for changing the behavior of social workers regarding the use of power.

Masking the Power Motive

Because power-motivated behavior is potentially threatening to the social order, McClelland noted, "there is no type of behavior that society regulates more carefully than expressions of power."[10] This attitude is particularly true for American society, where the exercise of power is viewed with more suspicion and distrust than in probably any other country in the world.[11] Ours is a society that places individual liberty at the top of its list of national values and provides a myriad of legal safeguards, beginning with the Constitution and the Bill of Rights, to protect the freedoms of its citizens. In a society that subscribes to the legal and philosophical doctrine that all people are created equal, Broyard suggested,

> there is no longer any way to live compatibly with authority. The coherent civilizations of earlier centuries depended on a universal respect for inequality, and we have lost forever that kind of innocence. We are all legally as good as one another now and every difference is an indictment.[12]

Besides being a democratic society, we are also a scientific one. As noted earlier, Americans are more likely to accept another's authority if it is based in — or claimed to be based in — scientific expertise.

For social workers, as both Americans and members of an occupation that aspires to professional status based on scientifically derived skills and expertise, the exercise of power violates a number of values. Even though the use of power may be alien to political and professional ideologies, social workers *do* exercise power in their work. Since the passage of the Social Security Act in 1935, policy analysts have been concerned with the discrepancy between the powerlessness of the clients applying for benefits and the power of the people who control benefit distribution. The critical issue has been how to fit a professionalized activity like social work, which assigns a central role to discretionary decision making by professionals, with the formal requirements of public administration, especially the concerns with due process and equitable treatment for all citizens. The nub of the issue, Keith-Lucas argued, was that

> the legal rights established in the [Social Security] Act presumed recipients to be self-directing, rational beings. Casework, despite its apparent acceptance of these rights, was learning largely from a psychology that held man to be basically irrational.[13]

These early concerns about power imbalances between welfare providers and recipients, and their potential abuse, have been borne out in studies on how social workers' use of power shapes the ways in which services are provided.[14] Social workers often control resources that clients need and cannot get elsewhere. This conformance to the concept of a power-dependence relationship is why psychologists define the giving of help as one expression of the power motive. For help to be given, McClelland argued,

> help must be received. And in accepting a gift, or help, the receiver can be perceived as acknowledging that he is weaker, at least in this respect, than the person who is giving him help. Thus, giving and receiving may have a "zero sum" quality analogous to winning and losing. To the extent that one person wins or gives, the other must lose or receive.[15]

This win-lose quality is true whether the parties to the relationship recognize and define it as such, or whether they give more socially desirable names to the interaction.

Thus, the exercise of power is not unknown to social workers, although they are more likely to define their control over resources needed by clients as part of the professional authority granted by their community mandate to offer services. The profession's code of ethics, in addition, provides strictures governing social workers' relationships with clients and clearly states that the social worker's primary responsibility is to clients. The argument that social workers only use their authority (or power) on behalf of their clients becomes blurred, however, when we consider that much of social work practice involves strong elements of social control. The provision of resources that clients want (money, day care, public housing) often is contingent upon clients changing their behavior to conform to standards set by the social worker, who is acting on behalf of the agency and the community. In these instances, the question of who the client is, Specht pointed out,

> is not always obvious. Professionals work with and for individuals, families, groups, organizations, and communities; it is sometimes difficult to determine in whose interest the professional is working and to whom the professional has ultimate accountability.[16]

The reluctance of social workers and other professionals to recognize the extent to which the use of power is part of their work is magnified when we look at their interactions with people other than clients. In addition to working with clients, human service professionals must establish relationships with organizational and professional colleagues and with administrative and political superiors.[17] Power relationships with clients have received the most attention because they are the clinical social worker's primary concern and, perhaps more importantly, because a framework exists that enables the use of power with clients to be rationalized in terms acceptable to the professional. This framework consists of practice principles regarding the use of authority with clients and normative guidelines set by the profession's code of ethics.[18]

When it comes to relationships with colleagues and superiors, however, professionals are more reluctant to examine the nature of these interactions, particularly the power dynamics involved. In their relationships with clients, professionals have the authority and autonomy to define the form and content of the interaction and to control its direction. This role is less true in their interactions with colleagues, and even less so when they interact with superiors. For professionals to exercise influence with peers and superiors, they must often engage in overt political activities. Those who do so are reluctant to admit it because of the perceived incompatibility of such activities with professional values and standards of practice. Others who might be inclined to adopt a more political approach to their work are dissuaded from doing so because of the value strain it would create.

Legitimizing Power

For the power motive, or any motive, to express itself in action, there must be opportunities for taking action and norms that legitimize the action. The normative question is critical, since professional social workers tend to view participation in organizational or community power processes in a negative light. One area in which the profession comes close to endorsing power acquisition as a legitimate part of professional practice is client advocacy. The Code of Ethics contains a number of provisions governing the social worker's "ethical responsibility to society" and holds that social workers should act to "ensure that all persons have access to the resources, services, and opportunities which they require…[and] expand choice and opportunity for all persons, with specific regard for disadvantaged or oppressed groups or persons."[19] Although social workers are expected to advocate on behalf of their clients, the profession is generally silent about how they should do that, and the professional schools do little to prepare their graduates for this kind of work. The profession's ambivalence about the role of advocacy in professional practice is due, in part, to the fact that advocacy entails the use of political influence tactics as a major component of practice.

It is through client advocacy, however, that participation in the power process can most realistically be legitimated as part of social work practice. The idea that the exercise of power is justified when used on behalf of others is the major argument for legitimating the use of power in all spheres. Since Aristotle, political and social theorists have distinguished between rulers who use power to pursue their own interests and rulers who use power to promote the well-being of the community. Exercising power on behalf of others is seen as an essential quality of leadership and a sign of individual maturity. It is what distinguishes the mere politician from the statesperson, the leader from what Kelly called the "destructive achiever."[20] Seen from this perspective, power means efficacy and capacity. Power in societies and organizations, Kanter suggested,

> is analogous in simple terms to physical power: it is the ability to mobilize resources…to get things done. The true sign of power, then, is accomplishment — not fear, terror, or tyranny. Where the power is "on," the system can be productive; where the power is "off," the system bogs down.[21]

While the use of power theoretically can be seen as a positive, constructive activity, people differ in their estimations of the likelihood of something positive being realized in practice. Our beliefs about whether power is a force for good or evil depend on how seriously we heed Lord Acton's caution that "power corrupts and absolute power corrupts absolutely." For those who view power negatively, the nub of the matter seems to be that in order to *have power* one must first *seek power*. From this perspective, it is not the possession of power that is necessarily the corrupting force, but the actions that must be taken to acquire it. To participate in the power process, one must engage in activities which in many people's eyes are morally and ethically suspect. If social workers are to exercise influence over peers, subordinates, or superiors, they must often engage in interactions that may demand the exchange of resources "that are inappropriate and undesirable in the professional's view, such as money, status, prestige, and even love in return for organizational resources."[22] The exercise of political influence in organizations means, as we saw in previous chapters, that professionals must manage the flow of information, ingratiate themselves with powerful people, manage impressions, form coalitions, and influence the order and content of issues that come before key decision makers. These tactics are all instances of a general kind of behavior that Brager called "artfulness," or the "conscious rearranging of reality to induce a desired...outcome."[23]

For many, however, artfulness is another word for manipulation and therefore cannot be part of ethical professional practice. Even though the ethical dilemmas are deep and significant, many social workers do choose to engage in the power process when they deem it the only feasible strategy for realizing their goals. Professional support for these individuals and their work has waxed and waned over the history of social work, largely because of shifts in the climate surrounding the provision of social services. Gilbert and his colleagues suggested that the context within which social services operate are influenced by the competing values of participation, leadership, and expertise.[24] Each value is associated with different approaches to planning and providing services. Participation entails broadening of democratic processes in policymaking and service delivery; leadership emphasizes the importance of upper- level managers and influential community members; and expertise looks to professionals and technicians as key actors. These values cycle in and out of favor, causing shifts in attitudes toward the most desirable approach to policy development, program planning, and service provision.

The leadership variable is most closely allied with the use of power and participation in the political process, both within organizations and community. The role assigned to leadership by the social work profession, however, has declined in recent years. This decline is in marked contrast, Brilliant noted, to the profession's early history, when social workers

> manifested leadership both within and outside the profession. We have had leaders of great significance to the development of the profession and of professional expertise, and we have had some who achieved a prominent place in the community at large....Jane Addams, Edward T. Devine, and Florence Kelly...earned reputations beyond the social work community, influencing the course of social welfare and the quality of life in our country in a broader sense.[25]

During the 1930s, and again in the 1960s, a number of social workers played influential roles in the New Deal, the civil rights movement, the War on Poverty, and the Model Cities program. Since the 1970s, however, the role of leadership has given way to an emphasis on developing the technical core of the profession and consolidating social work's claims to expertise in the design and provision of social services.

The profession's receptivity to involvement in organizational and community political processes as a legitimate part of practice is largely a result of the emphasis given to leadership and advocacy at any given time. Much of the social work literature on power, influence, and advocacy was written during the late 1960s and early 1970s, when the emphasis on leadership for social reform was the strongest in recent history. Social work's current de-emphasis of the role of leadership is in sharp contrast to fields like business and public administration, where the preparation of graduates to assume leadership positions is given high priority. There are indications, however, that this attitude is changing as social work practitioners and educators call for social workers to assume leadership roles in the human services and renew their commitment to advocating for the profession's vision of social welfare and social justice.[26] If the profession moves in this direction, we can once again expect to see the development of skills in exercising organizational and political influence recognized as an important part of professional practice.

Power Motivation Training

The third approach to social workers and organizational power accepts both the position that power is an important and legitimate part of professional practice and the argument that social workers generally have low power motivations. This approach assumes that power motivation, like other personality attributes, can be developed and looks to interventions for raising power motivation. This perspective has gained wide acceptance lately as previously excluded groups such as women and minorities pursue management careers in greater numbers and look to continuing education programs for training in a range of management skills, including acquiring and using power and managing organizational politics. As with other programs for changing individual behavior, power motivation training involves an assessment of an individual's current power motivation, discussion of alternative ways of thinking about power, presentation of specific skills for acquiring and using power, and opportunities to apply these skills in simulated training exercises and on-the-job situations.[27]

The presentation of alternative ways of thinking about power is particularly important because it provides individuals with an opportunity to look at power-oriented behavior in a framework that presents positive as well as negative reasons for why people might want to increase their power motivations. As noted earlier, the use of power is viewed by Americans in a mostly negative light. This attitude is probably even more widespread among social workers, since a leading theoretical discussion of the harmful aspects of power-oriented behavior comes from dynamic psychology, to which many social workers are attuned. Dynamically oriented psychologists view power motivation as an *irrational impulse*.[28] From this perspective, power motivation is defined as an individual's need to gain satisfaction from manipulating and influencing others; the act of manipulation becomes the means and the end in itself. According to Kipnis, the origins of this need are variously ascribed to either the developing individual's way of responding to an absence of love..., or to his feeling of inferiority..., or to continual anxiety....[W]hen we talk of power motivations in terms of gaining satisfaction from influencing others many people see power needs as representing the irrational, neurotic, and perverted aspects of man's nature.[29]

The view of power seeking as neurotic behavior, while widespread, is only one of at least three explanations of why people seek power. The others are power motivation as *role behavior* and as *instrumental behavior*.[30] Much power-oriented behavior is due to the interdependent nature of modern organizations, which requires people to influence others in order to do their jobs. This factor, coupled with the fact that the dependence inherent in most jobs is greater than the formal authority given to people in those jobs, means that political dynamics are, as Kotter noted, "inevitable and are needed to make organizations function well."[31] Employees with little organizational experience often assume that the formal authority attached to their positions gives them the control over the people and events that is needed for them to do their jobs. New managers take it for granted that their formal authority will ensure that workers under their direction will perform their jobs in accordance with agency goals and policies. It doesn't take long, however, before they find out that the authority of a position does not translate automatically into the power of the incumbent to direct the actions of subordinates. "While appointments to positions come from above," Zaleznik commented, "affirmation of position comes from below. The only difference between party and organizational politics is in the subtlety of the voting procedure."[32] The situation becomes further complicated as managers realize not only that they are dependent on subordinates to get the job done, but that their dependencies extend to their immediate superiors and to people in other units or departments who are at their own, a higher, or a lower rank. In these instances, the manager has no formal authority over those who make up the task environment for the work for which he or she is responsible.

To get the compliance of those upon whom they are dependent, managers and other organizational members often have to engage in power-oriented behavior, even though it may be personally distasteful. At best, this approach to power sees it simply as one of many things a person must do to get the job done. At worst, it has the potential for serious abuses of one's organizational position. When power motivation is derived solely from organizational role requirements, people tend to see themselves as not responsible for their actions, believing that the organization has granted them "absolution" for their behavior.[33] When carried to an extreme, this attitude can lead to a syndrome that Nielsen called "Eichmann as manager." Eichmann, he argued, was a thoughtless man

who did not understand what was right or wrong about his role as a manager in an organization that harmed people. He was not able to distinguish right from wrong in his organizational context because he did not think about what he was doing and cooperating with.[34]

When people do not feel personally accountable for their behavior, the organizational equivalent of mob psychology begins to operate; individuals feel free to do things to others that they would find reprehensible in another context.

The third approach to power motivation sees it as *instrumental behavior*. Unlike the other approaches, which cast power-oriented behavior as neurotic aberrations or the irresponsible and thoughtless actions of petty bureaucrats, this perspective sees power motivation as a universal attribute of human beings. People seek to control resources in order to influence others, thereby accomplishing the things they want and gaining the rewards to which they aspire. When power is thought of in instrumental terms, individual orientations to power shift from How can I increase my personal control over others (whether for neurotic or bureaucratic reasons)? to How can I influence others so that, together, we can accomplish our goals? A critical element in this approach is the ability to identify and articulate goals toward which others can become committed. This tactic, paradoxically, leads to a concern with *increasing the power of others*, rather than seeking their submission to one's wishes. People cannot influence others, McClelland argued, unless they express "vivid goals" which the others want.

> [I]n no case does it make sense to speak as if his role is to force submission. Rather it is to strengthen and uplift, to make people feel that they are the origins, not the pawns, of the…system.…His message is not so much: "Do as I say because I am strong and know best…," but rather, "Here are the goals which are true and right and which we share. Here is how we can reach them. You are strong and capable. You can accomplish these goals."[35]

To be effective, power-motivation training, whether conducted in schools of social work or extracurricular training programs, must go beyond training in specific behaviors aimed at improving an individual's ability to influence others. People's thinking about the nature of power relationships in general, as well as within organizations, must be made explicit. Alternative conceptions of the role of power in human affairs, such as those described above, need to be addressed if participants in these programs are to develop an approach to power that goes beyond Machiavellian manipulation and crass political maneuvering.

CAPACITY FOR POWER

Power is the ability of one person to get another person to do something that he or she would not otherwise do. A person, A, is able to exercise power over another, B, when A can overcome B's resistance to doing what A wishes. To do that, A must control resources that B needs and has no alternative source of supply. A power relationship develops when one person complies with another's wishes in exchange for resources controlled by the latter. Capacity for power is the extent to which people control the resources that enable them to direct others. Capacity for power refers to the *what* of power, in contrast to the *why* (motivation) or *how* (opportunity) of power.

The kinds of resources that individuals control are critical to understanding power relationships because different resources give rise to different amounts and forms of power. A resource is anything people need to do their jobs, and the definition of what is or is not a resource depends on the job at hand. The value of any resource varies from job to job and, within the same job, from time to time as assignments change. For example, an important resource for a manager charged with setting up a monitoring system for foster care placements is expertise in management information systems and computer technology. If that resource is possessed by one staff member only, that person will be in a position to influence his or her superior through control of the resource. When that same manager's assignment changes to recruiting adoptive parents for minority children in foster care, the resource shifts to someone who has knowledge of the community and access to influential community leaders. In this example, the computer expert's influence with the boss will decline, while the community worker's increases.

Although anything is potentially a resource, there are general types of resources which form the bases for different kinds of power transactions. Polsby, for example, identified the following potential power bases: money and credit; control over jobs; control over the information of others; social standing; knowledge and expertness; popularity, esteem, charisma; legality, constitutionality, officiality, legitimacy; ethnic solidarity; the right to vote; time; and personal energy.[36] A widely used categorization of power resources is French and Raven's typology of *reward power, coercive power, legitimate power, referent power,* and *expert power.*[37] Each power base varies in strength, range, and the degree of dependence it commands on the part of another. The following discussion examines the general characteristics of these bases of power and how they are used in organizational power processes.

Reward Power

Reward power is based on A's ability to give benefits to B in exchange for B's compliance with A's wishes. These benefits can be tangible (salary increases, additional staff and secretarial help, opportunities for travel, well-appointed offices) and intangible (recognition, prestige, deferential treatment). The strength of reward power increases with the size of the rewards which B perceives that A controls, and with B's belief in the probability that A can actually deliver these rewards.

For rewards to work as a basis for influencing another's behavior, the incentives that A controls must be attractive enough to B to induce him or her to go along with A's wishes. Since people's needs vary over time, it is important to know what B's needs are at the time of A's influence attempt. Many approaches to understanding human needs adopt a temporal or developmental framework that assumes that people's needs change as they progress through the life cycle. One of the best known of these is Maslow's hierarchy of needs, with physiological and safety needs at the base, the need for love and esteem at the next level, and the need for self-actualization at the top.[38] Alderfer refined this approach in his "existence-relatedness-growth" (ERG) theory of human needs.[39] Existence needs are concerned with material objects (food, water, air, money). They may not even be noticed when there is no scarcity, but set off

> win-lose competition whenever there are not enough of the material objects to meet everyone's needs. Relatedness needs are concerned with significant others...and have the process of mutuality as the means to satisfy these needs....Individual growth proceeds in cycles of differentiation, during which people develop more complex awareness of themselves, and integration, during which people consolidate their many parts into a whole.[40]

The strength of these needs was found to be influenced by an individual's stage in the life cycle, as well as by his or her social background and gender. The desire for relatedness with supervisors followed an inverted U-shaped curve as young adults developed relationships with mentors and ended them as they entered the midlife transition. Strength of growth desires generally followed a downward slope from early adulthood, when needs for growth are highest, to the midlife stage, when these needs are lowest. There were, however, exceptions for those who sought renewed opportunities for growth in middle life. By contrast, strength of existence needs (desire for pay) showed no relationship with life cycle stages. Individuals with parents of higher educational levels had stronger needs for growth and weaker needs for relatedness with supervisors than those whose parents had lower educational levels. Men showed higher strength of existence desires and lower needs for relatedness to work groups than women. There was no significant difference between men and women in the strength of their needs for relatedness to supervisors or growth.[41]

To make the best use of rewards as a basis for influence, managers must be sensitive to the range of needs that people have at different points in their professional and personal lives. This point is particularly important for social administrators, since the amount of tangible rewards such as salary and other perquisites that they control is usually quite limited. They must, therefore, seek other benefits as a basis for influencing behavior.

Coercive Power

The basis of coercive power is the ability to inflict punishment upon others if they don't comply with your wishes. Historically, coercion has been the most widely used form of control; well into the twentieth century, employers had almost life-and-death power over employees. The use of coercion in contemporary organizations has declined, largely as a result of the protections afforded employees by unions, civil services, and other employee associations. Even when managers are able to use punishment, or the threats of punishment, as a means of control, they are often dissuaded from doing so by the growing body of psychological evidence which suggests that punitive behavior is not as effective in inducing compliance as are positive rewards, particularly when trying to get another to engage in complex behaviors to produce positive results.[42]

Even though coercion is no longer regarded as an effective or ethical means of motivating workers, it is nevertheless an important part of an organization's political life. The use of coercion as a power resource brings us into the twilight zone between "clean" and "dirty" politics, whether in an organizational or community context. The punishments which form the basis of coercive power range from the use of physical force, to taking away valued things (pay, perquisites, autonomy), to psychological harm through insults and degradations. While the use of physical force is increasingly rare, the other forms of punishments are often resorted to when political struggles intensify.

One way that coercion enters into organizational politics is through what O'Day called "intimidation rituals."[43] This strategy is used to suppress dissenting opinions and, in its most extreme form, to discredit and eliminate "whistle blowers," the name given to people who seek to bring information about actual or possible wrongdoings by organizational elites to the attention of regulatory bodies or the general public. The goal of intimidation rituals is to control the dissenter so he or she cannot gain additional support and to exercise this control in ways that absolve those using coercion from any wrongdoing.

Intimidation rituals consist of four steps: *nullification, isolation, defamation,* and *expulsion*. Nullification occurs when dissenters are told by their superiors that their accusations of wrongdoing or suggestions for alternative policies or practices are invalid. If the dissenter is not immediately awed by bureaucratic authority, the superior will agree to conduct an "investigation," the results of which will "convince the reformer that his accusations are groundless and that his suggestions for enhancing organizational effectiveness or revising organizational goals have been duly noted by the appropriate authorities."[44] If dissenters persist in their efforts, higher management may try to isolate them from their peers, subordinates, and superiors, making it difficult for them to mobilize support. This step is done through closing communication links, restricting freedom of movement, reducing resources, and, most importantly, systematic unresponsiveness to the dissenter's criticisms or suggestions. Unresponsiveness can build up enormous psychological pressures in the dissenter due to mounting feelings of frustration and impotence. These feelings can cause a person to overreact by pressing claims in ways that violate organizational policies or norms, thus confirming management's depiction of the dissenter as irresponsible or psychologically unstable.

If the dissenter is still undaunted, the intimidation ritual moves into the defamation stage, in which the dissenter's character and motives are impugned. Dissenters are cut off from a potentially sympathetic following by attributing their suggestions or criticisms to questionable motives, psychopathology, or gross incompetence. One tactic is to accuse the dissenter of

> acting out his Oedipal conflicts. Such a personalization of a subordinate's reform efforts (especially a younger subordinate) permits his superior to present himself as a harassed "father" faced with a troubled "son," and blocks any examination of his conduct that might reveal provocation on his part.[45]

The final step in the process, should the dissenter continue in his or her opposition, is expulsion from the organization. In order to be effective, however, the dissenter should leave the organization voluntarily. In this way, management can avoid the public and formal proceedings that often accompany an official request for dismissal of an employee. Voluntary resignation is particularly important when organizational elites are reluctant to air their dirty linen in public.

While intimidation rituals are not the kind of practices that one would expect of professional social workers, or any other responsible managers, the differences between their elements and many practices that managers feel are legitimate and ethical tend to be matters of degree rather than kind. For example, there's a fine line separating the actions of managers who use human relations skills to direct employees' attention away from what may be substantive requests or complaints to an examination of their motives for raising these concerns, from the nullification and defamation tactics described above.[46] Similarly, under some circumstances it is perfectly acceptable for managers to control information to prevent adversaries from learning about their goals and strategies, while under other conditions this tactic would amount to coercion through isolation. The context and circumstances within which the action takes place determine whether it is within the bounds of acceptable behavior. It is circumstances, Edmund Burke remarked, that "render every civil and political scheme beneficial or noxious."

Legitimate Power

Legitimate power is based in a person's beliefs regarding another's right to direct his or her behavior. In Weber's classic analysis, legitimate power is synonymous with authority, which can be traditional, charismatic, or rational-legal (see Chapter Two). These forms of power are based in cultural norms, extraordinary individual characteristics, and belief in the rightness of existing social structures. Of the three, the rational-legal authority that comes from an individual's organizational position has been the most important source of power because, unlike other forms of power, it is *renewed when it is exercised.* The use of reward or coercive power, for example, involves using scarce resources (money, promotions, threats) to gain another's compliance. By contrast, when a subordinate complies with a superior's orders in the belief that the superior's position establishes a *right* to issue orders, the superior's authority is strengthened rather than depleted.

Although legitimate authority is the most efficient form of power, its use in contemporary organizations has become problematic. As noted earlier, there are indications of a growing reluctance on the part of employees to accept the legitimate power of organizational leaders in both the public and private sectors. In their review of research on public attitudes toward business and governmental leaders, Mitchell and Scott found that the public's confidence in their leaders has been declining since the mid-1960s and that "Americans no longer feel that it is their obligation or responsibility to believe what their leaders tell them or to do what their leaders ask of them."[47] This change in attitude does not mean that leaders are no longer able to control their employees, but it has made it necessary for leaders to develop sources of power separate from their formal authority. Individuals holding high organizational positions have, in addition to authority, other sources of power. They control rewards and punishments, are often acknowledged experts in their fields, and may have command presence by dint of their forceful personalities. They are thus able to exercise control through reward, coercive, referent, and expert power.

It may seem like hair splitting to dwell on the difference between legitimate power and other forms, but the distinction is important. Legitimate power is the power of position; all a person needs to do to exercise that power is to gain the position. As people's willingness to comply with those in positions of authority declines, however, position power loses its strength and the incumbents of those positions must develop other sources of power to do their jobs. This distinction is central to organizational politics because, for many people, legitimate power is the only appropriate form of power within an organization. All other forms of control are seen as one or another form of politicking, and thus as illegitimate.

Even though there may be a decline in people's willingness to comply with authoritative directives, the power of position is still a major force in organizational life. People in important organizational positions have a lot of influence over what happens within the organization.[48] Of course, it may be true that people who attain high rank within an organization had other sources of power (expertise, control over resources, personal dynamism) which propelled them upward. Nevertheless, having an important position is a major asset in any organizational influence process.

The use of legitimate power has become problematic for social work managers as they occupy fewer and fewer middle- and upper-management positions in the major agencies responsible for income transfers and services for children, the mentally and physically disabled, and the elderly. Since the mid-1970s, managers trained in business and public administration have made significant inroads in positions previously held by social workers. Social work managers are considered to be out of step with the growing conservatism that makes cost containment the sole measure of program effectiveness. Ideologies aside, social workers are seen as having neither the technical skills nor the personal traits needed to manage large organizations. If social workers want to correct this situation, the professional schools must offer opportunities for social workers to acquire the skills required for the effective performance of middle- and upper-level management roles. In addition, social workers must have a more realistic orientation to career mobility, including ways to cope with the conflicts between identification as a professional social worker and managerial career aspirations.

Referent Power

Referent power is based in the desire of one person to identify psychologically with another. People want to be closely associated with individuals to whom they are attracted. Identification can become the basis of a power relationship because

> P's [the person influenced] identification with O [the influencer] can be established or maintained if P behaves, believes, and perceives as O does….A verbalization of such power by P might be, "I am like O, and therefore I shall behave or believe as O does," or "I want to be like O, and I will be more like O if I behave or believe as O does."[49]

The qualities that make people attractive include a pleasing physical appearance, high activity level, emotional stability, skill in developing relationships, good humor, and optimism in the face of adversity. Attractive characteristics specific to organizational roles include a record of successfully carrying out difficult assignments, the possession of unique skills and competencies, and a reputation for reliability and impartiality.

An important basis for referent power is an individual's perceived ability to cope with the uncertainties facing the organization. A central feature of social agencies is the degree of uncertainty and indeterminacy that surrounds their operations. While these organizations are able to accomplish things and have an impact on their clients and the community, it is often unclear just how they did what they did and what factors led to one set of outcomes rather than another. All organizations exist, moreover, within a sociocultural context which assumes that organizations are rational, purposeful systems that pursue goals and use means explicitly chosen by the people formally charged with their operations. This discrepancy between relatively low levels of understanding of how organizations work, and society's expectation that organizations are under the rational control of those responsible for them, is resolved, Meindl and his colleagues argued, by a biased preference to understand important but causally indeterminate and ambiguous organizational events and occurrences in terms of leadership. Accordingly, in the absence of direct, unambiguous information that would allow one rationally to infer the locus of causality, the romanticized conception of leadership permits us to be more comfortable in associating leaders — by ascribing to them control and responsibility — with events to which they can be plausibly linked.[50]

The rational response to a problem is to analyze the problem's components to find the correct solution. But the problems that social workers deal with are so complex and ambiguous that rational analysis is of limited use. The variables that make up the problem are so numerous as to be incalculable, and the ones that are identified are often things about which little is known. The AIDS epidemic, for example, raised the question of instructing school-age children in the use of condoms as a public health measure. The establishment of permanency planning as a national policy for children in substitute care and the growing number of minority children needing foster and adoptive families raised the question of the appropriateness of transracial adoptions and the use of nontraditional foster placements such as single-parent families. Finding correct answers to these questions is a difficult (some would say impossible) task because of the number of issues each approach raises and our limited understanding of their likely consequences. People who present clear and convincing arguments for taking action in situations where knowledge is limited or absent will be influential in shaping the thinking and behavior of others. Their influence, moreover, comes from their intense convictions and strongly held beliefs, qualities that people wish to identify with in ambiguous and amorphous situations. An important source of referent power in social agencies, then, is a manager's ability to convey his or her beliefs about what should be done about baffling and complex problems. Individuals who can act forcefully not only when they *know* what is the right course of action, but when — in the absence of knowledge — they *believe* in a course of action, will be looked to for leadership.

Expert Power

This form of power is based on a person's possession of knowledge that others do not have but need in order to do their work. Both components of this power base are difficult for social workers to establish. Social work's knowledge base is seen by many outside the field as general information about human relation skills, the social-psychology of individual and family behavior, and public policies for dependent populations — information that is readily available to the average educated person. Even when social workers can demonstrate that they have specialized knowledge not available to others, the utility of this knowledge for solving problems is often disputed.

Expert power is available to social work managers, but they must think about expertise in different ways. The problems that organizations face are often specific to their situations and require expertise in an organization's unique characteristics, its services, environment, and clientele. There is a permanent tension, Pruger argued,

> between the organization's need to deal with the world as it is and its inability to command the technical skills this requires. Equally permanent is the opportunity for the ambitious, prescient bureaucrat to acquire some of the needed expertise and the benefits this will bring him and the organization he serves.[51]

In business management, for example, there is a growing uneasiness with general managers who, based on their professional education in schools of business administration and management science, claim to be able to step into any organization and run it well. Research indicates, rather, that successful managers have substantial knowledge of the businesses in which they are involved, including the specific products, competitors, markets, customers, technologies, unions, and governmental regulations associated with their respective industries.[52]

Managerial styles vary depending on how strongly managers identify with their organizations, as opposed to external groups such as professional associations. Gouldner referred to the former as "locals" and the latter as "cosmopolitans," a distinction used in the analysis of management styles in social agencies.[53] Managers with a local orientation are knowledgeable about all aspects of the agency's operations, its history, its relationships with the community, the idiosyncrasies of the staff, and anything else that is relevant to how the organization goes about its work. A newly appointed executive director of an agency, for example, read the minutes of agency staff meetings for as far back as records were kept. At his first staff meeting, he not only impressed the staff with his detailed knowledge of how agency practices had evolved (thus avoiding the liabilities of newness that come with not knowing the territory), but commanded their respect because of the esteem he showed for the organization, its history, and culture.

Expert power is acquired not only through detailed knowledge of an organization and its operations, but also through specialized knowledge about the unique problems facing an agency. For example, for most social agencies competition for clients and money will continue to intensify as more and more organizations enter the human service field and the amount of public — particularly federal — dollars declines. Important areas of expertise in this situation are the ability to develop, implement, and manage innovative approaches to service and to identify and secure funds from nonpublic sources, particularly the business community. Although there are general guides to program innovation and fund raising, the important issues that agencies have to deal with will be unique to their organizational structure and culture, the point in time in their developmental history, and the specific political, social, economic, and cultural conditions that surround their operations. People with expertise in how to deal with these situations will play influential roles in decision making.

POWER OPPORTUNITIES

Politically oriented managers are always alert to opportunities to use their power and influence to advance their interests and those of their units. They also are able to create opportunities for exercising influence where none appears to exist. The way they think about problems, interact with others, and perform their jobs advances their interests. The cognitive, behavioral, and organizational techniques used to create power opportunities are summarized in Figure 7-2. The purpose of this section is to examine these techniques in detail and suggest how they can be used by social work managers.

Thinking Politically

Most professionals develop an ideology about their work in the form of a body of systematically related beliefs about what they do. Mental health professionals, for example, usually subscribe to a psychological world view that sees events as caused primarily by people's psychological makeup and predispositions. Social reformers, by contrast, are more likely to have a sociological world view that sees the operations of social and economic systems as the primary explanation of why things are the way they are and why people behave the way they do. If there is a political world view, its central tenet would be the inevitability and ubiquitousness of conflict in human affairs. Politically oriented individuals assume that

FIGURE 7-2.   Categories of Political Behavior in Organizations.

Cognitive-Analytical
   Analyze power structures and vested interests
   Recognize and appreciate conflicts of interest
   Control agendas
   Control decision premises and alternatives

Personal-Interpersonal
   Develop personal and interpersonal intelligences
   Adjust mode of communication to audience and situation
   Build networks of relationships

Organizational-Programmatic
   Be sensitive to organizational norms
   Reduce organizational uncertainties
   Manage impressions

people's interests differ, and they approach any proposal from the perspective of the impact it is likely to have on others' interests. They also know that people's abilities to promote their interests vary with the amount of power and influence they have. Thus, a critical political skill is the ability to understand the interests represented in a given situation, the relationship between others' interests and your own, and the power of different actors to promote their interests and to block yours.

Diagnose Interests. The organizational chart provides a starting point for identifying the interests of organizational members. As the saying goes, "Where you stand depends on where you sit." People's organizational interests are heavily influenced by their positions, both hierarchically in terms of rank and functionally in terms of the work they do. People can be expected to take actions to protect and enhance their positions and the importance of their work to the organization as a whole. Another factor that shapes individual interests is a person's stage in the life cycle. The interests of people starting their careers will be different from those consolidating or ending their careers. The former are likely to be responsive to innovative proposals that can help them establish their own reputation and niche in the organization, whereas the latter will be more interested in conserving their positions and are likely to oppose innovations. Personal characteristics (gender, age, race, ethnicity) also play important roles in shaping organizational interests, particularly with the heightened awareness of, and resistance to, discriminatory practices based on these characteristics.

A factor unique to social workers is the tendency to develop an interest in a particular aspect of the social problem with which they are concerned. Contemporary social problems are complicated, multidimensional phenomena, and any one facet of a problem can become an organizing theme for thinking about the entire problem. Substance abuse, for example, can be looked at from the perspectives of its effects on an individual's mental and physical health, its contribution to the crime rate, its drain on public resources, and its impact on the quality of life in society generally.[54] Professionals working in this area are likely to develop an interest in one aspect of the problem, and that aspect becomes their major concern.

Based on their analysis of others' interests, managers should be able to estimate the number of people who will be in favor of, opposed to, or neutral toward their proposals. This assessment becomes the basis for how to proceed with a proposal. Specific questions that must be answered include, How much time should be spent consolidating the support of allies versus trying to win over neutrals? Are the objections of those opposed the kind that can be accommodated by incorporating elements of their interests into the proposal? If not, how much of a threat does the opposition pose relative to your own power to overcome it? The answers to these questions require, in addition to an understanding of people's interests, an assessment of their power in the organization.

Assess Power.

Assess Power. The organizational chart is also a good starting point for assessing power. Although the formal structure does not always reflect the actual distribution of power, it is still the best single indicator of an organization's power structure. In general, people in high organizational positions will have commensurately more power than those in lower positions. There are a number of exceptions to this generalization, but until they are shown to be true, the political manager must operate under the assumption that an organization's formal structure reflects people's actual power.

Power may also be assessed by the consequences of its use. An analysis of who benefits, and to what extent, from contested issues gives a clue to the relative power of the parties involved. Such things as budget allocations, assignment of personnel, and policy choices that are favored by, and favorable to, certain units are all reflections of the relative power of organizational members and units. Managers are powerful if they can intercede favorably on behalf of someone in trouble in the organization; get desirable placements or above-average salary increases for subordinates; get approval for expenditures beyond their budgets; get items on the agenda at policy meetings; get regular, frequent, and fast access to top decision makers; and get early information about decisions and policy shifts.[55]

A frequently used method of assessing organizational power is to ask people who the powerful are. There are serious limitations to this approach, however, because it assumes that the people asked actually know where power lies and are willing to tell what they know. Because it is based on people's subjective impressions, this approach is less reliable than the first two, which draw on an organization's official structure and on empirical data about the outcomes of major decisions. Another approach is to look at the sources of power that organizational members have. As discussed earlier, these include formal authority as well as coercive, reward, referent, and expert sources of power. This approach becomes an important strategy when there is evidence that the possession of these sources of power by organizational members is not accurately reflected in the official hierarchy. This situation often occurs in professional organizations like social agencies where individuals lower in the hierarchy may possess special skills or expertise that enable them to exert influence beyond their official positions.

The accuracy of a power assessment increases with the number of approaches used. When different indicators converge on the same person or unit, one can be confident that a reliable description of the distribution of power has been found. The cardinal thing to remember is that individuals, groups, or units are powerful if their opinions are heeded by decision makers. That is, those with power tend to have their views prevail.

Control Agendas. The importance of agenda setting in organizational politics has been highlighted by greater understanding of the use of "non-decisions" as a way of making decisions. This concept was developed by Bachrach and Baratz, who suggested that "power may be, and often is, exercised by confining the scope of decision-making to relatively 'safe' issues."[56] An important way in which political actors protect their interests is by preventing questions that can adversely affect those interests from being put on the agenda. Individuals who support the organizational status quo, for example, will want to keep items off agendas, whereas those seeking to introduce changes will be eager to bring issues to the attention of decision makers. From the perspective of the defenders of the status quo, a nondecision is, after all, a decision — namely, a decision to continue doing things in the same way.

An effective tactic for determining which issues are placed on the organizational agenda is to define who can attend meetings at which decisions are made. In order to bring an issue to the attention of decision makers, someone has to present it and advocate for it. The surest way of preventing an issue from coming up is to exclude the person associated with it from meetings where it can be acted on. Controlling participation in meetings is quite difficult, however, since participation is the organizational equivalent of enfranchisement, and interested parties will exert considerable efforts to ensure their presence. When the manager is unable to keep an issue off the agenda, the next tactic is to control the order in which items appear on the agenda.

Items at the beginning of an agenda frequently perform what Cohen and March called the "garbage can" function by becoming the vehicle for a discussion of a number of unrelated issues.[57] Meetings provide a setting for publicly recognizing and confirming the statuses of the participants. They are a stage upon which the organizational cast can be identified and the organizational drama played out. The first items on the agenda, consequently, are often used by participants to establish their place in the hierarchy by speaking authoritatively and at length about an issue and to show — regardless of the issue's substantive content — how it is related to major organizational concerns.

Managers who want an item that is inimical to their interests defeated, tabled, or significantly changed should encourage the issue's proponents to present it in terms of its broadest ramifications for the organization. An item about adequate parking facilities, for instance, can be escalated to the more general question of the distribution of perquisites within the organization and to the even larger issue of whether the agency subscribes to the principles of distributive justice. Managers should also insist that such items appear early in the meeting so there will be sufficient time for discussion. Items that they want passed, on the other hand, should be presented in as specific and noncontroversial a way as possible and placed near the end of the agenda, but not too near for fear that they won't be covered at this meeting and will be carried over to the next, where they will occupy the dreaded first place.

Control Decision Alternatives and Premises.   A decision can be thought of simply as a choice among alternatives. From this perspective, power rests with the person making the choice. A more complex view of decisions, however, sees decision makers as people who are *presented* with alternatives among which they must choose. In this conception, power is shared between those making the choice and those presenting the alternatives. The analysis of decisions has been refined further by pointing out that decision makers must abide by a set of constraints, or requirements, that their decisions must satisfy.[58] This refinement adds an additional complication to the question of who has the power to make decisions by introducing the people who set the constraints on the decision maker.

For example, a manager of a program for deinstitutionalized psychiatric patients must develop services for maintaining these clients in community residences. One alternative for doing this is to involve local residents in the creation of a community-sponsored halfway house that would be an integral part of the life of the community. This proposal requires a lengthy community organization process and involves sharing decision-making authority with neighborhood residents. The second alternative is to purchase a low-rise apartment house with funds provided jointly by the state department of mental health and by a consortium of business people. This proposal would take much less time to implement, and the control of the program would stay with agency staff, although they would be generally accountable for the use of the funds to the state agency and the consortium. Besides having to choose between these alternatives, the manager must interpret the meaning of the state law mandating deinstitutionalization. Many of the law's provisions are stated in general terms, and it is not clear what is meant by the terms "community residence" or "independent community living." These phrases have been variously interpreted by agencies throughout the state, leaving considerable latitude for individual managers to define them in specific terms.

While the manager ostensibly has the power to make the decision, a number of other people have the opportunity to play influential roles in this process. The advocates of the competing proposals can sway the manager's thinking by the information that they bring to bear in support of their proposals and, equally important, by their criticisms of the other proposal. In addition to factual arguments, program proponents can present arguments based on the competing values that underlie the two approaches. For social programs in particular, value arguments often override factual ones because of the ideological nature of most social services — in this case the value of community participation versus program efficiency and management control — and the reality that factual information about program effectiveness is usually scarce and of dubious quality. Another way in which people can influence the formal decision maker is by providing interpretations of what the constraints on the decision actually are. Thus, someone familiar with the legislative history of the deinstitutionalization law and the past practices of the state agency responsible for its administration can play a significant role in shaping the manager's sense of what is or is not permissible.

This example illustrates the crucial role that shaping decision alternatives and interpreting decision premises play in the organizational political process. To be effective in this role, the social worker as political actor must adopt an advocacy stance. The classic model of the advocate is the lawyer, and it is no coincidence that lawyers play such an important part in political life. Their approach to facts and argumentation is one-sided: building a case that will promote the interests of their clients and negate the arguments of the opposition. This approach requires analytical skills in finding the right information and organizing it in a logically persuasive manner, as well as rhetorical skills in presenting arguments in a convincing manner. In addition, the advocate must have a thorough knowledge of procedures and an acute sense of timing. Many battles have been lost because the arguments — well researched and logically impeccable — have been presented to the wrong person, in the wrong place, at the wrong time.

Behaving Politically

It is said that inside every politician lurks an amateur psychologist. At a basic level, politicians must understand people's motivations, interests, needs, and goals in order to assess support for and opposition to their positions. Understanding individual psychology is also essential for establishing interpersonal relationships and exercising influence. Lyndon Johnson, for example, was known for the extent and depth of his knowledge of people's psychological makeup. Johnson demonstrated this in an interview with Arthur Schlesinger, Jr., when Johnson was majority leader of the Senate.

> Saying, "I want you to know the kind of material I have to work with," he ran down the list of forty-eight Democratic Senators, with a brilliant thumbnail sketch of each — strength and weakness, openness to persuasion, capacity for teamwork, prejudices, vices....[I]n the course of this picturesque and lavish discourse, Johnson met in advance almost all the points I had in mind. When he finally paused, I found I had little to say.[59]

Interpersonal relationships are essential for the use of referent power through which people obtain the compliance of others on the basis of the quality of their relationships. Referent power is often the only kind of power that people have when they are trying to influence their peers or superiors. Networks of relationships are also important in obtaining information about developments which can affect one's interests. Finally, interpersonal relationships play a critical role in building coalitions.

Knowledge of personal and interpersonal psychology should include an understanding of one's own psychological characteristics, the ways in which relationships are established and maintained, how relationships are affected by the organizational setting, and how to use relationships to accomplish different ends. Political managers must be knowledgeable about interpersonal dynamics, know how to communicate with different people, and be skilled in building networks of relationships.

Political Behavior as Interpersonal Intelligence. Many psychologists question whether intelligence is a single human characteristic of the kind measured by I.Q. tests. They argue instead that there are a number of intelligences, each serving a different purpose. Gardner, for instance, developed a theory of six "multiple intelligences," of which one, "the personal intelligences," involves "access to one's own feeling life" and "the ability to notice and make distinctions among other individuals."[60] While organizational politicians are unlikely to disclose their inner feelings to others, they must not keep them from themselves. Self-knowledge in a political context involves understanding the nature and depth of one's commitments — to policies, programs, and people — and an awareness of the characteristic ways, or styles, in which people perform their jobs. A theme of this book has been that organizational politics arise when people are unclear about how to act because of a lack of knowledge or because of disagreements over value or ideological issues. An important strength that organizational politicians bring to such situations is their conviction about, and commitment to, a course of action.

There is nothing as convincing as a convinced person, the saying goes. To be convincing, however, organizational politicians must know what their convictions are, why they hold them, how far they will go to protect and promote them, and which aspects of a position they are willing to negotiate. Managers quickly acquire a reputation for having, or not having, integrity with regard to their stated positions. Managers who eloquently and passionately argue for a policy at a staff meeting and then offer to compromise at the first sign of opposition will lose whatever potential for influence they might have had because of their original strong stand. The positions that managers take must be carefully thought through and reflect their actual interests and values. Managers must be sufficiently introspective to know what they believe in and why, and be sufficiently candid (with themselves) to assess objectively their organizational, personal, and professional interests.

Self-knowledge must also extend to awareness of one's work style, particularly how one takes in information and thinks about it. Much of social psychological research confirms the Chinese proverb that "two thirds of what we see is behind our eyes." In the same way that psychotherapists should understand their own psychological makeup in order to be more objective about their patients, political actors need to know their own biases and preferences if they are to assess other people's interests and goals accurately. There are a number of ways in which people's thinking can be biased. Psychological factors include the tendency to identify with and be influenced by prestigious and powerful reference groups outside the organization. Social work managers who identify with business managers, for example, might systematically misread events and people in their organizations in their desire to use sophisticated management technologies in situations where they are inappropriate.

Personality factors also affect how we think. For example, people vary in the extent to which emotionality versus objectivity is a key element in their personalities. Emotionality refers to the degree to which preconscious feelings and defensive needs of which we have no awareness affect our conscious behavior. Defensive needs have been defined by Katz and Kahn as

> weaknesses in basic character structure which are such a threat to the ego that they are not consciously recognized by the person but nevertheless overdetermine his behavior....They can block out or distort the analysis of the problem, or the assessment of consequences, or they can overweight a given type of solution....Threatening and unpleasant facts are often denied, ignored, or distorted.[61]

In the case of upper-level managers, these distortions will often be reinforced by subordinates who are reluctant to bring bad news to their attention. Dramatic examples of this process at work are found in the elaborate systems of misinformation created during the Watergate and Iran-contra affairs of the Nixon and Reagan administrations, respectively. Political actors should be aware of their biases and prejudices and take steps to ensure that all sides of an issue are presented, not just the ones that they want to hear.

Communication Skills. If one randomly selects a moment in a manager's day, it is almost certain that the activity engaged in at that time is talking. Chance encounters in the hallways, face-to-face interviews, formal staff and committee meetings, presentations to community groups, and numerous phone conversations are the usual ways in which administrative work is conducted. A study of influence patterns among administrators (aptly entitled "Talk as the Work") identified the important role of verbal communications by showing how

> first, talk does things for the speaker, making known his or her version of something to others that must be attended to; second, talk gets others to do things, not only to take note or account of what is said, but to be influenced by what is said.[62]

Political managers must be attentive to both the content of their communications and the impact that their messages have on different audiences.

Most public figures live by the rule that you don't say anything to a reporter that you don't want to see in print. The organizational counterpart to this rule is that whatever a manager says to someone else sooner or later becomes common knowledge in the organization. Managers at every level are the focus of considerable attention by subordinates, peers, and superiors, as well as interested parties outside the organization. There are a number of reasons for this interest. Managers are the symbolic embodiments, or, as Mintzberg called them, the "figureheads," of the units or organizations that they head.[63] When managers speak, it is assumed that they speak on behalf of the organization or unit, whether or not that was their intention. Managers are also assumed to have the power to act on their words, so more importance and consequence are attributed to their utterances than to those of other organizational members. Finally, managers are assumed to be privy to important information, so whatever they say, no matter how pedestrian, is invested with great meaning. (Peter Sellers' brilliant portrayal of Chauncey Gardner in the movie *Being There* dramatizes the ludicrous situations that arise when these assumptions are carried to their logical extremes.)

Managers thus are denied the luxury of casual talk and must approach situations with a high degree of premeditation and purposefulness. This is especially true for political managers, since much of political communication involves convincing listeners that the course of action being advocated is superior to any other and that their interests will be enhanced by supporting this position. To accomplish the first of these goals, political managers must have highly developed rhetorical skills that they use to depict the existing situation in a negative light, while highlighting the positive aspects of their proposals. And although their communications accentuate the positive, managers must also be aware of weaknesses in their positions and anticipate potential opposition.

One way in which political managers seek to convince listeners that it is in their best interests to support a proposal is through manipulation of its symbolic meaning. Policy proposals contain both tangible and symbolic elements. A proposal to add a new unit to an agency is high on the tangible dimension since new jobs will be created as well as promotion opportunities for existing staff. A change in treatment strategies for working with clients, on the other hand, may have only symbolic meaning for the participants. The latter is an example of what Cohen and March called the "exchange of substance for status," which occurs when the people affected by a policy proposal

> care less about the specific substantive outcome than they do about the implications of that outcome for their own sense of self-esteem and the social recognition of their importance....[Managers] should find it possible to accomplish some of

the things they want by allowing others to savor the victories, enjoy the pleasures of involvement, and receive the profits of public importance.[64]

Consequently, much of the communication work of political managers is aimed at judiciously mixing the tangible and symbolic rewards of their proposals in ways that maximize support.

Another vital communication skill is the ability to assess the impact of one's messages on different listeners. Political managers must be as good at listening as they are at speaking. We hear with our ears, Forester suggested, but

> we listen with our eyes and bodies as well, we see gestures, expressions, postures — bodies speak and we listen and understand....[T]here is more to listening than meets the eardrum, far more than the hearing of words. Listening to what someone says can be as dependent on our knowing *them* as upon our hearing of their *words*.[65]

Gronn assessed how well administrators listened by analyzing how they responded to someone speaking to them. The possible reactions included a direct response to what was said ("talk to"); a response that was not in direct reference to what was said ("talk at"); a response given while someone was speaking that supported what was being said ("talk with"); a response given while someone was speaking that was not in reference to what was being said ("talk over"); an interrupting response which gave the listener the floor ("talk instead of"); and a response that repeated what was said either while the speaker was talking or after he or she had finished ("talk again"). People who talked to, with, and again were described as listeners, and those who talked at, over, or instead of were "more concerned with dictating rather than being dictated to."[66]

Another asset of the good listener is the ability "to speak the specialized languages of the organization, however haltingly."[67] In the same way that social workers seek to empathize with their clients by "starting where the client is," managers can strengthen their relationships with superiors, subordinates, and peers by familiarizing themselves with the details of different functional specialties. Managers should understand the technical aspects of a unit's work, the jargon used to describe specialized tasks, the unique issues and tensions within units, and the work cultures that develop in different parts of the organization.

Building Influence Networks. Networks refer to organizational patterns of communication and influence that follow lateral, horizontal lines, as opposed to the vertical lines of the formal hierarchy. They provide opportunities for organizational members to communicate with people in different divisions within their own organization, as well as people outside their organizations. They are also an important mechanism for informal contacts with superiors and subordinates in one's own unit. Networks can be formal bodies, such as task forces or interagency committees, or informal systems of mutual consultation and influence. Networks play a number of essential roles in organizational politics. They are a major informal communications channel for getting information that cannot be gotten through official means. This role is especially significant in organizations that rely heavily on hierarchical systems of communication. Managers need to know what is happening in the organization generally, as well as in their own units; obtaining this information requires access to a number of information sources. Networks, however, are useful not only for bringing information *to* the manager, but also for transmitting information *from* the manager on an unofficial basis. Managers use networks when they want to introduce new proposals but are unsure of what the reactions will be in different parts of the organization. Informal networks are good "trial balloons" for testing the receptivity to a proposal without having to commit oneself formally.

Networks are an important element in coalition building when the manager looks to the strength of numbers as a source of power. Organizational coalitions tend to be issue specific, with their composition changing as the issues change. The manager's general network of relationships cannot be expected to be the basis of a coalition for every issue. While some members of the network often will be involved in a coalition, the network as a whole serves as a sounding board for managers to explore who their potential allies and opponents are around a particular issue. Networks can be a source of political strength when the members ally themselves with the manager. They are, however, more likely to be a significant source of political information that the manager later translates into political strength.

Networks of relationships in organizations, like friendship networks in general, are built around exchanges of valued "things," ranging from tangible benefits like helping someone get a job or a promotion to intangible items like enhancing another's self-esteem. Wright, for example, suggested that friendships are built around the exchange of the values of stimulation, utility, and ego support.[68] Stimulation refers to the ability to introduce others to new ideas and activities that expand their knowledge and outlook. Utility refers to a person's willingness to use his or her time and resources to help others satisfy their needs and attain their goals. Ego support involves helping others maintain their impressions of themselves as competent and worthwhile people. The more of these values that are exchanged, the stronger the bonds within the network.

Once a network of relationships has been established, managers often forget that the same amount of effort and skill that went into its creation must be expended on *maintaining* it. The maintenance work, moreover, has to be done on a routine basis, not just when one individual in the network whom the manager has not talked to for several months suddenly becomes important because of his or her relation to an issue with which the manager is concerned. The job of maintaining relationships comes easiest, of course, to those who are naturally gregarious and enjoy the company of others. As Crossman suggested in his observations of British members of Parliament, the characteristics of a good politician are

> First, a tradition of public services; then a dash of vanity and another of self-importance and, added to these, a streak of rebelliousness, a pleasure in good talk for its own sake, and in gregarious living. These, much more than the desire for personal power, are the qualities of the individual member.[69]

For the shy, or those who value their privacy, the work of maintaining relationships will be more difficult, but no less important.

Working Politically

Managers engage in political activities in order to acquire the resources and influence needed to pursue the goals they deem important. At the same time, the way that managers perform their assigned tasks and carry out their official duties has political consequences in terms of increasing or diminishing their influence within the organization. Thus, working politically is both an end in itself and a means to that end. Jansson and Simmons' discussion of the need for social work managers in host settings (hospitals, schools, industries) to acquire power highlighted the dual nature of political work.

> A social work unit that obtains power is able to meet unaddressed needs in the host organization precisely because it has obtained resources and service mandates. Furthermore, powerful units often can be more effective than weak units in advocating for the needs of clients, patients, employees, and students because staff members and officials in the host organization are more likely to heed the suggestions of social work units with a high status.[70]

Managers can increase the positive political consequences of their work by carefully adhering to organizational norms, particularly those concerning the proper exercise of power and authority; identifying tasks that their units can do which are considered important to the overall organizational mission; and seeing that their accomplishments and those of their units are accurately and fully conveyed to others within and outside the organization.

Play by the Rules. Every organization, like every social system, has a "constitution" which provides rules for determining acceptable behavior on the part of its members. Constitutions can be formal documents (bylaws, charters of incorporation, Roberts' *Rules of Order*) or unwritten collective understandings. The purpose of organizational constitutions, Zald suggested, is to establish a set of agreements and understandings which define the limits and goals of the collectivity as well as the responsibilities and rights of participants standing in different relations to the organization....An organization's constitution defines both the constraints on and opportunities for the exercise of power.[71]

Constitutions set forth the rules of the political game in terms of who the players are, what plays are fair or foul, and how to know when the game is over and who won.

The overt exercise of power is generally frowned upon in social agencies where people are expected to act solely on the basis of professional or technical grounds. Political managers have to be careful that their actions are seen as properly within the norms of the organization. Actions that are perceived as arbitrary or that disregard accepted procedures will be discredited as dictatorial or as playing politics. In order to be powerful, Biggart and Hamilton argued, an organizational member must limit acts of power

> to the norms of his or her role, or convince others that he or she is exercising power within the limits of the role....[T]he ability to get things done, to be powerful, actually diminishes when a person steps outside the normative bounds of his or her position. Interpersonal power is in important measure a matter of getting others to view one's acts of power as acts of obedience of role obligations.[72]

An example of how organizational rules regulate the exercise of power is found in the procedures for determining who can attend meetings. As previously noted, participation in meetings defines the organizational polity, or governance structure, and is the organizational equivalent of enfranchisement. Whether an organization is run along autocratic, oligarchic, or democratic lines, whatever rights organizational members are entitled to are accorded by their inclusion in certain organizational groups. Participation also provides individuals with the opportunity to present and advocate for their interests. For instance, the ways in which staff are grouped in an agency that offers residential services for disturbed children and outpatient family therapy have important implications for policy and administrative choices. Should the nonprofessional residential staff, who are many, be included in the same meetings with the professional therapists, who are few? A decision to separate them and the organizational and programmatic matters they can act on will have a significant impact on their influence over policy and administrative decisions.

Political managers attempting to manipulate organizational rules in order to promote their interests and goals must use procedures that have been legitimated within the organization. Politicization occurs when people cannot agree about the goals that they should pursue in common. In such a situation, *the way in which a decision is made* assumes primary importance. While people may not agree with the outcome of a decision, they will accept it as legitimate and agree to be bound by its terms if the process of reaching it conformed to formal organizational rules and informal norms.

Perform a Useful Function. Organizations can be thought of as systems of interdependent activities for producing a service or product. Thinking in system terms has an equalizing or leveling effect since all organizational activities and the people performing them are viewed as equal contributors to the end product. This can be misleading, however, since some activities often are more important than others, even when a number of functions are involved in the completion of a task. An organizational function assumes added importance when the people able to perform it are in high demand because they are in short supply. Qualified people are scarce when their skills are the product of technological breakthroughs which training and educational facilities lag behind, or when supply is purposely restricted by occupational and professional associations to prevent a glut on the market.

A function also gains in significance when it contributes to dealing with critical uncertainties faced by the organization. An activity is uncertain when the technology for performing it is underdeveloped and unreliable, or when it is subject to external forces beyond management control, or both. Individuals or units that can reduce uncertainties by developing new techniques for dealing with problems, or bring external factors under organizational control, assume influential positions. A critical uncertainty for acute-care hospitals, for example, is a patient's length of stay. Hospital administrators are under increasing pressure to limit the length of stay as the cost of hospital care mounts and insurance carriers ration the number of hospital days for different conditions. Research has shown that directors of hospital social work departments increased their influence and that of their units by developing strategies that enabled hospital administrators to deal with this contingency.[73] Social workers' skill and experience in working with individuals and their families around discharge planning, plus their knowledge of and contacts with community agencies, were valuable resources to hospital administrators who needed to maintain a rapid turnover of beds.

The fact that power tends to flow to organizational units that contribute to the reduction of critical uncertainties, presents, Salancik and Pfeffer argued,

> an appealing picture of power. To the extent that power is determined by critical uncertainties and problems facing the organization and, in turn, influences decisions in the organization, the organization is aligned with the realities it faces. In short, power facilitates the organization's adaptation to its environment — or its problems.[74]

Situations in which people's actions simultaneously benefit themselves and others are the bases for non-zero-sum games, in which all players are winners. This accounts for the willingness of top managers to share their power with lower-level unit managers. The same situation, however, can become a zero-sum game, in which one person's gains are another's losses, when unit managers allow the goal of increasing unit power to displace program goals or professional values. In the same way that individuals have to seek power to have it, organizational units interested in becoming more powerful have to adjust their activities to accommodate upper management's goals. This process will be mutually rewarding as long as there is sufficient agreement between the goals of upper management and the interests of a particular unit.

When these goals diverge, however, the manager must decide how important it is for the unit's integrity and survival to compromise its own values and interests in order to accommodate those of upper management. In the case of hospital social work directors, for example, at what point do they resist the demands of fiscally oriented administrators to limit the number of bed days when it is questionable that this action is in the patient's best interest? If managers lose sight of their program and professional goals in their quest to increase their unit's power, they find themselves in the paradoxical position of having greater power to do what they are told to do, but less autonomy to do what they think they ought to do. On the other hand, if they are no longer of service to the organization's dominant coalition, they and their units will be left out of the "power loop."

Manage Impressions. A basic requirement for all organizational members is adequate performance of their jobs. This is even more true for those who wish to be effective in organizational political processes, since competence and expertise are major sources of power for professionals. More importantly, incompetence is a basis for dismissal. The assessment of individual competence is a difficult task in any organization because of the obstacles to identifying any one person's contribution to achieving an organizational goal. It is even more difficult in social agencies, where goals often are poorly defined, ambiguous, and difficult to specify. Consequently, managers must be skilled in controlling the impressions and perceptions that others within and outside the organization have of their abilities and accomplishments, as well as those of their units.

A number of mechanisms have been identified that managers use to manage impressions: self-descriptions, accounts, apologies, entitlements and enhancements, flattery, favors, and organizational descriptions.[75] Self-descriptions are managers' presentations of such personal characteristics as traits, abilities, behavioral patterns, feelings, and opinions; they can include positive, negative, or neutral information. Accounts are explanations designed to minimize the severity of a difficult situation by justifying the actions the manager took. Apologies seek to convince others that an undesirable event associated with a manager is not a fair representation of the manager's overall abilities. Conversely, entitlements are designed to maximize a manager's apparent responsibility for an event, and enhancements seek to maximize the favorability of the event itself. Flattery involves complimenting others about their virtues in an effort to make oneself appear perceptive and likable; favors are done in order to gain another's approval. Organizational descriptions are used to legitimize decisions, processes, and policies. The way that managers describe organizational activities, personnel, and accomplishments has key implications for their own images since they are typically viewed as the symbolic heads of their units.

In their research on how managers used these techniques in practice, Gardner and Martinko found that the administrators in their sample used self-descriptions and organizational descriptions more frequently, and for more time, than other types of verbal self-presentational behaviors.[76] They interpreted their findings in terms of Mintzberg's theory of managerial roles, particularly the roles of disseminator and spokesperson.[77] As a disseminator of information, the manager sends external information into the organization and relays internal information from one subordinate to another and from one unit to another. This role is particularly influential when the information conveyed is not factual but deals with values and preferences. In the latter case, the manager can shape the meaning that the information has for organizational members and thus influence their behavior. In the spokesperson role, the manager transmits information out to the organization's or unit's environment. This tactic affords the manager the opportunity to influence how important external audiences view the organization and its accomplishments.

NOTES

1. Douglas Yates, Jr., *The Politics of Management: Exploring the Inner Workings of Public and Private Organizations* (San Francisco: Jossey-Bass, 1985), pp. 54–55.
2. Chester I. Barnard, *The Functions of the Executive* (Cambridge, Mass.: Harvard University Press, 1968), pp. 168–69.
3. Larry Hirschhorn, "The Stalemated Agency: A Theoretical Perspective and a Practical Proposal," *Administration in Social Work*, 2, no. 4 (Winter 1978), 425–38.
4. Lillian Ripple, "Motivation, Capacity, and Opportunity as Related to the Use of Casework Service: Theoretical Base and Plan of Study," *Social Service Review*, 29, no. 2 (June 1955), 172–93.
5. Harold D. Lasswell, *Power and Personality* (New York: Viking Press, 1962), pp. 21–22 (emphases in original).
6. David C. McClelland, *Power: The Inner Experience* (New York: Irvington, 1975), pp. 7–8.
7. Allen Feld and Ronald Marks, "Self-Perceptions of Power: Do Social Work and Business Students Differ?" *Social Work*, 32, no. 3 (May-June 1987), 225–30.
8. Barry R. Cournoyer, "Assertiveness among MSW Students," *Journal of Education for Social Work*, 19, no. 1 (Winter 1983), 24–30.
9. Rino Patti et al., "From Direct Service to Administration: A Study of Social Workers' Transitions from Clinical to Management Roles — Part I: Analysis," *Administration in Social Work*, 3, no. 2 (Summer 1979), 151.
10. McClelland, *Power*, p. 22.

11. David Riesman, *The Lonely Crowd* (New Haven: Yale University Press, 1961).
12. Anatole Broyard, "On Authority," *The New York Times Book Review*, January 3, 1983, p. 27.
13. Alan Keith-Lucas, "Political Theory Implicit in Social Case-Work Theory," *American Political Science Quarterly Review*, 47, no. 4 (December 1953), 1082–83.
14. Richard A. Cloward and Frances Fox Piven, "The Professional Bureaucracies: Benefit Systems as Influence Systems," in *Readings in Community Organization Practice*, ed. Ralph M. Kramer and Harry Specht (Englewood Cliffs, N.J.: Prentice Hall, 1969), pp. 359–72; Joel F. Handler, *The Coercive Social Worker* (Chicago: Markham-Rand McNally College Publishing, 1973); Patricia Yancey Martin, "A Critical Analysis of Power in Professional-Client Relations," *Areté*, 6, no. 3 (Spring 1981), 35–48; Yeheskel Hasenfeld, "Citizen Encounters with Welfare State Bureaucracies," *Social Service Review*, 59, no. 4 (December 1985), 622–35; Yeheskel Hasenfeld, "Power in Social Work Practice," *Social Service Review*, 61, no. 3 (September 1987), 469–83.
15. McClelland, *Power*, p. 18.
16. Harry Specht, "Managing Professional Interpersonal Interactions," *Social Work*, 30, no. 3 (May-June 1985), 229; see also Burton Gummer, "Competing Perspectives on the Concept of 'Effectiveness' in the Analysis of Social Services," *Administration in Social Work*, 11, no. 3/4 (Fall-Winter 1987), 257–70.
17. Specht, "Managing Professional Interpersonal Interactions"; Richard S. Bolan, "The Social Relations of the Planner," *Journal of the American Institute of Planners*, 37, no. 6 (November 1971), 386–96.
18. Elizabeth D. Hutchinson, "Use of Authority in Direct Social Work Practice with Mandated Clients," *Social Service Review*, 61, no. 4 (December 1987), 581–98.
19. National Association of Social Workers, *Code of Ethics of the National Association of Social Workers* (Silver Spring, Md.: National Association of Social Workers, 1980), p. 9.
20. Charles M. Kelly, "The Interrelationship of Ethics and Power in Today's Organizations," *Organizational Dynamics*, 16, no. 1 (Summer 1987), 5–18.
21. Rosabeth Moss Kanter, "Power Failure in Management Circuits," *Harvard Business Review*, 57, no. 4 (July-August 1979), 66.
22. Specht, "Managing Professional Interpersonal Interactions," 228.
23. George A. Brager, "Advocacy and Political Behavior," *Social Work*, 13, no. 2 (April 1968), 8.
24. Neil Gilbert, Armin Rosenkranz, and Harry Specht, "Dialectics of Social Planning," *Social Work*, 18, no. 2 (March 1973), 78–86.
25. Eleanor L. Brilliant, "Social Work Leadership: A Missing Ingredient?" *Social Work*, 31, no. 5 (September-October 1986), 326.
26. Rino J. Patti, "Who Leads the Human Services? The Prospects for Social Work Leadership in an Age of Political Conservatism," *Administration in Social Work*, 8, no. 1 (Spring 1984), 17–29; Brilliant, "Social Work Leadership"; Burton Gummer and Richard L. Edwards, "The Enfeebled Middle: Emerging Issues in Education for Social Administration," *Administration in Social Work*, 12, no. 3 (Fall 1988), 13–23.
27. See, for example, David C. McClelland, Stephen Rhinesmith, and Richard Kristensen, "The Effects of Power Training on Community Action Agencies," *Journal of Applied Behavioral Science*, 11, no. 1 (January-February-March 1975), 92–115; David Kipnis, Stuart M. Schmidt, and Ian Wilkinson, "Intraorganizational Influence Tactics: Explorations in Getting One's Way," *Journal of Applied Psychology*, 65, no. 4 (August 1980), 440–52; Leonard D. Goodstein, "Getting Your Way: A Training Activity in Understanding Power and Influence," *Group & Organization Studies*, 6, no. 3 (September 1981), 283–90; Daniel Goleman, "Influencing Others: Skills are Identified," *New York Times*, February 19, 1986, p. C1.
28. David Kipnis, *The Powerholders* (Chicago: University of Chicago Press, 1976), p. 18.

29. Ibid., pp. 18–19.
30. Ibid., pp. 19–20.
31. John P. Kotter, *Power in Management* (New York: AMACOM Division of American Management Association, 1979), pp. 16–17.
32. Abraham Zaleznik, "Power and Politics in Organizational Life," *Harvard Business Review*, 48, no. 3 (May-June 1970), 49.
33. Kipnis, *The Powerholders*, p. 19.
34. Richard P. Nielsen, "Arendt's Action Philosophy and the Manager as Eichmann, Richard III, Faust, or Institution Citizen," *California Management Review*, 26, no. 3 (Spring 1984), 194.
35. McClelland, *Power*, p. 260.
36. Nelson W. Polsby, *Community Power and Political Theory* (New Haven: Yale University Press, 1963), pp. 119–20.
37. John R. P. French, Jr., and Bertram Raven, "The Bases of Social Power," in *Group Dynamics: Research and Theory*, 3rd ed., ed. Dorwin Cartwright and Alvin Zander (New York: Harper and Row, 1968), pp. 259–69.
38. Abraham H. Maslow, "A Theory of Human Motivation," *Psychological Review*, 50, no. 4 (July 1943), 370–96.
39. Clayton R. Alderfer and Richard A. Guzzo, "Life Experiences and Adults' Enduring Strength of Desires in Organizations," *Administrative Science Quarterly*, 24, no. 3 (September 1979), 347–61.
40. Ibid., 347.
41. Ibid., 354–55.
42. Henry P. Sims, Jr., "Further Thoughts on Punishment in Organizations," *Academy of Management Review*, 5, no. 1 (January 1980), 133–38.
43. Rory O'Day, "Intimidation Rituals: Reactions to Reform," *Journal of Applied Behavioral Science*, 10, no. 3 (July-August-September 1974), 373–86.
44. Ibid., 375.
45. Ibid., 377–78.
46. Richard Sennett, *Authority* (New York: Vintage Books, 1981), pp. 97–104.
47. Terrence R. Mitchell and William G. Scott, "Leadership Failures, the Distrusting Public, and Prospects of the Administrative State," *Public Administration Review*, 47, no. 6 (November-December 1987), 445.
48. Gerald Zeitz, "Hierarchical Authority and Decision-Making in Professional Organizations: An Empirical Analysis," *Administration & Society*, 12, no. 3 (November 1980), 277–300; Donald C. Hambrick and Phyllis A. Mason, "Upper Echelons: The Organization as a Reflection of Its Top Managers," *Academy of Management Review*, 9, no. 2 (April 1984), 193–206.
49. French and Raven, "The Bases of Social Power," p. 266.
50. James R. Meindl, Sanford B. Ehrlich, and Janet M. Dukerich, "The Romance of Leadership," *Administrative Science Quarterly*, 30, no. 1 (March 1985), 80.
51. Robert Pruger, "The Good Bureaucrat," *Social Work*, 18, no. 4 (July 1973), 30.
52. John P. Kotter, *The General Managers* (New York: The Free Press, 1982).
53. Alvin W. Gouldner, "Cosmopolitans and Locals: Toward an Analysis of Latent Social Roles — I," *Administrative Science Quarterly*, 2, no. 3 (December 1957), 281–306. For an application of this concept to social work management, see William E. Berg, "Evolution of Leadership Style in Social Agencies," *Social Casework*, 61, no. 1 (January 1980), 22–28.
54. Mark H. Moore, "Anatomy of the Heroin Problem: An Exercise in Problem Definition," *Policy Analysis*, 2, no. 4 (Fall 1976), 639–62.
55. Kanter, "Power Failure in Management Circuits," 67.
56. Peter Bachrach and Morton S. Baratz, "Two Faces of Power," *American Political Science Review*, 56, no. 4 (December 1962), 948.

57. Michael D. Cohen and James G. March, *Leadership and Ambiguity*, 2nd ed. (Boston: Harvard Business School Press, 1986), pp. 211–12.
58. Herbert A. Simon, "On the Concept of Organizational Goal," *Administrative Science Quarterly*, 9, no. 1 (June 1964), 1–22.
59. Arthur M. Schlesinger, Jr., *A Thousand Days: John F. Kennedy in the White House* (Greenwich, Conn.: Fawcett Publications, 1965), pp. 18–19.
60. Howard Gardner, *Frames of Mind: The Theory of Multiple Intelligences* (New York: Basic Books, 1983), p. 239.
61. Daniel Katz and Robert L. Kahn, *The Social Psychology of Organizations* (New York: John Wiley and Sons, 1966), pp. 292–93; see also Joel Brockner et al., "Escalation of Commitment to an Ineffective Course of Action: The Effect of Feedback Having Negative Implications for Self-Identity," *Administrative Science Quarterly*, 31, no. 1 (March 1986), 109–26.
62. Peter C. Gronn, "Talk as the Work: The Accomplishment of School Administration," *Administrative Science Quarterly*, 28, no. 1 (March 1983), 17.
63. Henry Mintzberg, *The Nature of Managerial Work* (New York: Harper and Row, 1973), pp. 58–60.
64. Cohen and March, *Leadership and Ambiguity*, pp. 208–9.
65. John Forester, "Listening: The Social Policy of Everyday Life (Critical Theory and Hermeneutics in Practice)," *Social Praxis*, 7, no. 3–4 (1980), 222 (emphases in original).
66. Gronn, "Talk as the Work," 12–13.
67. Robert K. Kaplan, "Trade Routes: The Manager's Network of Relationships," *Organizational Dynamics*, 12, no. 4 (Spring 1984), 47.
68. Paul H. Wright, "A Model and a Technique for Studies of Friendship," *Journal of Experimental Social Psychology*, 5, no. 3 (1969), 295–309.
69. Richard H. S. Crossman, *The Charm of Politics* (New York: Harper, 1958), p. 9.
70. Bruce S. Jansson and June Simmons, "The Survival of Social Work Units in Host Organizations," *Social Work*, 31, no. 5 (September-October 1986), 342.
71. Mayer N. Zald, *Organizational Change: The Political Economy of the YMCA* (Chicago: The University of Chicago Press, 1970), pp. 23–24.
72. Nicole Woolsey Biggart and Gary G. Hamilton, "The Power of Obedience," *Administrative Science Quarterly*, 29, no. 4 (December 1984), 540.
73. Bruce S. Jansson and June Simmons, "Building Departmental or Unit Power within Human Service Organizations: Empirical Findings and Theory Building," *Administration in Social Work*, 8, no. 3 (Fall 1984), 41–56.
74. Gerald R. Salancik and Jeffrey Pfeffer, "Who Gets Power — And How They Hold on to It: A Strategic-Contingency Model of Power," *Organizational Dynamics*, 5, no. 3 (Winter 1977), 5.
75. William L. Gardner and Mark J. Martinko, "Impression Management: An Observational Study Linking Audience Characteristics with Verbal Self-Presentations," *Academy of Management Journal*, 31, no. 1 (March 1988), 43–44.
76. Ibid., 53–58.
77. Mintzberg, *The Nature of Managerial Work*, pp. 71–77.

8

Managing Organizational Politics II: Negotiating and Bargaining

Managers use their power and influence to promote their interests and those of their units. With enough power, managers can resolve organizational conflicts by imposing their preferences upon those less powerful than themselves. Rarely, however, will managers be able to amass sufficient power to act unilaterally. As discussed earlier, social agencies are likely to have multiple power centers. Even when agencies have centralized administrative structures, the people at the top of the hierarchy — while more powerful than their subordinates — will usually not be able to act on important issues without the support of others. Instead, most political conflicts within organizations are dealt with by negotiations and bargaining.

Power is nevertheless a crucial asset in the negotiation process, since those with more power have better bargaining positions than those with less. When one party to a negotiation has greater resources than the other, the former is in a better position to walk away from a negotiation without a settlement, whereas the latter will have a greater need to arrive at a settlement, even when the terms of the agreement are more beneficial to the other side. The relative power of the parties to a negotiation, however, is only one of several factors that shape the outcomes. Other factors include the substance of the issue that prompted the negotiation, the form the negotiations take, the strategies and tactics that the parties use, and who the parties to the negotiation are. This chapter will examine these elements and show their applicability to the social administrator's role.

THE ISSUE TO BE NEGOTIATED

Negotiation is a process whereby positions that are initially divergent become identical; parties who initially disagree with each other reach an agreement. Negotiations represent, Kochan and Verma pointed out,

> a special form of social interaction or decision making that (1) involves more than one party, (2) who hold some potentially conflicting interests as well as sufficient common interests or interdependence to motivate each to remain within the relationship or complete the exchange, and (3) involves reciprocity.[1]

Since negotiations are centrally concerned with reconciling competing interests, it is important to understand the nature of the interests that can separate people in organizations. As previously noted, the ability to identify the interests affected by an issue is an essential skill for the political manager. In addition to identifying which actors hold what interests, the manager must understand the substance of these interests and the meaning they have for those who hold them. Two concepts that contribute to such an understanding are the *objective or subjective* nature of interests and whether the interests address *integrative or distributive* issues.

The Objective-Subjective Dimension

The conflicting interests that people negotiate over can be based in the objective conditions of their different economic interests, policy preferences, or structural roles in the organization. They can also reflect subjective, psychologically based differences. Coser referred to the first kind of conflict as *realistic* and the second kind as *nonrealistic*.

> Conflicts which arise from frustration of specific demands within the relationship and from estimates of gains of the participants, and which are directed at the presumed frustrating object, can be called realistic conflicts....Nonrealistic conflicts, on the other hand,...are not occasioned by the rival ends of the antagonists, but by the need for tension release of at least one of them.[2]

The classic example of a realistic conflict situation is labor-management negotiations in which both sides focus on the goal of maximizing their respective economic positions. Because the focus is on goals, each side has flexibility with regard to the means for attaining those goals. This context characterizes most formal negotiations, where the parties engage in a series of offers and counteroffers until each side feels it has maximized its gains or minimized its losses. Popple presented a hypothetical example of realistic conflict in a social agency in which a union set a goal of a 10 percent pay increase that averaged out to $2,000 per worker per year.

> The current contract includes an insurance package that costs $1,000 per year for each worker, the company paying one-half, and sixteen days per year paid vacation/holiday. The union negotiating team has assigned a value of $100 per day to vacation/holidays. If the company proposes a 6% increase ($1,200 per worker) and refuses to go higher, the union can quickly formulate a counterproposal of 6% pay increase plus full insurance coverage, plus five extra vacation days, for a total package of $2,200 per worker. This allows the union room for $200 in concessions while still achieving the goal of a 10% increase.[3]

Nonrealistic conflict, on the other hand, has its source in individual psychological and social predispositions and is concerned less with achieving a specific goal than with the conflictual relationship itself. The goal in nonrealistic conflict is for one or both parties to release pent-up tensions, rather than to reach agreement over objective conditions such as differences in salary or benefit levels. A group of workers, for example, confronts their supervisor with a complaint about what they perceive to be the supervisor's unwillingness to involve workers in decisions affecting the unit. These workers make up less than one-quarter of the workers in the unit, and their position is not shared by the rest. Participation in decision making does not lend itself to objective measurement and often reflects subjective preferences for one management style over another. These preferences stem from people's attitudes toward, and feelings about, authority relationships.

The workers in our example are, indeed, individuals who bridle under bureaucratic control. They are using the complaint about worker participation in decision making to express their frustrations about work generally, rather than to reach agreement about a way to share in this activity. This is borne out when the supervisor, after agreeing to set up a committee for getting worker advice on certain decisions, sees that, after one or two meetings, the advisory committee ceases to function because of lack of worker interest, including among those who originally brought the complaint. Furthermore, the supervisor is confronted by the same group of workers a few months later with the demand that workers be given the discretion to decide whether or not they will accept referrals of clients with certain kinds of problems. In negotiations over realistic, objective conflicts, the focus is on goals, and the negotiating process is a means for coming to a mutually agreeable settlement. By contrast, negotiations over nonrealistic, subjective conflicts tend to be situations where the negotiating process becomes an end in itself. The goals sought are often ill-defined and amorphous, and the settlements reached are likely to be unstable.

The distinction between objective and subjective conflicts sensitizes managers to what outcomes they can expect from specific negotiations. Managers will avoid considerable frustrations and wasted efforts if they use different strategies and have different expectations as to outcomes when negotiating over subjective, nonrealistic conflicts than they would when negotiating over concrete, objective issues. At the same time, thinking about conflicts as *either* objective *or* subjective can lead to certain abuses, since all conflicts have *both* objective and subjective dimensions. Social workers often complain that supervisors "casework" them by reducing their concerns about agency practices or policies to the level of the worker's psychological problem. When carried to an extreme, this takes on the quality of the coercive tactic of nullification that was discussed earlier. In this respect, negotiators are subject to a variant of the Type II error that plagues researchers (accepting a hypothesis as false when it is true). Managers sometimes approach a negotiation assuming that the issues are subjective ones, when, in fact, the other parties view the issues as objective problems. The manager will tend to treat the specific demands of the other parties as less important than the opportunity that the negotiation situation itself provides for airing personal frustrations. The same problem arises when the manager mistakenly assumes that the issue to be negotiated reflects objective, realistic interests. There is no easy way for negotiators to avoid this bind. Detailed knowledge of the parties to the negotiations, past experience in dealing with issues and individuals, and careful attention to what the other side says and does can help managers develop an accurate sense of what is at stake in a particular negotiation.

The Distributive-Integrative Dimension

All objective conflict situations concern competing goals between two or more parties. Conflicts can be over policies and programs or over the allocation of valued things such as money, power, prestige, and career opportunities. The distributive-integrative dimension refers to whether the conflict is over values that are in short supply, such that one party's gains are the other's losses, or whether a way can be found to reconcile the interests of both parties. The first type of conflict involves what Walton and McKersie called distributive issues. In "zero-sum" or "win-lose" situations, the issue is framed in a way that leads to agreements that make one party a winner and the other a loser.[4] The second type of conflict involves integrative issues, known as "positive-sum" or "win-win" situations, in which an agreement can be reached that both parties feel is to their advantage.

The condition that makes an issue a distributive rather than an integrative one is scarce resources. Resources are scarce when there are not enough to go around. If an agency has only one new personnel line that two department heads are competing for, the outcome to the negotiations over the line will involve one winner and one loser. But resources can also *appear* to be scarce because of how people think about them. The same situation often can be thought of in either distributive or integrative terms, depending on the information available to the negotiators and the way in which they frame the issue. An example of such a situation is two people fighting over one orange. In what appears to be a classic zero-sum situation, the only solution seems to be dividing the orange in half, leaving both with only half of what they wanted, and both dissatisfied with the outcome. The first person takes her half of the orange and squeezes it for the juice that she wanted, while the second uses the rind from his half in the cake that he is baking. If the parties had been privy to the uses that each intended for their halves prior to the beginning of the negotiations, they would have been able to negotiate a win-win situation by giving the first person *all* of the juice and the second *all* of the rind.

There will be many negotiating situations in which the parties have no choice but to view the conflict in win-lose terms. However, there are a number of advantages to be gained from finding ways to transform distributive issues into integrative ones, particularly when negotiating over internal organizational conflicts. Fisher and Ury argued that any method of negotiation may be judged by three criteria:

> It should produce a wise agreement if agreement is possible. It should be efficient. And it should improve or at least not damage the relationships between the parties. (A wise agreement can be defined as one which meets the legitimate interests of each side to the extent possible, resolves conflicting interests fairly, is durable, and takes community interests into account).[5]

Integrative agreements are more likely to meet these criteria than ones that create winners and losers. When people negotiate over issues that are of central concern to them, moreover, finding an integrative agreement may be the only way that negotiations can take place and stalemate avoided, since neither party is likely to make major concessions, as is required when negotiating over a distributive issue. Distributive agreements are apt to be unstable since the losing side is likely to bring the issue up again at a later time. Also, because they are mutually rewarding, integrative agreements tend to strengthen the relationship between the parties. Most issues, Pruitt argued, have more integrative potential than is commonly assumed. Pruitt identified five ways for achieving integrative agreements: expanding the pie, nonspecific compensation, logrolling, cost-cutting, and bridging.[6]

Expanding the Pie.   Since resource shortages are what force the parties to think of issues in win-lose terms, integrative agreements can be devised by increasing the available resources, when possible. A supervisor may be negotiating with a worker over how the worker will use the funds that the agency makes available for professional development. The supervisor wants the worker to attend a workshop on grant development, but the worker wants to attend a workshop on family therapy. The supervisor can expand the pie by offering the worker the opportunity to attend both workshops. This strategy will work, however, only if the worker rejected the original offer because he would have had to forgo the opportunity to attend the family therapy workshop. It will not lead to an integrative agreement if the worker has a strong aversion to working on grant proposals.

Nonspecific Compensation.   Negotiations nearly always involve, as Bacharach and Lawler pointed out, "heteromorphic exchanges, that is, the exchange of qualitatively different commodities."[7] This characteristic presents obstacles to working out mutually satisfactory agreements, since what is exchanged often has qualitatively different meanings to the parties, making it difficult for each side to know whether it is getting fair value for what it is giving. This same characteristic, however, is the basis for reaching integrative agreements through nonspecific compensation, in which one party gets what he or she wants and the other is repaid in some unrelated coin. In the negotiation over which workshop the worker will attend, the supervisor may offer the worker the supervision of a unit of student interns, something of interest to the worker, in exchange for the worker's agreement to attend the grant development workshop. Nonspecific compensation involves the use of reward power for the party making the compensation. As previously discussed, the use of reward power requires information about what is valuable to the other party, including information about how badly the other party would be hurt by making the concession. If such information is not available, Pruitt suggested, "it may be possible to conduct an 'auction' for the other party's acquiescence, changing the sort of benefits offered or raising one's offer, in trial-and-error fashion, until an acceptable formula is found."[8]

Logrolling.   Some negotiations involve single issues, but most deal with complex agendas where several issues of varying priorities are under consideration. Logrolling involves concessions by each party on low-priority issues in exchange for concessions on issues of higher priority. Solutions by logrolling can also be developed by a trial-and-error process in which the parties test each other's reactions to different proposals until an alternative is found that is acceptable to both. The negotiation between the supervisor and the worker over workshop attendance might come up during a general discussion about the worker's job assignment in which a number of other issues are addressed. It might be a matter of relative indifference to the worker as to which, if any, workshop he attends. A high-priority issue for him, on the other hand, might be a flexible work schedule. For the supervisor, having staff expertise in grant development may be of high priority, whereas allowing workers latitude in setting their schedules is a low-priority item. When these preferences become known to the two parties, the bargain will be made.

Cost Cutting.   In solutions by cost cutting, one party gets what he or she wants and the other's costs are reduced or eliminated. Costs in this sense refer to whatever hardships the party making the concession antici- pates as a result of the concession. In the case of the grant development workshop, the worker is reluctant to accept this assignment because he fears that, once he completes the training, he will be expected to spend most of his time writing grants, thus taking him away from his primary interest of working with clients. The supervisor explains that her goal is to have the worker disseminate the information he gets at the workshop to the agency staff through a number of mini-workshops in the agency. The worker was asked to attend the workshop, she continues, not because he was slated to take over the grant development responsibilities for the agency but because of his reputation as a teacher and workshop leader. The recognition of the worker's skill as a teacher and group leader might be sufficient payment to compensate for his agreeing to attend the workshop. If not, the supervi- sor might further reduce the worker's costs by offering other payments such as compensatory time off.

Bridging.   In bridging, neither party achieves its initial demands, but a new option is devised that satisfies the most important interests underlying these demands. Bridging, Pruitt pointed out,

> typically involves a reformulation of the issue(s) based on an analysis of the underlying interests on both sides....This new formulation becomes the basis for a search model..., which is employed in an effort to locate a novel alternative.[9]

The supervisor and worker in our example both are concerned with the fiscal well-being of the agency. They both recognize that it is in their mutual interest to help the agency deal with reductions in funds by identifying and acquiring new sources of money. The worker points out that the strategy that the supervisor chose is but one of several ways of reaching their common goal. As their discussion of the issue continues, they identify a number of other strategies, such as bringing in a consultant or developing a consortium of agencies that can pool their expertise in grant development. It is finally agreed that the worker will draw on his contacts with other agencies to coordinate the development of an interagency technical advisory committee on grant development.

THE FORM OF THE NEGOTIATION

When we think about negotiations, the picture that usually comes to mind is a formal setting where diplomats argue over the terms of a treaty or represen- tatives from union and management confront each other over salaries and fringe benefits. The two parties are seated opposite each other along a conference table, surrounded by lawyers, economists, and other experts who advise them on what offers to make and how to respond to the other side's offer. This form of negotiation, what Schelling called "explicit" negotiations, is one where the parties define the relationship as a bargaining one, have open lines of communication with each other, and consent to consider compromise.[10]

Negotiations, however, are not always explicit. Negotiations can also be "tacit," when the parties do not publicly acknowledge the bargaining relationship. The negotiations remain tacit, or what Holloway and Brager called "implicit," because the parties are unaware that what they are doing is negotiating an agreement, or, although conscious that negotiations are occurring, one or both parties has an interest in not openly acknowledging them.[11] The give-and-take of tacit negotiations, Bacharach and Lawler suggested, "involves few explicit offers or counteroffers; instead, parties attempt to outmaneuver and manipulate each other, often using subtle influence tactics or rewards and punishments."[12] Explicit negotiations are more likely to occur in bargaining between organizations, whereas tacit negotiating takes place more often within the organization, among people at both different and the same hierarchical levels. Each has advantages and disadvantages that administrators should be familiar with in order to increase their effectiveness as negotiators.

Tacit Negotiations

More than any other action, the use of bargaining and negotiating is identified with a political approach to work and is likely to violate a number of organizational norms. Most bureaucratic organizations have an organizational culture that assumes that subordinate members of the hierarchy are, Moore argued, "*technically, strategically, cognitively,* and *morally passive,* have *limited motives* (if any) in executing their duties, and are *dependent* in their relations to their superiors, to technical routines, rules, and other features that make up their work."[13] By contrast, a desire to negotiate over issues, particularly directives that come from organizational superiors, introduces what Bacharach called the "calculating free actor" and a politicized organizational culture in which we assume that

> actors have different interests; we assume that actors think; we assume that actors calculate; we assume that actors coalesce; we therefore assume that they make strategy and bargain. The application of bargaining in organizations is a simple acceptance of the fact that actors are no less political in their organizational life at work than they are in life outside their organizations.[14]

Tacit negotiations offer the opportunity for organizational actors to engage in political activities without labeling them as such. Most organizational members approach their work with a definition of the situation that is not always shared by those with whom they work. A manager in charge of human resource development, for example, might take an economizing, cost-cutting approach to a job that is assumed to be primarily oriented to developing staff potential. The political actor will approach many situations with an agenda that differs from official organizational policies. Tacit negotiations allow the political actor to function without appearing to be outside the general organizational culture. They are particularly useful when one is attempting to negotiate with superiors. Tacit negotiations permits, Holloway and Brager suggested, the

> softening of what might otherwise seem a demand and mitigates the potential charge that the worker is "too pushy." More importantly, when the negotiation remains implicit, a high power person (or any involved party) is more able to accede without appearing to lose face, and to prevent the loss of face is often a requirement for a favorable settlement.[15]

Tacit negotiations offer the parties room to maneuver. As noted earlier, attempts to transform divisive issues into ones that integrate competing interests often involve a period of trial-and-error offers and counteroffers in which the parties feel each other out over what terms are acceptable or unacceptable. By keeping the definition of the negotiating situation vague, the parties are freer to experiment with a variety of possible agreements without committing themselves in advance to any one. When the parties feel that they have to reject or accept an offer when it's made, as is often true in formal negotiations, they don't have the time to think through the ramifications of an offer that on the surface looks unacceptable but might in the long run benefit all concerned. Also, since research has suggested that stated commitments tend to intensify the commitment of speakers to their point of view, Holloway and Brager pointed out,

> it is good organizational practice for the worker to forestall the expression of an opinion or decision until there is some indication that the response will be a favorable one. Furthermore, the "sounding out" of implicit negotiations allows the negotiator-practitioner a graceful exit if it appears that destructive conflict will ensue or if the timing turns out to be wrong. When demands are only hinted at, they lend themselves to deniability.[16]

Tacit negotiations create problems, however, when only one of the parties to an interaction is thinking in those terms. When two managers come together to work on a problem, one may treat the meeting as a tacit negotiating session in which the two sides will probe each other's interests and positions with no serious intention of coming to a resolution of the problem at that time. The other may come to the meeting expecting to solve a straightforward administrative problem within the context of formal organizational policies and procedures. In such a situation there is a high likelihood of misunderstandings at best and charges of duplicitous and manipulative behavior at worse. If such a situation unfolds, not only will the problem at hand not be solved, but the working relationship between the parties is likely to be damaged. Tacit negotiations are most effective when they are a preliminary phase of what will ultimately become explicit negotiations. For this to happen, however, both parties must accept bargaining as a legitimate way to solve organizational problems, even though they do not publicly acknowledge it at the time.

Explicit Negotiations

The move from tacit to explicit negotiations involves more than a change in the form of the negotiations. When people openly acknowledge that negotiating is an acceptable method for deciding about organizational issues, they legitimize a political model of organizational behavior. Cohen and March argued that administrators and other organizational members employ an assortment of metaphors to describe the kind of organized system in which they work and the appropriate ways for making decisions.[17] The decision to make negotiations explicit involves a change from what the authors called "the administrative metaphor" to "the collective bargaining metaphor." The administrative metaphor assumes that organizational members agree to be bound by administrative rules and regulations in exchange for payments in the form of salaries, status, and prestige. Differences of opinion are resolved through rational analysis or the invocation of bureaucratic authority. The collective bargaining metaphor, by contrast, assumes that there are fundamentally conflicting interests within the organization that can be resolved only by bargaining and formal agreements among representatives of the major interests.

Managers who view their work in political terms must engage in "meta-negotiation work" that involves getting organizational members to recognize each other as parties with legitimately conflicting interests and to accept formal, explicit bargaining as an appropriate means for their resolution. Meta-negotiation work seeks to create the conditions that are necessary for explicit negotiations to take place. The first of these conditions is the acceptance of the *legitimacy of conflict* within the organization. As noted earlier, much of organization and administrative theory is based on a harmony of interest theme which assumes that organizational members and units work cooperatively toward a common goal. These theories either underplay the role of conflict or treat it as an aberration, a temporary breakdown in the otherwise smooth functioning of the organization. From a political perspective, however, conflict is a normal and legitimate part of organizational life that must be dealt with directly and explicitly if the organization is to function effectively. There should be no embarrassment, Yates argued,

> about the existence of even bitter disagreements and hostility between bureaucratic units. No effort should be made to preserve any existing organizational myth about solidarity and shared interests. Rather, conflict should be viewed as inevitable and even healthy, provided that it is dealt with openly.[18]

One way in which conflict is made a normal part of organizational life is the creation of organizational norms that prescribe ways in which disputes can be resolved, or what amounts to an agreement about how to disagree. Although the specifics of these agreements will vary from organization to organization, there are elements that must be present in all such compacts. The first is the expectation that the parties to a dispute will consider the possibility of *making concessions*. People's strategies for dealing with conflicts tend to range along a continuum that consists of competition, compromise, collaboration, accommodation, and avoidance.[19] Morley and Shockley-Zalabak provided illustrations of each of these styles: "There is no question that this is the way it has to be" (competition); "We need to find middle ground on this problem" (compromise); "Let's look at all sides of this issue recognizing everyone has a right to their opinion" (collaboration); "Because it is important to you, I'll agree" (accommodation); and "I don't want to be involved" (avoidance).[20] For negotiations to take place, the parties have to deal with the ambiguity and tension that come with the middle ground of compromise. They must avoid the temptation to adopt a competitive, combative stance in which they try to reduce their opponents to submission, as well as the impulse to completely give in to their opponents' demands or avoid the situation altogether. Capable negotiators, Mastenbroek noted,

> do not like to deal with inexperienced opponents, whose toleration for the stress and ambiguity connected with the dilemmas is generally too low. They become emotionally upset, start fighting, or naively get themselves into a predicament before the attainable limits have been explored. Negotiating is the subtle handling of the delicate balance between cooperation and fighting.[21]

A third condition necessary for explicit negotiations is *open lines of communication*. Explicit negotiations require free-flowing communications that allow the parties to examine, discuss, debate, and make proposals regarding all areas or issues in the conflict. Open lines of communication, however, are not to be confused with open communications, or the full disclosure of information about one's interests and goals. Negotiations can take place, Bartos pointed out, "only if each participant is at least partially ignorant of his opponent's true interests."[22] Negotiations involve mixed motives: the parties have conflicting interests as well as sufficient common interests or interdependencies to motivate each to reach an agreement that is acceptable to all. Successful negotiations occur within a paradoxical framework in which the individual parties believe that they are better off by reaching an agreement than by quitting the negotiations, and the parties collectively feel that the negotiations have been conducted fairly and equitably. The key to this paradox is that each party was at least partially ignorant of what the other party's true interests were.

Communications in a negotiation situation present a dilemma between presenting too much information about one's aims and not presenting enough information to keep the other side involved in the process. The skill in negotiating, Mastenbroek suggested, "lies in carefully bringing about a step-by-step exchange of information that gradually gives shape to realistic expectations on both sides."[23] One way for accomplishing this, Pruitt observed, is through use of the "dual concern model":

> This postulates that problem solving and hence…high joint benefit will arise to the extent that bargainers are concerned about their own and the other party's outcomes. If they are mainly concerned about their own outcomes, they will engage instead in contentious behavior designed to elicit concessions from the other party….If they are concerned primarily about the other party's outcomes, they will be overly flexible with respect to ends….[24]

An agency administrator related an account of a negotiation he had with representatives of his staff that failed to come to an agreement because the other side, in the administrator's words, "didn't know that they were winning." The issue was over workload and the assignment of cases. The administrator, an experienced and skillful negotiator, sympathized with the staff's position and was willing to make concessions, but he was constrained by state regulations connected to purchase-of-service contracts, as well as by a number of board members who were concerned about strict administrative procedures. The administrator attempted to convey to the staff representatives what these constraints were, but they were either unable or unwilling to hear them. Their concern was exclusively with presenting their demands as forcefully as possible, with no appreciation of the problems facing the administrator. The staff representatives assumed, as Fisher and Ury put it, that "solving their problem is their problem," and failed to understand that to reach a satisfactory agreement both sides must present viable alternatives, or alternatives that satisfy each party's limits.[25]

Negotiators are helped in establishing and maintaining open lines of communications by adhering to norms of *mutual respect and civility*. These norms include having consideration of the personal needs of others; paying attention to what others say and respecting their arguments; avoiding personal attacks, badgering, and other forms of verbal insult; maintaining a sense of humor and the ability to see one's position in perspective; and ensuring that all parties have sufficient time to present their arguments. A specific requirement in negotiations over technical matters is what Yates called "establishing a neutral language of discourse."[26] To the extent possible, the parties to the negotiation should express their arguments in ordinary language. When ordinary language is not possible because of the complexity of the issues, technical language should be translated into terms that are understandable to nonspecialists. In a negotiation over the distribution of fringe benefits to agency staff, one side argued that the median salary should be used as the cutoff point for determining who would receive a particular benefit. The other side was willing to go along with this until it was explained that the median salary meant that half of the employees would receive the benefit.

An obstacle to using ordinary, nontechnical language arises when employees are negotiating with their superiors or other upper-level managers. An important, and often only, source of power of lower-level employees is the highly specialized information uniquely in their possession. By making that information available to others, they reduce their access to informal influence within the organization and thereby weaken their negotiating position. By contrast, upper-level managers who are required to translate the technical information in their possession into terms understandable by all still retain considerable power through their hierarchical positions of authority.[27]

Creating the conditions for explicit negotiations is a costly effort. Aside from the tangible costs of time and energy, there are intangible costs involved in moving to a more open recognition of the existence of organizational conflicts and the acceptance of a political approach for resolving them. There are, however, a number of benefits that justify these expenditures. On a practical level, agreements arrived at through explicit negotiations are likely to be more stable, less ambiguous, and more enforceable than those achieved through informal negotiations. Equally important, the acceptance of the legitimacy of other positions and interests creates an organizational climate which recognizes that people have a right to disagree over administrative and programmatic issues and that these disagreements are best resolved through mechanisms that are fair and open.

NEGOTIATING STRATEGIES AND TACTICS

Whether negotiations are explicit or implicit, experienced bargainers decide before the negotiation session how they will present their demands and develop alternative responses to the demands that the other side is likely to make. Strategy refers to the overall negotiating plan, and tactics are the specific actions taken to implement the plan. Strategies are what negotiators think; tactics are what they do. Strategy, as Bacharach pointed out, "is not simply what negotiators think; it is a way of thinking that involves consideration of one's power, one's objectives, and how the one can most effectively be used to secure the other, given that one's opponent has objectives and sources of power of his own."[28] The objectives that negotiators can achieve are directly linked to the amount and kinds of power they have. An agency staff member who has detailed knowledge of program operations will be in a relatively good negotiating position over issues relating to program changes. That same person, however, would be in a weaker position when negotiating issues concerning the board of director's prerogatives in personnel matters, since his or her specialized knowledge does not extend to this area.

Strategic thinking is the operational expression of the political world view. It entails detailed knowledge of the interests involved in a negotiation, the relative power of the parties, and the ability to think of ways in which negotiators can most effectively use his or her power to maximize the achievement of his or her goals. Different strategies are needed for different phases of the negotiation process. Negotiations are generally viewed as consisting of a "pre-conference stage," in which the parties do background research and work out the logistics of time, place, and agenda, and the negotiation session itself, referred to as the "conference stage."

The Pre-Conference Stage

Prior to facing each other in a negotiating session, each party engages in a number of activities aimed at strengthening its bargaining position. Each side will gather information about the demands that the other side is likely to make, as well as the other side's probable reactions to one's own demands; identify the goals it wants to attain and frame them in the most advantageous way; and create a favorable climate within which the negotiations will take place. People generally focus on the actual bargaining session as the most important part of the negotiation process. These sessions are often tense and dramatic, with two people facing each other across a table, carefully weighing each other's words and gestures, where the slightest mishap can have disastrous consequences. The activities that make up the pre-conference stage, by contrast, are more prosaic, involving careful research on the issues, sizing up the other party's interests, and worrying about where to hold the meeting. Nevertheless, the success of a negotiation is often as dependent on the care with which negotiators prepare for their confrontation with their opponents as it is on what takes place in the negotiating room.

Gathering Information. Information is power, and in negotiations, information about the other side's intentions affords a number of advantages. If one side knows in advance of the negotiating session what the other side hopes to achieve, that side will have a better idea of what it can realistically demand. In addition, a party can adjust the concessions it will make to exactly what the other side hopes to get, or less, thus avoiding making more concessions than are needed. All parties to a negotiation know the value of such knowledge and therefore will be cautious about releasing information. As a result, the parties will have to use informal and indirect ways for gathering information about the other's goals and interests. These techniques are the same as those discussed in the previous chapter for identifying interests and assessing power.

Acquiring information about the other side's interests and power assumes added significance in light of research which suggested that most negotiators tend to be overly confident about their chances of success. One of the primary goals of a negotiation is to convince one's opponent of the fairness of one's offer and the unfeasibility of the opponent's offer. One probable result of this, Neale and Bazerman pointed out, is that negotiators may well convince themselves that their particular offers are obviously more equitable....Unless negotiators are able to take their opponent's perspective, they are likely to underestimate the value of their opponent's position.[29]

Negotiators who are overly confident about their chances for success are less likely to seek information about the other side's position before the negotiation and less likely to make concessions during the negotiation session. They usually make the mistaken assumption that if the negotiations reach an impasse and a third party is brought in to mediate, their position is the one that is likely to be chosen.

In addition to having information about the other side's goals, negotiators should have information about the issue itself. If a director of a hospital social service department intends to negotiate with a hospital administrator over the educational and professional qualifications for social work staff, the director will want to know as much as possible about personnel standards in hospitals in that community and around the country. Other relevant information would be research that demonstrated the superiority of trained social workers for these positions to those without training. Negotiators are particularly interested in identifying objective criteria that can be used as a basis for an agreement. At a minimum, Fisher and Ury pointed out,

> objective criteria need to be independent of each side's will. Ideally,...objective criteria should be...both legitimate and practical. In a boundary dispute, for example, you may find it easier to agree on a physically salient feature such as a river than on a line three yards to the east of the riverbank. Objective criteria should apply, at least in theory, to both sides.[30]

Possible sources of objective criteria include market value, scientific judgment, professional standards, what a court of law would decide, moral standards, and generally accepted community practices.

Setting Goals. The parties to a negotiation usually have a number of goals they want to achieve. It is therefore critical that negotiators order their goals in terms of their importance. Hermone, for example, suggested that goals be categorized as "essential, desirable, and tradeable."[31] Equally significant is the need for negotiators to develop alternative ways for achieving their most important goals. One strategy is to think of any specific negotiating session as part of a long-term process that will continue into the future. Negotiations over complex issues are rarely one-time events and usually involve a series of negotiations that can extend over several years. Within this context, negotiators can adopt a "two steps forward, one step backward" strategy which enables them to make incremental steps toward long-term ends. Advocates for publicly financed health insurance, for example, have been involved in a series of legislative negotiations that began with the passage of disability insurance under the Social Security Act in the mid-1950s. This legislation set the stage for the enactment a decade later of health insurance for the elderly and the medically indigent. The negotiations continue on through the present day with proposals to broaden Medicare coverage, provide health insurance for the unemployed, and establish a national health insurance program.

Once goals have been identified and ranked in terms of their importance, negotiators look for ways of presenting, or framing, their goals in the most advantageous way. Research on negotiation behavior has shown that people's reactions to a conflict situation are significantly affected by whether the issue is framed in terms of avoiding losses as opposed to obtaining gains. Tversky and Kahneman asked one group of college students how they would respond to the following situation:

> Imagine that the U.S. is preparing for the outbreak of an unusual Asian disease, which is expected to kill 600 people. Two alternative programs to combat the disease have been proposed. Assume that the exact scientific estimate of the consequences of the programs are as follows:
> If Program A is adopted, 200 people will be saved.
> If Program B is adopted, there is 1/3 probability that 600 people will be saved, and 2/3 probability that no people will be saved.
> Which of the two programs would you favor?[32]

Seventy-two percent of the respondents chose Program A, and 28 percent chose Program B. The prospect of being able to save 200 lives for certain was more attractive than a risky prospect of a one-in-three chance of saving all 600 lives. A second group of students was given the same cover story, but with the options reframed as follows:

> If Program C is adopted, 400 people will die.
> If Program D is adopted, there is 1/3 probability that nobody will die, and 2/3 probability that 600 people will die.
> Which of the two programs would you favor?[33]

Twenty-two percent of the respondents chose the certain outcome of Program C, and 78 percent chose the risky outcome of Program D. The prospect of 400 people dying for certain was less acceptable than a 2/3 probability that 600 people will die. These findings suggest that individuals are reluctant to take risks when options are framed in terms of gains (Program A) and more likely to take risks when options are framed in terms of losses (Program D). When negotiators present their demands in terms of losses they want to avoid, Neale and Bazerman pointed out, they adopt a negative frame,

> exhibit risk-seeking behavior, and increase the likelihood of their reaching impasse because of a general reduction in concessionary behavior....Conversely,

a risk-averse orientation — such as that resulting from evaluating the prospect of gains — will lead to an increased likelihood of reaching a negotiated settlement.[34]

A second dimension of goal framing that is particularly relevant to negotiations within organizations is whether goals are presented in terms of their importance for the negotiator's unit or their value for the institution as a whole. In a study of how departments in colleges and universities negotiated for budgetary allocations, Hackman divided units into "core" and "peripheral" in terms of how closely a unit's purposes matched the central mission of the institution.[35] The core units were the academic departments, and the peripheral units included admissions, administrative computing, student affairs, and counseling. The author compared the strategies used by core and peripheral units that were successful in their negotiations with those used by core and peripheral units that failed to get the budget allocations they asked for. She found that core units were most successful when they focused on their own needs, because their needs were most often allied with the mission of the organization. In contrast, peripheral units were most successful when they focused on broader institutional needs and then showed how they contributed to that. These findings suggest ways in which social work managers in host settings such as hospitals and schools should approach negotiations with upper-level managers in those institutions. They should also be instructive for managers of community-based social agencies that have to negotiate with local and state funding sources for funds that are also being pursued by other community services, such as corrections, education, and health.

Creating a Favorable Climate.   Negotiating is a form of interaction and, like any interaction between people, is affected by the climate within which it takes place. Climate includes such factors as whether the interaction is friendly or hostile, whether mutual respect and trust develop between the parties, and whether the negotiators adopt a competitive or cooperative stance toward one another. During the pre-conference stage the parties engage in what Walton and McKersie called "attitudinal structuring" as they attempt to shape interaction patterns in ways that each party sees as most advantageous to its position.[36]

Frequently, the parties will engage in a form of psychological warfare prior to the conference stage. There may be considerable verbal fireworks when, as Mastenbroek noted,

> both parties make firm statements in which they present their demands and conditions as completely fixed and unassailable....[T]his often takes the form of speeches in which a statement of principle is coupled with the great righteousness of the demands. Thoroughly bolstered with facts, the proposals are presented as reasonable and fair.[37]

This tactic gives the other side the message that it is confronting a tough bargainer with a firm position; it reassures the negotiator's constituents that their representative has their best interests at heart; and it sets the parameters of one's position, thus providing a starting point for the probes and counterprobes that will follow as each side presses for concessions. Under other circumstances, such as when one party is more desirous of negotiating than the other or one party is clearly less powerful than the other, the negotiator may seek to create a cooperative climate by stressing the mutual gains to be attained through negotiations.

Whether negotiators seek to create a tough, competitive climate or a softer, more cooperative one, they are always faced with the dilemma that results from the strain between their desire to come to an agreement with the other side and their desire to reach an agreement that is as favorable as possible to their individual interests. To cope with these contradictory demands, negotiators need to adopt a policy of what Pruitt called "firm flexibility," in which one is firm with respect to one's ends but flexible with respect to the means to those ends.[38] Negotiators use the pre-conference stage not only to make pronouncements about their commitment to their goals, but also to show their willingness to be flexible by indicating possible alternative means through which those goals can be realized.

One concrete way in which the negotiating climate is set is the selection of the site for the negotiating session. The options are to meet in the offices of one or another of the parties or, if this can't be arranged, in some neutral place. Generally, it is considered advantageous to have the negotiating sessions in one's own office. If the other party comes to you, you may interpret that to mean that the other party is anxious to reach an agreement or that it is willing to defer to you because of what it perceives as your more powerful position. Going to another's office is akin to going to another's house, and a kind of guest law operates. The convener is in a position to be a generous host or hostess, providing refreshments and genial hospitality, or, conversely, to set a stark, no-nonsense atmosphere. The convener also has the advantage of immediate access to files when issues require documentation for their resolution, thus giving the convener control over the kinds of information considered during the meeting.

On the other hand, one's agreeing to go to the other's office can be taken as an initial, albeit minor, concession that creates the expectation that the other party will reciprocate with some other concession, such as agreeing to the other party's request for the date and time of the meeting or the order in which items on the agenda will be considered. Also, the visiting side can use being away from its home office as a tactic for timing the release of critical information ("We have to consult our own files") or to ward off pressure from the other side to accept or reject an offer ("We have to return to our organization to consult with superiors or constituents").

The Conference Stage

The negotiating process is driven by how much each side is willing to concede before reaching the point at which no settlement is preferable to a negotiated agreement. The point at which negotiators are willing to accept no settlement is what Greenhalgh and his colleagues called the negotiator's "resistance point" and defined as "the point within the hierarchy of possible outcome packages at which the negotiator is indifferent about accepting the deal or reaching an impasse."[39] The resistance point is not the point at which the benefits to be gotten from a negotiated settlement have fallen to zero, but the point at which these benefits are less than what the parties had prior to the negotiation or what they can hope to get from dealing with a third party.

Researchers and practitioners have identified a number of strategies that negotiators use to identify the limits to which the other side can be expected to go. These strategies range from ones based on mathematical models that purport to identify the best agreement possible in a given situation, or the point at which the interests of both sides are maximized, to those that are much less precise but do not make the assumptions that the former do. The mathematical approaches come mainly from game theory and use the economic concept of utility functions to develop fair solutions that identify the point in the bargaining process in which the utilities of both sides are maximized. An example of such a model is the Nash solution, which, as Greenhalgh and his colleagues pointed out, is the only settlement that satisfies the following requirements for a fair solution:

> Pareto optimality, equal payoffs if the game is symmetric, independence of irrelevant alternatives, and independence of the settlement with respect to utility function scale. For example, Pareto optimality requires that the prescribed settlement be such that no other settlement provides better payoffs to both negotiators.[40]

Formal models of negotiating have stringent assumptions which must be met if the models are to work. They assume that the positions of the opposing sides can be translated into quantitative terms, such as dollar amounts, and subjected to sophisticated economic analyses; that there are a limited number of issues involved; and that each side has a precise idea of what it wants to accomplish as well as complete information on what the other side wants. Most importantly, these models prescribe how the parties to the negotiation would act *if they were completely rational*. In the context of game theory, Rapoport pointed out,

> the players are not endowed with any psychological characteristics except those that may be reflected in the description of the game itself, for example, what each of the outcomes is worth to each of the players. Therefore, the desirable properties of the proposed solution cannot depend on any personal characteristics

of the players beyond the utilities ascribed to the outcomes which are assumed to be known.[41]

While some of the issues that social administrators negotiate meet these assumptions, most do not. The issues that come up for negotiations within social agencies usually involve multiple and conflicting goals; reflect ambiguity and uncertainty on the part of the opposing sides about exactly what they hope to accomplish; do not readily lend themselves to quantification; and are part of larger political conflicts that involve efforts to manipulate and distort information. In these situations, the preferred negotiating strategies are ones that have evolved from the experiences of practitioners and research on negotiating behavior within organizations. One such approach is derived from the "level-of-aspiration" theory developed by Siegle and Fournaker.[42] This strategy starts with the assumption that level of aspiration, or what each party hopes to achieve through negotiations, is inversely related to concession level, or the compromises each party is willing to make. Put simply, the more that negotiators expect to get, the harder they will bargain. This theory suggests that a negotiator can extract more concessions from an opponent by presenting very high aspirations to which the negotiator appears to be irrevocably committed. Moderate or low aspirations, Bacharach and Lawler argued,

> will raise the opponent's aspiration level and reduce the opponent's yielding, while tough tactics will decrease the opponent's level of aspiration and, thereby, increase the opponent's yielding....The best overall stance is to make no or only very small concessions or conciliatory gestures early in the bargaining or until the opponent stops making concessions.[43]

The basic problem with this strategy is the potential for reaching an impasse. The level-of-aspiration theory is subject to what logicians call the fallacy of exception. The classic example of this fallacy is the spectator at a parade who stands on his or her tiptoes in order to get a better view. This tactic can work only if *no one else does it.* If everyone stands on his or her tiptoes, the person is no better off than before. Similarly, if setting a high aspiration level will work for one side, we can expect the other side to adopt the same approach, thus increasing the likelihood that the negotiation will end in a stalemate.

Even with the risk of stalemate, tough bargaining, or setting one's demands at a high level and making as few concessions as possible, is generally seen as the most effective negotiating strategy. There are, however, a number of factors which constrain negotiators to moderate their demands and increase their conciliatory responses to the other side's demands. Negotiations, as noted earlier, involve mixed motives on the part of the participants. If the parties' interests did not conflict, there would be no need for negotiation. What is equally true, however, is that if the parties did not have some common interests, there would also be no need to negotiate since they would be free to engage in unfettered competition as a means of achieving their goals. When people agree to negotiate, they agree to be held to the expectation that they will make concessions.

From a strategic point of view, however, people will make concessions only if it is in their interests to do so. That is, while negotiators are expected to play the game by making sufficient concessions to keep the other party involved, it is also expected that each side will play to win, that is, to maximize its gains and minimize its losses. It is in people's best interest not to make concessions when they judge the outcome of a negotiated agreement to be worse than returning to the status quo prior to negotiations or taking their chances and going to a third party for arbitration.

There are two ways for judging the success or failure of a negotiation. The first evaluates the negotiating process itself and asks the question, Did the negotiators succeed in reaching an agreement? The second looks at the outcome, or payoff, for each of the parties and asks, How good is the agreement? Negotiators thus can fail in two ways: they can fail to reach an agreement, or they can agree to a settlement that is not in the best interests of their constituency. People negotiate when they expect to produce something better than the results they could obtain without negotiating. Negotiations which fail in the first sense because one or both parties refused to lower their demands or increase their concessions, can still be a success in the second sense if it was in the interests of the parties not to come to agreement. Conversely, many negotiations succeed in producing an agreement but fail because one (and sometimes both) of the parties is worse off than it was prior to the negotiations.

The ability of a negotiator to know when to lower demands and increase concessions will in large part be dependent on the quality of the work that was done in the pre-conference stage. Negotiators who have done their homework will have a precise understanding of the nature of their own preferences and an accurate assessment of what the other side hopes to gain. This knowledge enables them to make skillful assessments of when to stand firm and when to be flexible. Other factors also play a part in determining the success of a negotiation, notably the relative power of the two sides and the personalities of the negotiators, but research has shown that an in-depth understanding of one's own goals and those of one's opponents is the most important variable.[44]

THE NEGOTIATING PARTIES

The people who conduct the actual negotiations are critical actors in the process. Researchers have studied the role of the individual negotiator from the perspectives of how the negotiator's personality and other individual characteristics affect negotiating style; the relationship between negotiators and the constituencies that they represent; and the dynamics of third-party negotiations.

The Negotiator as Individual

Studies of the relationship between individual characteristics and negotiating style have shown how people with different attributes typically approach negotiations and have pointed to the conditions under which one
negotiating style is likely to be more successful than another. Negotiating style
is generally taken to mean how people are apt to behave in a negotiating
situation and how they characteristically think about the issues before them.
An influential framework for thinking about negotiators' behavioral styles is
Rubin and Brown's concept of *interpersonal orientation* (IO).[45] A person with a
high IO is someone who is

> responsive to the interpersonal aspects of his relationship with the other. He is
> both interested in, and reactive to, variations in the other's behavior. Such
> variations provide the high IO individual with the important information he
> seeks about the other party: what the other prefers and expects, how he intends
> to behave, and what he is really like.[46]

By contrast, a person at the low end of the IO continuum is characterized by
nonresponsiveness to interpersonal aspects of his or her relationship with
others. The low IO person's interest is

> neither in cooperating nor competing with the other, but rather in maximiz-
> ing his own gain — pretty much regardless of how the other fares. He is not
> interested in discovering the other party's true nature. The other, for him, is
> a nonperson, a "machine" — wholly rational, perhaps, or simply a person
> who can be expected to reason and behave just as he himself does.[47]

High IO negotiators view the relationship between the parties as the
most important variable in the negotiating process. They attribute
changes in the other side's negotiating position to personality factors
rather than to external conditions. For example, high IO negotiators are
likely to perceive the other side's refusal to compromise over a particular
point as a reflection of psychological rigidity rather than a rational strategy
for advancing their interests. Rather than search for alternatives that take
into consideration the objective factors that impinge on the other side's
position, they are likely to concentrate on the other negotiators' motives
and try to get them to be more flexible. Low IO negotiators, on the other
hand, are less likely to view variations in the negotiating situation as a
result of the other side's idiosyncratic way of behaving, and they will view
changes in negotiating positions as a result of changes in external conditions. Regardless of the other's behavior or disposition, "the low IO's
behavior is simply designed to achieve as much tangible or intangible gains
for himself as he can."[48]

A low IO will be an asset when negotiators judge that they are in a better
bargaining position than their opponents and therefore adopt a distributive,
or win-lose, strategy in which they maintain a firm stand, regardless of the

losses that the other side may sustain. A low IO is also an advantage when game theory or economic models of negotiations are used: negotiators are bound by predetermined positions derived from formal analytical models and cannot be affected by the interpersonal dynamics of the moment. A high IO, conversely, is useful when negotiators seek to develop integrative agreements that maximize the benefits to both parties. The strategies for reaching integrative agreements discussed earlier all require a high degree of interpersonal responsiveness for their success. Negotiators with a high IO will also be better able to distinguish conflict situations based on nonrealistic, subjective issues from those that are more objective in nature.

The second element of negotiating style is how people think about issues. As the issues in a negotiation increase in complexity and the goals that each party wants to achieve multiply, negotiators' cognitive styles assume greater importance. The negotiators will have to assimilate large amounts of information and make complex trade-off decisions. Mitroff developed a framework for describing cognitive styles based on the work of Carl Jung.[49] The two dimensions of the framework are (1) the way in which people typically take in data from the outside world and (2) how they make decisions based on these data. According to Jung, people can take in data by either *sensation* or *intuition*. Sensing types attend to the details of any situation. They feel most comfortable

> when they have gathered some hard facts that pertain to the situation. In contrast, intuitive types typically take in information by looking at the situation as a whole. They concentrate their attention on the hypothetical possibilities in a situation rather than getting bogged down and constrained by details and an endless array of hard facts.[50]

Jung also posited that people reach decisions either through *thinking* or *feeling*. Thinking types base their decisions on impersonal, logical modes of reasoning. They do not feel comfortable unless they have

> a logical or an analytical...basis for making a decision. Feeling types, however, make their decisions based on personal considerations, for example, how they *feel* about the particular person or situation, whether they *like* the person or *value* the situation....Thinking types, on the other hand, want to depersonalize every situation, object, and person by "explaining" them and having rules for correct conduct.[51]

The combination of these two dimensions creates four cognitive styles, as shown in Figure 8-1. The sensing-thinking type is the classic rational actor who deals with facts in a systematic, analytical manner. This style would be most effective when negotiating over complicated issues and when formal negotiating models are used. The intuition-thinking type tends to be more interested in hypothetical possibilities and is more likely to come up with innovative alternatives to problems. This style would be an asset when negotiations have reached

FIGURE 8-1.   Jungian Typology of Cognitive Styles. (*Adapted from:* Ian I. Mitroff, *Stakeholders of the Organizational Mind* (San Francisco: Jossey-Bass Publishers, 1983), p. 58. Reprinted by permission of Jossey-Bass, Inc.)

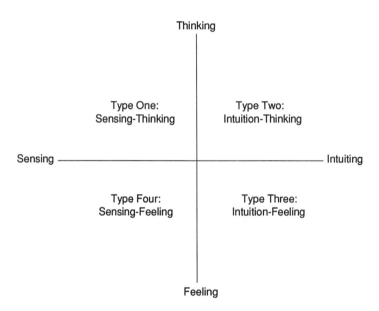

an impasse and new ideas are needed to move the parties to agreement. The intuition-feeling type, in contrast, is more concerned with the human aspects of a problem but, like the second type, tends to think about human problems in global or conceptual terms. The sensing-feeling type is also concerned with people but thinks about issues in terms of their specific effects on particular people. Both styles would be helpful when negotiators are concerned about the future relationship between the parties and must be sensitive to the impact that an agreement will have on their relationship.

While the negotiator's behavioral and cognitive styles have important consequences for the outcomes of negotiations, it may not be immediately clear how administrators can use this knowledge to improve their effectiveness as negotiators. If an administrator assesses himself or herself as having a high interpersonal orientation with an intuitive-feeling cognitive style, what good is it to know that these traits are likely to be a liability in negotiations over complicated issues that call for tough bargaining? People's behavioral and cognitive profiles are fairly stable, and a person with a high IO, for example, cannot easily or quickly adopt a more detached, impersonal style. This knowledge can be helpful, however, if the administrator uses it as a guide in the selection of the most appropriate person, or persons, to negotiate a particular issue.

Organizational issues are often negotiated by the people who are directly involved with the problem. They may or may not have the behavioral and cognitive characteristics most appropriate for that particular negotiation. If the issue is important enough, however, and if the negotiations are to be conducted in a formal, explicit manner, the conduct of the negotiations can be delegated to people with the necessary characteristics or skills. Different issues will require negotiators with different combinations of personal attributes and skills. These attributes include substantive knowledge of the issues, the ability to relate to people in a variety of ways, the ability to come up with creative solutions to knotty problems, and the ability to assess quickly and accurately the implications of the other side's proposals and counterproposals. The ideal negotiator, Ilich suggested, should be

> a confident person, confident in his own abilities and his ability to persuade. He must be flexible....His mind must be quick and alert, and he must possess mental toughness....He must be thoroughly prepared and he must be enthusiastic.[52]

Rarely, however, will these characteristics be found in one person, particularly when that person is selected on the basis of his or her incumbency in a particular organizational position.

One way of dealing with this problem is to create negotiating teams whose members are assigned to different aspects of the negotiating situation. Ideally, such a team would include someone who is knowledgeable about the issues and who would be responsible for framing demands and counterdemands. Another member with the personal characteristics most appropriate for the bargaining strategy that has been adopted would be responsible for presenting the team's position to the other side and responding to their counterproposals. Another member of the team would be the person with the formal authority to accept or reject the other side's offer. Of course, the realities of life in a social agency will present few opportunities to create negotiating teams for every issue that comes up. However, in those instances when managers can plan for a formal negotiating session, such as in renewals of union contracts or negotiations over grant applications, the team approach has many advantages.

One of the disadvantages of using negotiating teams is that, as with any group, extra work must be done to maintain the team as a cohesive unit with one goal and one approach to the problem. Dissension within the team could create an opening that the other side could exploit to its advantage. Careful attention should be given to selecting team members to ensure that they have the needed skills, are committed to the team's goals, and can be trusted to abide by group decisions. After the team has been formed, ongoing group maintenance work is necessary to deal with disagreements that arise among members in the course of the negotiations.

The Negotiator as Representative

The need for negotiating teams to maintain group cohesion and the commitment of its members to a single position is part of a general category of issues that arise because most negotiators act on behalf of the units, organizations, or constituencies that they represent. Although there are instances when organizational members negotiate solely on their own behalf, most issues reflect the interests of some group or unit, which then selects one of its members to conduct the actual negotiations. Even issues that originally come up as an individual matter, such as a worker negotiating with a supervisor about his or her work evaluation, will likely end up as a group issue as other workers hear of the negotiations and want to be included.

People who negotiate on behalf of others are confronted with the dilemma that is created by the conflict between the roles of being a good representative and being an effective negotiator. Constituents tend to have higher aspiration levels than their representatives and are tougher in terms of what they are willing to concede. Constituents talk mostly to each other, confirming each others' beliefs in the rightness of their position and the wrongness of the other side's. They have little or no contact with the other side and are likely to view the opposition in negative, stereotyped ways. Representatives, on the other hand, regularly meet with each other, get to know each other as individuals, and acquire an appreciation for each other's interests, goals, and the constraints that each side faces. Their role as negotiator, moreover, means they must find ways of resolving conflicts; their constituents, however, often are more interested in highlighting differences than in finding common grounds.

The dilemma is expressed in the conflict between being responsive to the wishes of one's constituents and retaining the autonomy and flexibility needed to maneuver in the negotiating situation. The pressures that constituents exert on their representatives tend to produce, Deutsch suggested, a narrowing of vision in negotiations.[53] This narrowing results from a reduction in the search for alternative ways of resolving issues, a lowering in the quality of communications, and a lessening of the representative's ability to interpret issues from the other side's point of view. Dramatic examples of this process at work are seen daily in legislative arenas around the country as single-issue interest groups pressure their representatives to take strong, uncompromising stands on controversial topics such as abortion-on-demand, the death penalty, or nuclear energy. The same degree of intransigence is often reached within organizations when departments square off against each other over questions of policy and organizational turf, preferring stalemate to compromise. Being a good representative often means being a poor negotiator, as representatives give in to constituent pressures to maintain a hard line.

If negotiators want to reduce the pressure from their constituents, they must understand the conditions under which this pressure is transmitted. These conditions include, Bacharach and Lawler pointed out, the degree of constituent involvement in the negotiating process, the accountability of representatives to their constituents, and the representative's commitment to the coalition and its goals.[54] The degree of constituent involvement can be assessed through use of what Dachler and Wilpert called the "influence-power-sharing" continuum.[55] Adapted to negotiating behavior, the low-involvement end of this continuum is when no advance information is given to constituents about impending decisions in the negotiations. The next point is when constituents are informed in advance of a decision. This is followed by the situation in which constituents' opinions about how an issue should be decided are solicited by representatives. These opinions are given more weight when constituents have the power to veto a potential action by their representative or when the representative is required to obtain constituent concurrence prior to acting. The high-involvement end of the continuum is the point at which constituents retain complete power to approve or disapprove all actions taken by the representative, whose role is reduced to transmitting messages between the sides. The greater the involvement of constituents, the more they can limit the range of options that their representatives can consider. High involvement ties representatives to positions set in advance by constituents and reduces the representative's discretion to respond to unexpected elements of the bargaining process.

Accountability refers to the degree to which constituents can make representatives account for their actions. The extent of accountability is determined by the frequency of contacts between representative and constituents, the level of constituents' knowledge about the negotiations, and the degree to which constituents can apply sanctions against the representative. The greater the accountability, the less latitude representatives have in the negotiating session. Walton and McKersie identified a number of tactics that negotiators use to reduce the degree of their accountability to constituents and increase their flexibility in the negotiation session.[56] These tactics include avoiding a strict mandate or precise terms of reference by allowing a short time for constituents to consider the issues or by keeping the subject unclear; moderating constituent demands by underestimating what concessions are attainable; reporting the results of negotiations in vague or complicated terms; and exaggerating the opponent's concessions.

The negotiator's commitment to the goals of the group for which he or she is a representative is largely determined by whether the representative is a member of that group. A representative who is a member of the group will be more adamant in defense of the group's goals and more resistant to compromise than an outsider. Negotiators who are brought in from outside the unit or organization are less likely to be committed to the group's point of view and more likely to make concessions to the opposition in order to reach a satisfactory agreement. This will be particularly true for negotiators whose professional reputations depend on their ability to bring a negotiation to a successful conclusion.

The relationship between representatives and their constituents, like the relationship between the opposing sides, involves mixed motives. The negotiator often shares the goals of the group that he or she represents and will share in whatever gains and losses that come out of the negotiations. At the same time, the negotiator has an interest in establishing a sufficiently harmonious relationship with the other side in order to facilitate the negotiation process. As noted earlier, negotiations are successful when the parties feel that they have gotten what they wanted *and* when the negotiating process is judged to have been conducted in an efficient and effective manner. Constituents are primarily interested in the first kind of success, whereas the negotiator — whether a professional arbitrator or a member of the unit who has been temporarily assigned to this role — has an interest in both kinds of success. Conflict management is an important management function, and organizational members who temporarily assume the role of negotiator know that their performance is being evaluated and that the way in which they handle themselves in this role will affect their reputation within the organization.

Third-Party Negotiations

Third parties frequently become involved in negotiations when the opposing sides have reached an impasse but still wish to look for ways to reach an agreement. In formal negotiating situations, third-party intervention is usually conducted by professional negotiators and takes the form of mediation, fact-finding, or arbitration. In mediation, the third party works directly with both sides, helping them reach an agreement. Social workers are most likely to be familiar with this role in family counseling and divorce mediation. In fact-finding, the third party listens to arguments from both sides and produces a set of nonbinding recommendations. Arbitration is like fact-finding except that the recommendations are binding.

Negotiators within organizations also make use of third-party intervention, although it is not usually referred to by that name. In one sense, the hierarchical structure of an organization serves as a system for third-party negotiations, since many disputes between organizational members are resolved by the intervention of someone at a higher level. When upper-level managers intervene in disputes among subordinates, they often assume the role of a mediator whose goal is to create the conditions under which the contending parties are more likely to reach an agreement. Failing this, the manager can invoke his or her authority to direct the terms of a resolution, in much the same way that an arbitrator would. Many of the strategies used by professional mediators and arbitrators thus find their parallels within organizations.

Analysts of negotiating behavior have identified two types of mediation, *process* and *content*. Process mediation is directed toward improving the conditions under which the negotiations take place, as well as the skills of the individual negotiators. Content mediation addresses the substance of the issues under discussion, with the third party suggesting solutions or trying to persuade the bargainers to move in certain directions.[57] In process mediation, the third party assumes the role of honest broker, or facilitator. To be effective in that role, the conflict manager must be viewed, Yates argued,

> as a neutral and personally disinterested party to policy debate....The goals of honest brokers are that they be viewed as fairminded in their management of policy-making procedures, that they not have "hidden agendas" of their own, and that they treat competing interests seriously and with respect.[58]

Often, the mere presence of a third party will improve the negotiating climate, since people tend to be on their best behavior in the presence of outsiders. When emotions between the parties heat up and communications break down, the mediator often takes on, Pruitt observed, a psychotherapeutic role, in which he or she serves as a "surrogate target for emotion, allows catharsis, and then leads the client to a more realistic interpretation of the situation."[59] This strategy is especially helpful when the issues under discussion are subjective in nature (the "nonrealistic" conflict discussed earlier) and affect strongly held values or philosophies. When emotions run high, people are not as likely to think clearly and are apt to overinterpret each other's behavior as indications of hostile intentions. If left unchecked, these situations can deteriorate into what Yates called "negative symbolic politics" in which the contending parties "feel (or come to feel) that the issue at hand signifies a far more important and sensitive value or principle."[60] Third parties can bring a measure of disinterestedness and common sense to bear on these situations by helping the opposing sides to see each other in a more realistic light and by moving the discussion away from symbolic and global concerns to concrete and specific problems to be solved.

Another function that process mediators perform is to educate the parties about the dynamics of conflict and to foster negotiating skills. This role is particularly important in negotiations within organizations since both parties are likely to be inexperienced negotiators who are not explicitly aware that they are involved in a bargaining situation. This situation was faced in the earlier example of the administrator who commented that the other side didn't know that it was winning. His efforts to educate the other side about trade-offs and constraints were unsuccessful, however, since he was a party to the conflict, and his advice was seen not as education but as a ploy to get the other side to moderate its demands. The dynamics involved in process mediation are similar to those that social workers see in their work with couples and families, and mediators need the same authority and credibility that family and marital counselors do to get their message across. The analogy with family counseling can be taken a step further in that process mediators often seek to show the contending parties how to fight successfully with each other. For organizations with little experience in conflict management, the development of effective negotiating skills among the members is a major accomplishment in itself that can have benefits beyond the immediate negotiating situation.

In content mediation, third parties address themselves to the substantive issues under discussion and attempt to help the parties identify viable alternatives. An alternative is viable if it enables both parties to achieve their ends and takes into account the constraints with which each party must contend. In some circumstances, Pruitt pointed out,

> a viable alternative is among the options currently under consideration, but concession to that alternative is blocked for one or another reason. In other circumstances, it is possible to develop a viable alternative if imagination can be mobilized. In still other circumstances, development of a viable alternative is not possible, and one or both parties must change their limits if agreement is to be reached.[61]

One or another of the parties may resist conceding to a viable alternative because it thinks it can hold out for a more favorable agreement. This situation is often a result of negotiator overconfidence, rather than an objective assessment of the other side's willingness to make further concessions. Third parties can intervene in these situations by helping the parties gain a more accurate reading of the other side's strengths, thereby bringing each side's estimation of its chances of winning into realistic perspective. The parties may also be prevented from adopting a viable alternative when they fear that doing so will create a loss of face. Mediators can deal with this situation by suggesting a particular solution in a joint session. Concessions made in response to a suggestion from a respected mediator, Pruitt argued, "do not carry the implications of weakness that are inherent in concessions made to the other party."[62]

When viable alternatives are not present in the options under consideration, the third party's focus is on initiating a process leading toward an integrative agreement. This approach involves the strategies discussed earlier for transforming win-lose conflicts into win-win situations, with the difference being that the mediator assumes responsibility for thinking up such alternatives and persuading the parties to consider them. In this situation it is important that the mediator be thoroughly familiar with the parties in terms of their organizational interests and goals. One general strategy that conflict managers use is to get the parties to identify problems that they have in common. Organizational units are frequently insulated from each other, with little appreciation of what others are trying to accomplish and what they are up against. The key element in this situation, Yates suggested, is for the mediator to "emphasize *identification* with the organizational problems and condition of other participants rather than *comparison* of one's position with that of others."[63] One way that managers do this is to present an organizational mission toward which all units are working. In this way, short-term losses that one unit might incur can be weighed against long-term gains for the organization as a whole.

NOTES

1. Thomas A. Kochan and Anil Verma, "Negotiations in Organizations: Blending Industrial Relations and Organizational Behavior Approaches," in *Negotiations in Organizations*, ed. Max H. Bazerman and Roy J. Lewicki (Beverly Hills: Sage Publications, 1983), p. 14.
2. Lewis A. Coser, *The Functions of Social Conflict* (New York: The Free Press, 1956), p. 49.
3. Philip R. Popple, "Negotiation: A Critical Skill for Social Work Administrators," *Administration in Social Work*, 8, no. 2 (Summer 1984), 6.
4. Richard E. Walton and Robert B. McKersie, *A Behavioral Theory of Labor Negotiations* (New York: McGraw-Hill, 1965), pp. 4–5.
5. Roger Fisher and Willis Ury, *Getting to Yes* (Boston: Houghton Mifflin, 1981), p. 4.
6. Dean G. Pruitt, "Achieving Integrative Agreements," in *Negotiating in Organizations*, ed. Max H. Bazerman and Roy J. Lewicki (Beverly Hills: Sage Publications, 1983), pp. 37–41.
7. Samuel B. Bacharach and Edward J. Lawler, *Power and Politics in Organizations* (San Francisco: Jossey-Bass, 1981), p. 121.
8. Pruitt, "Achieving Integrative Agreements," p. 38.
9. Ibid., pp. 40–41.
10. Thomas C. Schelling, *The Strategy of Conflict* (Cambridge, Mass.: Harvard University Press, 1960).
11. Stephen Holloway and George Brager, "Implicit Negotiations and Organizational Practice," *Administration in Social Work*, 9, no. 2 (Summer 1985), 16.
12. Bacharach and Lawler, *Power and Politics*, p. 114.
13. Scott T. Moore, "The Theory of Street-Level Bureaucracy: A Positive Critique," *Administration & Society*, 19, no. 1 (May 1987), 78–79 (emphases in original).
14. Samuel B. Bacharach, "Bargaining within Organizations," in *Negotiating in Organizations*, ed. Max H. Bazerman and Roy J. Lewicki (Beverly Hills: Sage Publications, 1983), p. 373.
15. Holloway and Brager, "Implicit Negotiations," 17.
16. Ibid., 18.
17. Michael D. Cohen and James G. March, *Leadership and Ambiguity*, 2nd ed. (Boston: Harvard Business School Press, 1986), p. 30.
18. Douglas Yates, Jr., *The Politics of Management: Exploring the Inner Workings of Public and Private Organizations* (San Francisco: Jossey-Bass, 1985), p. 131.
19. K. W. Thomas, "Conflict Handling Modes in Interdepartmental Relations," Ph.D. diss., Purdue University, 1971.
20. Donald Dean Morley and Pamela Shockley-Zalabak, "Conflict Avoiders and Compromisers: Toward an Understanding of Their Organizational Communication Style," *Group & Organization Studies*, 11, no. 4 (December 1986), 400.
21. Willem F. G. Mastenbroek, "Negotiating: A Conceptual Model," *Group & Organization Studies*, 5, no. 3 (September 1980), 328.
22. Otomar J. Bartos, "Determinants and Consequences of Toughness," in *The Structure of Conflict*, ed. Paul Swingle (New York: Academic Press, 1970), p. 46.
23. Mastenbroek, "Negotiating," 329.
24. Pruitt, "Achieving Integrative Agreements," p. 44.

25. Fisher and Ury, *Getting to Yes*, p. 61.
26. Yates, *The Politics of Management*, p. 131.
27. Eric M. Eisenberg and Marsha G. Witten, "Reconsidering Openness in Organizational Communication," *Academy of Management Review*, 12, no. 3 (July 1987), 422.
28. Bacharach, "Bargaining within Organizations," p. 372.
29. Margaret A. Neale and Max H. Bazerman, "The Effects of Framing and Negotiator Overconfidence on Bargaining Behaviors and Outcomes," *Academy of Management Journal*, 28, no. 1 (March 1985), 37.
30. Fisher and Ury, *Getting to Yes*, p. 89.
31. Ronald H. Hermone, "How to Negotiate and Come out the Winner," *Management Review*, 63, no. 11 (November 1974), 20.
32. Amos Tversky and Daniel Kahneman, "The Framing of Decisions and the Psychology of Choice," *Science*, 211, no. 4481 (January 30, 1981), 453.
33. Ibid.
34. Neale and Bazerman, "The Effects of Framing and Negotiator Overconfidence," 37.
35. Judith Dozier Hackman, "Power and Centrality in the Allocation of Resources in Colleges and Universities," *Administrative Science Quarterly*, 30, no. 1 (March 1985), 61–77.
36. Walton and McKersie, *A Behavioral Theory of Labor Negotiations*, p. 5.
37. Mastenbroek, "Negotiating," 330.
38. Pruitt, "Achieving Integrative Agreements," p. 43.
39. Leonard Greenhalgh, Scott A. Nesline, and Roderick W. Gilkey, "The Effects of Negotiator Preferences, Situational Power, and Negotiator Personality on Outcomes of Business Negotiations," *Academy of Management Journal*, 28, no. 1 (March 1985), 12.
40. Ibid., 15.
41. Anatol Rapoport, "Conflict Resolution in Light of Game Theory and Beyond," in *The Structure of Conflict*, ed. Paul Swingle (New York: Academic Press, 1970), p. 11.
42. Sidney Siegel and Lawrence E. Fouraker, *Bargaining and Group Decision Making* (New York: McGraw-Hill, 1960).
43. Bacharach and Lawler, *Power and Politics in Organizations*, p. 125.
44. Greenhalgh, Nesline, and Gilkey, "The Effects of Negotiator Preferences."
45. Jeffrey Z. Rubin and Bert R. Brown, *The Social Psychology of Bargaining and Negotiation* (New York: Academic Press, 1975), pp. 158–60.
46. Ibid., p. 158.
47. Ibid., pp. 159–60.
48. Ibid., p. 160.
49. Ian I. Mitroff, *Stakeholders of the Organizational Mind* (San Francisco: Jossey-Bass, 1983), pp. 56–59.
50. Ibid., pp. 56–57.
51. Ibid., p. 57 (emphases in original).
52. John Ilich, *The Art and Skill of Successful Negotiations* (Englewood Cliffs, N.J.: Prentice Hall, 1973), p. 19.
53. Morton Deutsch, "Conflicts: Productive and Destructive," *Journal of Social Issues*, 25, no. 1 (January 1969), 7–41.
54. Bacharach and Lawler, *Power and Politics in Organizations*, pp. 131–36.
55. H. Peter Dachler and Bernhard Wilpert, "Conceptual Dimensions and Boundaries of Participation in Organizations: A Critical Evaluation," *Administrative Science Quarterly*, 23, no. 1 (March 1978), 14.
56. Walton and McKersie, *A Behavioral Theory of Labor Negotiations*, pp. 312–40.
57. Dean G., Pruitt, *Negotiating Behavior* (New York, Academic Press, 1981), p. 203.

58. Yates, *The Politics of Management*, pp. 160–61.
59. Dean G. Pruitt, "Kissinger as a Traditional Mediator with Power," in *Dynamics of Third Party Intervention: Interdisciplinary Perspectives on International Conflict*, ed. Jeffrey Z. Rubin (New York: Praeger, 1981), p. 3.
60. Yates, *The Politics of Management*, pp. 149–50.
61. Pruitt, *Negotiating Behavior*, p. 207.
62. Ibid., p. 209.
63. Yates, *The Politics of Management*, p. 133 (emphases in original).

9

The Ethics of
Organizational Politics

The practice of organizational politics raises a number of ethical and professional questions. Involving, as it does, the conscious manipulation of information, people, and events, organizational politics can lead to a cynical amorality that substitutes self-interest and organizational aggrandizement for the intended purposes of social programs. The ethical problems associated with organizational politics are compounded by the perception on the part of many that management practice in general lacks a solid ethical foundation. This perception proceeds from a conception of the managerial role as the epitome of modern rationalism; as such, it is no longer measurable by traditional ethical or moral standards. The growth of bureaucratic systems, Katz and Georgopoulos argued,

> helped to diminish absolutist values of a moral character....Pragmatism replaced tradition. Results and accomplishment were the criteria rather than internal moral principle....Rules and laws were the instruments of men to achieve their purposes and lacked any transcendental quality. They could be changed at will as situations and needs changed or they became ineffective.[1]

Viewed from this perspective, the politicization of managerial work is the logical extension of a self-interested, instrumental approach to work in general. The ethical problems that face social work managers are further complicated because these individuals often belong to a profession that requires its members to abide by a code of ethics that may conflict with the demands of their organizational roles.

Attempts to hold political behaviors — whether within organizations or in general — to ethical standards are often seen as naive or futile. This attitude is summed up in Walzer's comment that the moral politician is known by his dirty hands: "If he were a moral man and nothing else, his hands would not be dirty; if he were a politician and nothing else, he would pretend that they were clean."[2] A number of writers have addressed the difficult issue of an ethics for organizational politics, and some have developed guidelines for assessing the ethics of political behaviors. They were motivated by the realization that all forms of organizational life demand compromises of important values and that people cannot contribute to any organization until they have developed a way for dealing with those compromises. The significant ethical question, Rohr argued, "is not *whether* one should compromise but *when* one should do so — that is, how important are the values at stake?"[3]

The purpose of the present chapter is to distill from the work on ethics and organizational politics a set of ethical principles or guidelines that are relevant to the work of social work managers and other members of social agencies. The discussion begins with the question of whether one code of ethics can be used for all of social work practice or whether different ethical systems are needed for social workers engaged in different aspects of practice. It then proceeds to a discussion of the ethics of organizational politics and the ethical principles that have been suggested as guides to administrative practice.

THE ETHICS OF SOCIAL WORK PRACTICE: GENERIC OR SPECIFIC?

The social work profession has given considerable attention to the ethics of practice, and a significant literature on this topic exists. Most of this attention, however, has been directed to the ethical dimensions of work with clients, with only passing mention of the ethical issues that stem from one's organizational role. In the National Association of Social Worker's Code of Ethics, for example, the section on the social worker's ethical responsibilities to clients contains 20 ethical principles, compared to four in the section on the social worker's ethical responsibilities to employers and employing organizations.[4] It is generally assumed, moreover, that this general code of ethics should guide social workers in whatever form of practice they are engaged. Levy, for example, argued that the ethical conduct expected of social workers in their relationships to clients

> would be expected of administrators in their work with administrative groups. All of the humanistic and humanitarian considerations applicable to social workers in their relationships to clients apply to the administrator's

relationships with board members, committee members, and so on, although in form and operation there are appreciable differences.[5]

The question of whether social workers are bound by a common set of values has been debated throughout the profession's history and is actively debated today. A number of writers have sought to identify social work's common value base, and the results of their inquiries have pointed to central professional purposes as diverse as, for example, looking after those who have been categorized, for whatever reasons, as socially or economically redundant; providing personal care services for the chronically ill or disabled; enhancing the quality of life for middle-class individuals and families; and promoting the value of distributive justice.[6] Each of these arguments captures a segment of the social welfare enterprise, but none stands as a definitive statement of the mission of the profession as a whole. Social work is too varied an activity to fit into one category. This diversity is reflected in the profession's official pronouncements about values and ethics, which, rather than being a unified product of a systematic ethical framework, are the result of intraprofessional committee politics and compromises. While these efforts serve the important function of providing the profession with a single, general statement of its ideals and aspirations, it is questionable how much guidance they give to individuals facing specific ethical dilemmas that arise from the unique features of their organizational roles, work assignments, and the policies that they are expected to implement.

A number of writers have taken issue with the idea of a unitary ethical framework for all of social work practice, arguing that social workers who work in areas other than clinical practice must deal with situations and make decisions that create ethical problems which are qualitatively different from those arising from work with clients and require a different ethical framework for their resolution.[7] The social work profession has always encompassed functions that are sufficiently different to qualify as separate occupations (e.g., counselor, administrator, organizer, planner). As different subspecialities vie with each other to define standards and policies for the profession as a whole, a number of tensions in the field are created. During the last two decades, moreover, social work has consolidated its position as one of the mental health professions, and social work clinicians and clinical researchers have assumed a dominant position within the profession. As a result, nonclinical social work specialities like administration and planning are held to professional standards that are predominantly oriented to clinical practice. This orientation is particularly true in the area of professional ethics, where administrators are expected to conform to a code of ethics that is mostly concerned with the relationship between service providers and their clients.

One of the tenets of many ethical systems is the principle of distributive justice, which holds that "individuals who differ in a relevant respect should be treated differently in proportion to the differences between them."[8]

From this perspective, many professional codes of ethics are themselves unethical because of their failure to take into account the different circumstances of the members who are expected to abide by them. One result of this failure is what Maritain called "hypermoralism," or the moral stance that applies ethical norms suitable to one realm of action to another, unrelated area.[9] Maritain specifically referred to the practice of applying ethical norms suitable for interpersonal relations to political situations. He argued that hypermoralism is as dangerous as amoralism, for they both lead to moral cynicism. Holding people to standards of behavior which are unattainable invariably leads to disillusionment, frustration, and despair.

The unattainability of many ethical codes to which administrators are expected to conform, moreover, stems more from the inappropriateness of the standards than any characterological shortcomings of the individuals. Unless social workers become aware of the range of ethical systems that are used to evaluate behaviors of people in different situations, they will continue to see administration and other forms of nonclinical social work practice as ethically suspect. This situation has a number of negative consequences for the profession. It creates distrust between professional colleagues who must work closely with each other, and it discourages social workers from developing a positive attitude about administrative work at a time when the number of social workers involved in nonclinical practice is growing.

Divergent developments in the social work profession and the larger human services field have created a paradox. At the same time that the social work profession has consolidated its position in the mental health field and strengthened its emphasis on clinical practice, the broader human services field offers an increasing number of career paths that take social workers into nonclinical positions.[10] These people are likely to find themselves in situations which present ethical problems that their professional education and socialization have not prepared them to address. One way that social work managers can remedy this problem is to look to the literature on administrative ethics that comes from fields like public administration where administrative practice is a central concern. It is to this literature that we now turn.

ETHICAL DIMENSIONS OF THE PUBLIC PROFESSIONS

Most theories of professionalism take as their reference point the attributes of the traditional professions of medicine and law. A central feature of these professions is the degree of autonomy that society grants to their members in their relationships with their patients and clients. This autonomy, in turn, is predicated on the assumption that these practitioners should be free from as many nonprofessional considerations as possible so they can devote themselves wholeheartedly to their clients' problems. It is further assumed that the professional-client relationship is *private* and confined to the professionals' efforts to alleviate their clients' distress.

This model of professionalism has serious shortcomings, however, when applied to professions that are essentially *public* in nature. The main difference between private and public professions is how they are held accountable for their work.[11] Private professions, like medicine and law, are primarily responsible, at least in theory, to their clients, whereas public professions, like public administration and urban planning, involve work that has consequences that go beyond the clients who are in direct receipt of their services and affect the public at large. Public administration and medicine are examples of professions at opposite ends of the public-private continuum. The social work profession, however, historically has been conflicted over its appropriate place on this scale. Like doctors and attorneys, social workers profess a primary orientation to service to their clients. At the same time, the services that social workers provide are not — with some exceptions — strictly a matter between the social worker and the client. Social service organizations produce *public goods*, or goods that have a mixed public and private character. Their services, Austin pointed out,

> are assumed to have a collective or public benefit in addition to any benefits accruing to individual users or consumers....Because they produce outputs with a public goods element, human service organizations always involve some type of collective or public assessment of performance, in addition to or in place of individual user assessment.[12]

Within the social work profession, the kind of work performed influences the public or private orientation of the practitioner. Social workers who deal directly with clients will have less of a public orientation than those in administrative positions. (Even in direct services the degree of public accountability can be high when the services directly involve the public interest, such as aid to the economically dependent or interventions in cases of child neglect or abuse.) Generally speaking, the higher the position in the organization, the greater the incumbent's accountability to external bodies. The public nature of most administrative work creates unique ethical dilemmas and requires an orientation to professional ethics that takes this nature into account.

Frameworks for evaluating the ethical behavior of public officials can be profitably applied to social work administrators, since both are responsible for the implementation of public social policies. Wilbern, for example, identified six levels of public morality: basic honesty and conformity to law; conflicts of interest; service orientation and procedural fairness; the ethic of democratic responsibility; the ethic of public policy determination; and the ethic of compromise and social integration.[13] The first three levels deal mainly with the administrator's personal morality, and the latter three address the ethics of the administrator's decisions or actions. In a similar vein, Morgan suggested that concerns about an administrator's ethics fall into three categories that depend on whether "one wishes to prevent some form of administrative lying, cheating or stealing; whether one hopes to frustrate bureaucratic initiative to shape unclear policy directives; or whether one wants to punish a clear administrative departure from a previously adopted policy."[14] These studies suggest that an ethical framework for the political manager should address both personal ethics and the ethical issues that arise from one's organizational role and responsibilities for policymaking and implementation.

Personal Ethics

Most people assume that it is wrong for administrators to lie, cheat, or steal. It is also assumed that there is general agreement about what constitutes lying, cheating, or stealing. Bok, for example, defined lying as a form of manipulation, or an attempt to evoke an effect through revision of the reality of a matter.[15] Those who believe that ethical behaviors can be objectively determined argue that lying can be uncovered by getting out all the facts of the matter and holding them against the account that is in question. When put into practice, however, this approach is often overly simplistic and incapable of distinguishing among the complex variety of communications that occur among people.

Manipulation is ubiquitous in human communications. Social psychologists have documented the pervasiveness of people's efforts to present themselves in the most desirable ways. Consciously and unconsciously, we represent ourselves in partial, selected ways that, regardless of our motives or goals, constitute a variety of manipulation. Whether through the strength of one's ideas, Brager and his colleagues argued, "the passion of one's style, the appearance of objectivity or impartiality, the appeal to love, morality, family, or community, manipulation occurs to the extent that people seek to influence others."[16]

An example of the gray area that separates the artful use of language and outright lying is found in the literature on organizational cultures. Many organizations have sought to emulate the "excellent companies" lauded by Peters and Waterman by promulgating an organizational culture that places primary emphasis on excellence in products and services, respect for the individual, personal integrity, and concern for the welfare of all employees.[17] Frequently, however, there are gaps between an organization's aspirations and its day-to-day practices. These gaps may be the result of good intentions, such as setting high standards that serve as future goals for the organization, or they can be due to circumstances beyond management's control, such as unexpected cutbacks in funding that force cancellation of employee-oriented programs like parental leave or opportunities for professional development. Gaps between an organization's aspirations and practices may also result from cynical efforts to protect the organization from public scrutiny of shoddy or questionable practices by the creation of a socially acceptable facade behind which the organization is free to conduct business as usual.

At some point, management's efforts to change organizational policies by setting new goals or to ensure that the public is made aware of an organization's accomplishments can deteriorate into misrepresentation of the facts (that is, lying). Just when that point has been crossed has been the subject of a number of legal cases. One of the most important of these is the Michigan Supreme Court's decision in *Toussaint v. Blue Cross & Blue Shield of Michigan*.[18] Charles Toussaint held a middle management position with Blue Cross for five years before he was terminated. In a lawsuit challenging the termination, he alleged that Blue Cross had promised him in his pre-employment interviews that he would not be discharged "as long as I did my job." He also based the suit on statements in the company's 260-page policy manual that contained language such as the organization's promise to "provide for the administration of fair, consistent and reasonable corrective discipline" and "to treat employees leaving Blue Cross in a fair and consistent manner and to release employees for just cause only."[19] The court held that statements and practices forming the organization's culture may become legally binding employee rights.

> Unless the organization's policy statements are clearly identified as only aspirations or goals, and are understood to be such by employee's, the organization may be legally held to its published statements rather than its actual practices. Where there is such a gap, a court may focus on the employee's beliefs about what constitutes the terms of the employment contract, rather than on the employer's intention.[20]

Even when people seek to present the truth in an unadorned, straightforward manner, many situations are so complex that one person usually has only a narrow perspective that can lead to distortions of the truth of the overall situation. This is especially true in organizations, where people's perceptions are institutionally fragmented because of hierarchical and functional divisions of labor. Most organizational members are continually subjected to what McSwain and Wright called the Rashomon phenomenon: "From some possible viewpoint, any situation can be constructed in a way that will show a given lie to be a truth, or, conversely, an accepted true account to be inaccurate."[21]

Lying as misrepresentation of the facts confines the definition to acts of commission only. If we extend the definition to acts of omission — that is, not giving a full account of the facts — the ethical issues become even murkier. Research on communications in organizations has shown that, while most employees say they would like their superiors to communicate in an open and honest way, they rarely hold this as an expectation for themselves. At all levels, Eisenberg and Witten argued,

> members of organizations stand to gain from the strategic use of ambiguity....It can be especially useful...when coping with the multiple interactional goals associated with supervisory positions....Vague, metaphorical, and humorous

suggestions are methods of communicating multiple messages which could not be expressed as easily in a literal fashion.[22]

Cheating and stealing are other behaviors that, in the context of organizational life, present definitional ambiguities and complexities that make it difficult to establish unequivocally when the ethical injunctions against them have been violated. Cheating occurs when one makes gains by secretly not conforming to the rules of a situation. The rules that govern organizational life, however, are rarely as explicit and unambiguous as the rules for poker or Scrabble, and most organizational rules lend themselves to a variety of interpretations. Organizations have different cultures with regard to the literalness with which rules are interpreted. In many instances, the literal wording of a rule reflects only the tip of the iceberg in terms of the rule's meaning within the organization. A full understanding of a rule often involves knowing the administrative interpretations that have been made, as well as the informal practices that have developed in different parts of the organization.

Stealing, or taking another's property into one's own possession, is for many the clearest example of unethical and immoral behavior. Even so, our ability to clearly discern what constitutes stealing in contemporary society has been weakened by a number of developments. Foremost among these is the growing ambiguity about what constitutes ownership of public property. This ambiguity was first expressed in Reich's discussion of the "new property," in which the valuables distributed by government, such as entitlements to social benefits, licenses to perform work, and tax exemptions, have replaced traditional forms of wealth based in private property and have created a new field of legal and administrative law for settling disputes regarding their ownership.[23] The question of ownership is further complicated by the growth of "third-party" government and the increase in the amount of public funds that are dispersed through grants and contracts to private and quasi-public organizations. The complicated mechanisms through which public funds are now dispersed have blurred the distinction between public and private ownership and have compounded the legal and ethical issues that surround these activities.

The foregoing discussion is not intended as an argument against the possibility of any ethical code for evaluating administrators' behaviors. Rather, it is intended to highlight the difficulties in trying to judge ethical behavior solely on the basis of a list of rules or guidelines that are expected to cover every situation that administrators are likely to encounter. "No rule," Carl Jung suggested, "can cope with the paradoxes of life." Formal codes of ethics are the starting point for assessing the rightness or wrongness of an action, but they alone are rarely a sufficient basis for the final evaluation. They usually have to be supplemented by an individual's judgment about the right course of action to take in a particular situation. The choices that administrators have to make are often difficult and painful, involving a choice between competing goods or between the lesser of two evils. In the final analysis, the rightness of these choices will be judged by the force and persuasiveness of the arguments presented by the individual actor to justify the actions taken, rather than a mechanical application of a set of formal ethical rules or guidelines.

The difference between ethical behavior as conformity to a code of conduct and ethical reasoning about the rightness of a specific course of action is reflected in the distinction that students of ethics make between the content of an ethical system and the process by which ethical judgments are made. In the first approach, the rules of ethical conduct are assumed to be known; in the second, the rules are assumed to be open to further inquiry and discussion.[24] For the professional practitioner, being ethical means following right rules of conduct as set down in a code of ethics and making judgments about what those right rules of conduct *should be* when (1) ethical codes are too vague or too general to provide guidance in a specific situation; (2) the rules set forth in the code conflict with each other; or, most importantly, (3) in the individual's judgment, the rules should be suspended in order for other, more significant, values to be realized.

Several writers view the content approach to ethics as inferior, or at a lower stage of development, to the process approach. Kohlberg, for example, suggested that moral development proceeds through a series of stages in which people move from an early emphasis on compliance with a set of rules, to incorporation of norms, and finally to a realization of their own internal moral responsibilities.[25] Bosanquet argued that ethical behavior requires a "good" will and concrete understanding of moral difficulties, and that "your moral conclusions must issue from your whole self, and be inspired by the convictions which dominate your life and determine your special outlook on your special situation."[26] Writing specifically of ethics for public administrators, Rohr labeled the approach that addresses administrative ethics exclusively in terms of adherence to agency rules as the "low" road, in contrast to the "high" road of ethical reasoning based on a systematic set of principles.[27]

The process approach makes greater demands on those who aspire to be ethical. It requires training in ethical reasoning and sets the expectation of incorporating ethics into every decision that administrators make. Given that most educational programs for managers — whether in social welfare, public administration, or business — contain little or no training in ethical reasoning, the process approach can become another form of hypermoralism in which administrators are held to unrealistically high, or inappropriate, standards of conduct. Nevertheless, some exposure to what is involved in ethical reasoning is necessary for the manager who seeks moral guidance in the twilight zones of personal conduct into which the practice of organizational politics inevitably leads.

Cavanagh and his colleagues developed a framework for ethical reasoning about organizational politics based on the major approaches used by ethicians to study moral issues.[28] These approaches are the *utilitarian* approach, the *theory of moral rights*, and the *theory of justice*. Utilitarianism judges actions by their consequences and asserts that moral acts are those that produce the greatest good for the greatest number. Decision makers are required to estimate the effect of alternative courses of action on all concerned parties and to select the one that optimizes the satisfactions of the greatest number. This approach entails enormous decision complexities because of the difficulty in identifying all the parties affected by a single action and because of the need to calculate an action's consequences for each party.

The theory of moral rights asserts that people have certain moral entitlements that should be respected in all decisions. The rights most germane to political acts in organizations are the right to free consent, the right of privacy, the right to freedom of conscience, and the rights of free speech and due process. This approach defines as unethical any action that violates an individual's rights. The protection of the rights of employees is as important to the conduct of responsible political behavior within organizations as it is in society in general. Within the American political system, the moral justification for political actions rests almost exclusively on the means by which political decisions are made, rather than their outcomes. That is, decisions that adversely affect some segment of the society are justified on the grounds that the rights of all concerned parties to participate in the decision process were protected. The process is fair, although the outcomes may not be.

The theory of justice, by contrast, makes ethical judgments about processes in terms of whether or not they produce fair outcomes. This approach requires that managers be guided by fairness, equity, and impartiality. The canons of justice that are relevant to organizational politics are equal treatment, consistent administration of rules, and restitution. Equal treatment means that people who are similar in relevant respects should be treated similarly. Equally important is the principle that individuals who differ in a relevant respect should be treated differently in proportion to the differences between them. In order for rules to be consistently administered, they should be clearly written and communicated. Individuals should be held to consistent expectations, and their performances impartially judged. Restitution refers to the manager's responsibilities for dealing with injustices. People who commit an injustice upon another should be held responsible for the costs of the victim's suffering, and no one should be held responsible for matters over which they have no control.

The following example shows how this framework can be used to make ethical judgments about political behavior in a social agency. Margaret Locke was in charge of program development and obtaining grant and foundation funds for a large hospital and nursing home complex. For several months she had been working on raising money for the construction of a new hospital wing. The proposed funding arrangement involved public monies that had to be matched with money raised in the local community. For the latter, Margaret had applied to a local foundation whose board chairman was Frank Weston, the chief executive officer of a company in the community. The foundation was in the process of reviewing the nursing home's request, along with requests from several other community agencies.

Margaret was contacted by Larry Caldwell, an executive with Weston's company and a member of the foundation's board. Larry's 79-year-old mother was in the hospital recovering from surgery to repair a fractured hip. Larry was anxious to have her admitted to Margaret's nursing home as soon as possible because of its reputation for physical therapy and rehabilitation, but he had been told that there was a six-month wait for admissions. The director of the social work department, Ron Howard, said that Larry's mother was not likely to be given priority consideration. Ron's department handled admissions, and his recommendations were usually followed by the home's director. Larry met with Margaret to see if she could persuade Ron to place his mother at the head of the waiting list. In return, Larry said he would use his influence with Frank Weston and other members of the board to persuade them to decide in favor of the home's request for funds.

Margaret met with Ron Howard and presented Caldwell's proposition. She argued strongly in favor of admitting Caldwell's mother, basing her argument on the benefits that the construction of the hospital wing would provide to both the agency and the community. Time was of the essence. Public funds were scarce, and if the agency was unable to raise the matching funds, these funds would go elsewhere. There was no telling when new funds would be available. Margaret also mentioned the opportunities that the new wing would create for Ron to expand the resources of the social work department and to increase its importance in the overall operations of the facility. Ron agreed with Margaret's position and recommended immediate admission for Caldwell's mother. At their next meeting, the foundation board announced the award of a grant to the home.

The ethical framework discussed above highlights the moral dilemmas of the situation. Ron's decision was ethical from a utilitarian point of view, since it will benefit the largest number of people. From the moral rights perspective, the only right violated was the right to consent on the part of the other people on the waiting list. Hypothetically, all the people on the list could have been presented with the facts of the situation, and a vote taken on whether Mrs. Caldwell should be given top priority. From a justice perspective, however, the decision violated all three canons. The people on the waiting list were not treated equally, the administration of rules was inconsistent, and applicants who might have suffered from having their waiting period extended were not compensated.

There are no easy ways for reconciling conflicting ethical principles. Ultimately, it involves a form of moral *triage* in which individual actors set priorities that reflect their values and beliefs. There are, however, some guidelines for aiding people in this difficult task. Cavanagh and his colleagues referred to one of these as the *principle of double effect*, which holds that it is acceptable to make a decision that has two effects, one good and one bad, "provided that the decision maker's dominant motivation is to achieve the good effect and provided that the good effect is important enough to merit the bad effect....."[29] Brager and his colleagues argued that the decision to engage in political maneuvering should be weighed against the criterion of, among others, who benefits and who loses.[30] This standard requires that political behavior must not be used to enhance the professional's own interests.

> Manipulation should be eschewed *except* when it clearly supports another, overriding, value. The magnitude of the need, the powerlessness of the constituent, and the rules of the game as played by adversaries support the conclusion that manipulation is justified.[31]

It was noted at the beginning of this chapter that ethical politicians can be identified by their dirty hands. They can also be recognized by an overburdened conscience. The organizational politician who aspires to be ethical must assume the role of the independent moral agent. As such, the individual must ultimately decide the rightness or wrongness of a course of action and live with the consequences. For the organizational politician, as for all other politicians, what is decisive, Max Weber argued, "is the trained relentlessness in viewing the realities of life, and the ability to face such realities and to measure up to them inwardly."[32]

The Ethics of Administrative Policymaking

Many discussions of professional ethics begin and end with the issue of personal morality. Even in social work, where 90 percent of the work takes place within complex organizations, the profession's code of ethics is mostly concerned with issues that arise between individual social workers and their clients. Administrators, however, have as great a need for ethical guidelines for actions that result from their organizational roles as they do for those that come out of their personal or professional beliefs.

One aspect of administrative work that creates a number of ethical concerns is the amount of discretion that is inherent in most administrative roles. Through administrative discretion, managers participate in the policymaking process for social agencies. This defines an ethical issue peculiar to one's organizational role, since most conceptions of the administrative function separate policymaking from policy implementation. In the public sector, the responsibility for policymaking is assumed to reside with elected representatives, executives, and their appointees, and in the private sector with an agency's board of directors.

For the reasons discussed earlier (see Chapters Two and Six), this distinction between policymaking and policy implementation has broken down, and administrators are generally recognized as active participants in the policy process. While most administrators play an important role in determining what social programs will actually do, many do not admit to having this kind of power. They frequently resist the idea that they have an impact on policymaking, which, in their eyes, can only be done by those bodies duly authorized to do so. This line of reasoning is usually based on the fallacy that if legislatures and boards of directors have much power, then administrators have none. Not only is this reasoning fallacious, Rohr argued, it is dangerous as well, "for it is always dangerous when the powerful are unaware of their own power."[33]

Some administrators continue to maintain that they are technical specialists who dutifully implement the policies transmitted to them without modification. However, most admit that their work involves considerable latitude in shaping the programs they manage, and they recognize the ethical dilemmas that this creates. The ethical problems, moreover, often reflect different and irreconcilable conceptions of what constitutes ethical administration. In an examination of the administration of a disability program, for example, Mashaw found that criticisms of the program reflected different conceptions of ethical administration.[34] Some accused the program of not providing adequate levels of professional services. Others were concerned that the program did not produce consistent and predictable results. A third group accused administrators of not providing adequate due process protection to claimants.

Mashaw concluded that these criticisms were based in different models of administrative justice. Those who were concerned about service deficiencies were using a professional treatment model, which evaluates programs in terms of clients' access to qualified professional care. Those who accused the program of not producing predictable and consistent results were using a bureaucratic model, in which efficient processing of information is critical. Finally, those who accused the program of being arbitrary and unfair to clients were using what Mashaw called the "moral judgment" model, which sees justice in terms of giving each individual what he or she deserves. Moreover, while the bureaucratic and professional models view administrative decision making as the implementation of values that were previously determined by policy-setting bodies or professional societies, "the moral judgment model sees decision making as value defining."[35]

The moral judgment model poses the most serious ethical problems because it places the administrator in the role of the independent moral actor. A number of difficulties are created by the substitution of an administrator's judgments about the proper way to conduct a program for the judgments of elected and appointed officials or boards of directors. For administrators of public programs, it violates the norm of democratic responsibility, which holds that sovereignty resides in the electorate, who delegate the authority to set policy to their representatives and their appointees. The same problem faces administrators of nonpublic, community agencies, since these organizations are usually private in name only, with a substantial part of their funds coming from tax dollars. In addition, these administrators must deal with the ethical problems created by their acting independently of their boards of directors, who have been authorized by the community to set policies for the agency.

While most administrators publicly acknowledge that their actions are determined by the voice of the people, in actual practice there is no way they can escape the responsibility to make ethical choices based on their own values. The voice of the people will rarely be clear or univocal: "it will not be based on full knowledge, it will conflict in small or large degree with other persuasive and powerful normative considerations."[36] The conflicts will be most severe when the popular will conflicts with the administrator's professional expertise and that of the agency staff. Administrators often rationalize actions that differ from legislative or board directives on the grounds that they are doing what their superiors would want done if they had the same information available to them.

Cooper provided a useful framework for helping administrators think about these ethical dilemmas in his distinction between an organization's *internal and external goods*.[37] Internal goods are the valued end products that an agency seeks to create. Their achievement is assumed to be a good for the whole community, as well as for the individual recipients of an agency's services. The internal goods of social agencies include, as noted earlier, the promotion of distributive justice, care for the chronically dependent, and helping people reach higher levels of fulfillment as individuals and members of families and communities. External goods, by contrast, are those things that support the members of the organization in their work but do not contribute directly to the production of internal goods. They include money, prestige, status, position, and power.

The acquisition of external goods often becomes the dominant concern of organizations. Although they are needed for the survival of the organization, they often become an end in themselves as administrators seek to expand their own and their organization's influence and power. Considerable evidence has shown, as Cooper pointed out,

> that organizations do *tend* to corrupt the practices which they support as a result of their focus on external goods....Consequently, the internal goods of a practice are at risk in an organizational environment dominated by the external goods inherent in organizational survival and growth....The practice of organizational management can support or corrupt the integrity of practices which function under their purview.[38]

The most pressing ethical problem that administrators and other members of social agencies face is one of maintaining their commitments to the production of internal goods in the face of demands for personal or organizational loyalty rooted in acquiring external goods. "Perhaps the highest order of ethics in management," Levy argued, "is the resistance...to the siren call of tempting powers."[39]

The tension between using resources to produce quality services versus directing those resources toward organizational maintenance and enhancement projects invariably leads administrators and other agency staff into positions where they must either go along with agency policies and practices that violate their professional or social values or use their administrative discretion, combined with the personal and organizational influence and power they have developed, to modify policies to make them more consonant with their values. As was true with issues of personal morality, moreover, administrators must ultimately justify their discretionary and independent actions through ethical argumentation in defense of the rightness of those actions.

No matter how persuasive or eloquent these arguments are, however, the use of administrative discretion to modify or change agency policies inevitably raises questions of disloyalty or underhanded practices. Administrators often try to avoid this dilemma by working to influence the content of policies while they are being developed. The change in the conception of administrators from value-neutral technicians to policy and program advocates who actively seek to invest the programs they manage with their own beliefs, values, and professional philosophies, raises important questions of the ethical responsibilities for administrators in policy development.

The ultimate ethical test of a social program is what it accomplishes. Did the program produce benefits for its clients? Were the beneficiaries those most in need of the service? How were the costs of the program distributed? The way in which a program is administered will account for some of the variation in the answers to these questions. However, the most important determinant of the questions of who benefits and who pays is the substance of the policies upon which the program is based. This, in turn, raises what is for many the most crucial ethical issue for administrators, namely, their responsibility to play an active role in promoting the policies they believe are correct and opposing those they think are harmful. This role, as has been shown throughout this book, leads them into political arenas and necessitates the development of political skills. The ethics of organizational politics, then, is ultimately the ethics of people trying to promote their beliefs about the social good in an imperfect world.

NOTES

1. Daniel Katz and Basil S. Georgopoulos, "Organizations in a Changing World," *Journal of Applied Behavioral Science*, 7, no. 3 (May-June 1971), 347.
2. Michael Walzer, "Political Action: The Problem of Dirty Hands," *Philosophy & Public Affairs*, 2, no. 2 (Winter 1973), 168.
3. John A. Rohr, *Ethics for Bureaucrats* (New York: Marcel Dekker, 1978), p. 9 (emphases in original).
4. National Association of Social Workers, *Code of Ethics of the National Association of Social Workers* (Silver Spring, Md.: National Association of Social Workers, 1980), pp. 4–8.

5. Charles Levy, "The Ethics of Management," *Administration in Social Work*, 3, no. 3 (Fall 1979), 287.

6. These arguments are presented, respectively, in Bernard Beck, "Welfare as a Moral Category," *Social Problems*, 14, no. 3 (Winter 1967), 258–77; Robert Morris and Delwin Anderson, "Personal Care Services: An Identity for Social Work," *Social Service Review*, 49, no. 2 (June 1975), 157–74; Neil Gilbert, *Capitalism and the Welfare State* (New Haven: Yale University Press, 1983); Jerome Carl Wakefield, "Psychotherapy, Distributive Justice, and Social Work — Part 1: Distributive Justice as a Conceptual Framework for Social Work," *Social Service Review*, 62, no. 2 (June 1988), 187–210.

7. George Brager, Harry Specht, and James L. Torczyner, *Community Organizing*, 2nd ed. (New York: Columbia University Press, 1987), pp. 316–39; Burton Gummer, "Are Administrators Social Workers? The Politics of Intraprofessional Rivalry," *Administration in Social Work*, 11, no. 2 (Summer 1987), 19–31.

8. Gerald F. Cavanagh, Dennis J. Moberg, and Manuel Velasquez, "The Ethics of Organizational Politics," *Academy of Management Review*, 6, no. 3 (July 1981), 366.

9. Jacques Maritain, *Man and the State* (Chicago: University of Chicago Press, 1951), pp. 61–62.

10. Wayne A. Chess, Julia M. Norlin, and Srinika D. Jayaratne, "Social Work Administration 1981–1985: Alive, Happy and Prospering," *Administration in Social Work*, 11, no. 2 (Summer 1987), 67–77.

11. Elizabeth Howe, "Public Professions and the Private Model of Professionalism," *Social Work*, 25, no. 3 (May 1980), 179–91.

12. David M. Austin, "The Political Economy of Social Benefit Organizations: Redistributive Services and Merit Goods," in *Organization and the Human Services*, ed. Herman D. Stein (Philadelphia: Temple University Press, 1981), pp. 39–40.

13. York Wilbern, "Types and Levels of Public Morality," *Public Administration Review*, 44, no. 2 (March-April), 102–08.

14. Douglas F. Morgan, "Varieties of Administrative Abuse: Some Reflections on Ethics and Discretion," *Administration & Society*, 19, no. 3 (November 1987), 268–69.

15. Sissela Bok, *Lying* (New York: Pantheon Books, 1978).

16. Brager, Specht, and Torczyner, *Community Organizing*, p. 317.

17. Thomas Peters and Robert H. Waterman, Jr., *In Search of Excellence* (New York: Harper and Row, 1982).

18. Cited in Bruce H. Drake and Eileen Drake, "Ethical and Legal Aspects of Managing Corporate Cultures," *California Management Review*, 30, no. 2 (Winter 1988), 115–16.

19. Ibid.

20. Ibid.

21. Cynthia J. McSwain and Orion F. Wright, Jr., "The Case for Lying, Cheating, and Stealing — Personal Development as Ethical Guidance for Managers," *Administration & Society*, 18, no. 4 (February 1987), 423.

22. Eric M. Eisenberg and Marsha G. Witten, "Reconsidering Openness in Organizational Communication," *Academy of Management Review*, 12, no. 3 (July 1987), 422.

23. Charles A. Reich, "The New Property," *Yale Law Journal*, 73 (April 1964), 732–87.

24. Raziel Abelson and Kai Nielsen, "History of Ethics," *The Encyclopedia of Philosophy*, vol. 3 (New York: Macmillan and The Free Press, 1967), pp. 81–117.

25. Lawrence Kohlberg, *Stages in the Development of Moral Thought and Action* (New York: Holt, Rinehart and Winston, 1969).

26. Bernard Bosanquet, *Some Suggestions in Ethics* (London: Macmillan, 1918), p. 154.

27. Rohr, *Ethics for Bureaucrats*, pp. 52–55.

28. Cavanagh, Moberg, and Velasquez, "The Ethics of Organizational Politics."

29. Ibid., 370.

30. Brager, Specht, and Torczyner, *Community Organizing*, pp. 327–30.

31. Ibid., p. 322 (emphasis in original).
32. Max Weber, "Politics as a Vocation," in *From Max Weber*, ed. and trans. H. H. Gerth and C. Wright Mills (New York: Oxford University Press, 1958), pp. 126–27.
33. Rohr, *Ethics for Bureaucrats*, p. 40.
34. Jerry L. Mashaw, "Conflict and Compromise among Models of Administrative Justice," *Duke Law Journal*, 1981, no. 2 (April), 181–213.
35. Ibid., 188.
36. Wilbern, "Types and Levels of Public Morality," 105.
37. Terry L. Cooper, "Hierarchy, Values, and the Practice of Public Administration: A Perspective for Normative Ethics," *Public Administration Review*, 47, no. 4 (July-August 1987), 322-23.
38. Ibid., 323 (emphasis in original).
39. Levy, "The Ethics of Management," 281.

Bibliography

Abelson, Raziel, and Kai Nielsen. "History of Ethics," *The Encyclopedia of Philosophy*, vol. 3. New York: Macmillan and The Free Press, 1967.

Aberbach, Joel D., Robert D. Putnam, and Bert A. Rockman. *Bureaucrats and Politicians in Western Democracies*. Cambridge, Mass.: Harvard University Press, 1981.

Adrian, C. R., and C. Press. "Decision Costs in Coalition Formation," *American Political Science Review*, 62 (June 1968), 556–63.

Alderfer, Clayton R., and Richard A. Guzzo. "Life Experiences and Adults' Enduring Strength of Desires in Organizations," *Administrative Science Quarterly*, 24, no. 3 (September 1979), 347–61.

Arguello, David F. "Minorities in Administration: A Review of Ethnicity's Influence in Management," *Administration in Social Work*, 8, no. 3 (Fall 1984), 17–28.

Astley, W. Graham, and Paramjit S. Sachdeva. "Structural Sources of Interorganizational Power: A Theoretical Synthesis," *Academy of Management Review*, 9, no. 1 (January 1984), 104–13.

Astley, W. Graham, and Andrew H. Van de Ven. "Current Perspectives and Debates in Organization Theory," *Administrative Science Quarterly*, 28, no. 2 (June 1983), 245–73.

Austin, David M. "The Political Economy of Social Benefit Organizations: Redistributive Services and Merit Goods," in *Organization and the Human Services*, ed. Herman D. Stein. Philadelphia: Temple University Press, 1981.

Austin, Michael J. "Managing Cutbacks in the 1980s," *Social Work*, 29, no. 5 (September-October 1984), 428–34.

Bacharach, Samuel B. "Bargaining within Organizations," in *Negotiating in Organizations*, ed. Max H. Bazerman and Roy J. Lewicki. Beverly Hills: Sage Publications, 1983.

Bacharach, Samuel B., and Edward J. Lawler. *Power and Politics in Organizations*. San Francisco: Jossey-Bass, 1981.

Bachrach, Peter, and Morton S. Baratz. "Two Faces of Power," *American Political Science Review*, 56 (1962), 947–52.

Bardach, Eugene. *The Implementation Game*. Cambridge, Mass.: MIT Press, 1977.

Barfield, C. E. *Rethinking Federalism*. Washington, D.C.: American Enterprise Institute, 1981.

Barnard, Chester I. *The Functions of the Executive*. Cambridge, Mass.: Harvard University Press, 1968.

Bartos, Otomar J. "Determinants and Consequences of Toughness," in *The Structure of Conflict*, ed. Paul Swingle. New York: Academic Press, 1970.

Bass, Bernard M. "Leadership: Good, Better, Best," *Organizational Dynamics*, 13, no. 3 (Winter 1985), 26–40.

Baum, Howell S. "Autonomy, Shame, and Doubt: Power in the Bureaucratic Lives of Planners," *Administration & Society*, 15, no. 2 (August 1983), 147–84.

Beck, Bernard. "Welfare as a Moral Category," *Social Problems*, 14, no. 3 (Winter 1967), 258–77

Bellah, Robert N., et al. *Habits of the Heart*. New York: Perennial Library, Harper and Row, 1986.

Bendick, Marc. "Privatizing the Delivery of Social Welfare Service," in *Working Paper No. 6: Privatization*. Washington, D.C.: National Conference on Social Welfare, 1985.

Berg, William E. "Evolution of Leadership Style in Social Agencies: A Theoretical Analysis," *Social Casework*, 61, no. 1 (January 1980), 22–28.

Berg, William E., and Roosevelt Wright. "Program Funding as an Organizational Dilemma: Goal Displacement in Social Work Programs," *Administration in Social Work*, 4, no. 4 (Winter 1980), 29–40.

Berger, Raymond, and James J. Kelley. "Do Social Work Agencies Discriminate against Homosexual Job Applicants?" *Social Work*, 26, no. 3 (May 1981), 193–98.

Biggart, Nicole Woolsey, and Gary G. Hamilton. "The Power of Obedience," *Administrative Science Quarterly*, 29, no. 4 (December 1984), 540–49.

Bixby, A. K. "Social Welfare Expenditures, Fiscal Year 1980," *Social Security Bulletin*, 46 (1983), 9–17.

Bok, Sissela. *Lying*. New York: Pantheon Books, 1978.

Bolan, Richard S. "The Social Relations of the Planner," *Journal of the American Institute of Planners*, 37, no. 6 (November 1971), 386–96.

Boles, Janet K. "The Politics of Child Care," *Social Service Review*, 54, no. 3 (September 1980), 344–62.

Bombyk, Marcia J., and Roslyn H. Chernesky. "Conventional Cutback Leadership and the Quality of the Workplace: Is Beta Better?" *Administration in Social Work*, 9, no. 3 (Fall 1985), 47–56.

Bosanquet, Bernard. *Some Suggestions in Ethics*. London: Macmillan, 1918.

Bowman, James S. "Whistle Blowing: Literature and Resource Materials," *Public Administration Review*, 43, no. 3 (May-June 1983), 271–76.

Bozeman, Barry, and E. Allen Slusher. "Scarcity and Environmental Stress in Public Organizations: A Conjectural Essay," *Administration & Society*, 11, no. 3 (November 1979), 335–55.

Brager, George A. "Advocacy and Political Behavior," *Social Work*, 13, no. 2 (April 1968), 5–15.

Brager, George, Harry Specht, and James L. Torczyner. *Community Organizing*, 2nd ed. New York: Columbia University Press, 1987.

Brass, Daniel J. "Being in the Right Place: A Structural Analysis of Individual Influence in an Organization," *Administrative Science Quarterly*, 29, no. 4 (December 1984), 518–39.

Brilliant, Eleanor L. "Social Work Leadership: A Missing Ingredient?" *Social Work*, 31, no. 5 (September-October 1986), 325–31.

Brockner, Joel, et al. "Escalation of Commitment to an Ineffective Course of Action: The Effect of Feedback Having Negative Implications for Self-Identity," *Administrative Science Quarterly*, 31, no. 1 (March 1986), 109–26.

Brodkin, Evelyn, and Michael Lipsky. "Quality Control in AFDC as an Administrative Strategy," *Social Service Review*, 57, no. 1 (March 1983), 1–34.

Brown, Richard Harvey. "Bureaucracy as Praxis: Toward a Political Phenomenology of Formal Organizations," *Administrative Science Quarterly*, 23, no. 3 (September 1978), 365–82.

Broyard, Anatole. "On Authority," *The New York Times Book Review*, January 3, 1983, p. 27.

Bucher, Rue, and Anselm Strauss. "Professions in Process," *American Journal of Sociology*, 66, no. 3 (November 1960), 325–34.

Bunker, Douglas R., and Marion Wijnberg. "The Supervisor as Mediator of Organizational Climate in Public Social Service Organizations," *Administration in Social Work*, 9, no. 2 (Summer 1985), 59–72.

Burns, Tom. "Micro-Politics: Mechanisms of Institutional Change," *Administrative Science Quarterly*, 6, no. 3 (September 1961), 257–81.

Bush, James A. "The Minority Administrator: Implications for Social Work Education," *Journal of Education for Social Work*, 13, no. 1 (Winter 1977), 15–22.

Caplow, Theodore, *Principles of Organization*. New York: Harcourt, Brace and World, 1964.

Cavanagh, Gerald F., Dennis J. Moberg, and Manuel Velasquez. "The Ethics of Organizational Politics," *Academy of Management Review*, 6, no. 3 (July 1981), 363–74.

Chambers, Donald E. "Policy Weaknesses and Political Opportunities," *Social Service Review*, 59, no. 1 (March 1985), 1–17.

Chase, Gordon, and Elizabeth C. Reveal. *How to Manage in the Public Sector*. Reading, Mass.: Addison-Wesley, 1983.

Chess, Wayne A., Julia M. Norlin, and Srinika D. Jayaratne. "Social Work Administration 1981–1985: Alive, Happy and Prospering," *Administration in Social Work*, 11, no. 2 (Summer 1987), 67–77.

Cloward, Richard A., and Frances Fox Piven. "The Professional Bureaucracies: Benefit Systems as Influence Systems," in *Readings in Community Organization Practice*, ed. Ralph M. Kramer and Harry Specht. Englewood Cliffs, N.J.: Prentice Hall, 1969.

Cohen, Michael D., and James G. March. *Leadership and Ambiguity*, 2nd ed. Boston: Harvard Business School Press, 1986.

Cohen, Yinon, and Jeffrey Pfeffer. "Organizational Hiring Standards," *Administrative Science Quarterly*, 31, no. 1 (March 1986), 1–24.

Cooper, M. R., et al. "Changing Employee Values: Deepening Discontent?" *Harvard Business Review*, 57, no. 1 (January-February 1979), 117–25.

Cooper, Terry L. "Hierarchy, Values, and the Practice of Public Administration: A Perspective for Normative Ethics," *Public Administration Review*, 47, no. 4 (July-August 1987), 320–28.

Coser, Lewis A. *The Functions of Social Conflict*. New York: The Free Press, 1956.

Cournoyer, Barry R. "Assertiveness among MSW Students," *Journal of Education for Social Work*, 19, no. 1 (Winter 1983), 24–30.

Crocker, Jennifer. "Introduction—After Affirmative Action: Barriers to Occupational Advancement for Women and Minorities," *American Behavioral Scientist*, 27, no. 3 (January-February 1984), 285–86.

Crocker, Jennifer, and Kathleen M. McGraw. "What's Good for the Goose is Not Good for the Gander: Solo Status as an Obstacle to Occupational Achievement for Males and Females," *American Behavioral Scientist*, 27, no. 3 (January-February 1984), 357–69.

Crosby, Faye, "The Denial of Personal Discrimination," *American Behavioral Scientist*, 27, no. 3 (January-February 1984), 371–86.

Crossman, R. H. S. *The Charm of Politics*. New York: Harper and Brothers, 1958.

Crow, Richard T., and Charles A. Odewahn. *Management for the Human Services*. Englewood Cliffs, N.J.: Prentice Hall, 1987.

Crozier, Michael. *The Bureaucratic Phenomenon*. Chicago: University of Chicago Press, 1964.

Cyert, Richard M., and James G. March. *The Behavioral Theory of the Firm*. Englewood Cliffs, N.J.: Prentice Hall, 1963.

Dachler, H. Peter, and Bernhard Wilpert. "Conceptual Dimensions and Boundaries of Participation in Organizations: A Critical Evaluation," *Administrative Science Quarterly*, 23, no. 1 (March 1978), 1–39.

Davis, Kenneth. *Discretionary Justice*. Baton Rouge: Louisiana University Press, 1969.

Davis, Liane V., and Jan L. Hagen. "Services for Battered Women: The Public Policy Response," *Social Service Review*, 62, no. 4 (December 1988), 649–67.

Demone, Jr., Harold W., and Margaret Gibelman. "Reaganomics: Its Impact on the Voluntary Not-for-Profit Sector," *Social Work*, 29, no. 5 (September-October 1984), 421–27.

Denhardt, Robert B. "Toward a Critical Theory of Public Organization," *Public Administration Review*, 41, no. 6 (November-December 1981), 628–35.

Derthick, Martha. *The Influence of Federal Grants*. Cambridge, Mass.: Harvard University Press, 1970.

———. *Policymaking for Social Security*. Washington, D.C.: The Brookings Institution, 1979.

Deutsch, Morton. "Conflicts: Productive and Destructive," *Journal of Social Issues*, 25, no. 1 (January 1969), 7–41.

Donnison, David D. "Observations on University Training for Social Workers in Great Britain and North America," *Social Service Review*, 29, no. 4 (December 1955), 341–50.

Drake, Bruce H., and Eileen Drake. "Ethical and Legal Aspects of Managing Corporate Cultures," *California Management Review*, 30, no. 2 (Winter 1988), 107–33.

Drucker, Peter. "On Managing the Public Service Institution," *The Public Interest*, no. 33 (Fall 1973), 43–60.

Durkheim, Emile. *Suicide*, trans. John A. Spaulding and George Simpson, ed. George Simpson. New York: The Free Press, 1966.

Easton, David. *A Systems Analysis of Political Life*. New York: John Wiley and Sons, 1965.

Eisenberg, Eric M., and Marsha G. Witten. "Reconsidering Openness in Organizational Communication," *Academy of Management Review*, 12, no. 3 (July 1987), 418–26.

Elmore, Richard F. "Organizational Models of Social Program Implementation," *Public Policy*, 26, no. 2 (Spring 1978), 185–228.

Emerson, Richard M. "Power-Dependence Relations," *American Sociological Review*, 27, no. 1 (February 1962), 31–40.

Emery, F. E., and E. L. Trist. "Socio-technical Systems," in *Management Science, Models and Techniques*, vol. 2, ed. C. W. Churchman and M. Verhulst. London: Pergamon, 1960.

Ewing, David W. *Freedom Inside the Organization*. New York: E. P. Dutton, 1977.

Ezell, Hazel, Charles A. Odewahn, and J. Daniel Sherman. "Women Entering Management: Differences in Perceptions of Factors Influencing Integration," *Group & Organizational Studies*, 7, no. 2 (June 1982), 243–53.

Fabricant, Michael. "The Industrialization of Social Work Practice," *Social Work*, 30, no. 5 (September-October 1985), 389–95.

Fanshel, David. "Status Differentials: Men and Women in Social Work," *Social Work*, 21, no. 6 (November 1976), 448–54.

Feld, Allen, and Ronald Marks. "Self-Perceptions of Power: Do Social Work and Business Students Differ?" *Social Work*, 32, no. 3 (May-June 1987), 225–30.

Fisher, Roger, and Willis Ury. *Getting to Yes*. Boston: Houghton Mifflin, 1981.

Forester, John. "Listening: The Social Policy of Everyday Life (Critical Theory and Hermeneutics in Practice)," *Social Praxis*, 7, no. 3/4 (1980), 219–32.

French, Jr., John R. P., and Bertram Raven. "The Bases of Social Power," in *Group Dynamics*, 3rd ed., ed. Dorwin Cartwright and Alvin Zander. New York: Harper and Row, 1968.

Friedson, Eliot. "Dominant Professions, Bureaucracy, and Client Services," in *Organizations and Clients*, ed. William R. Rosengren and Mark Lefton. Columbus, Ohio: Charles E. Merrill, 1970.

Galbraith, Jay R. "Designing the Innovating Organization," *Organizational Dynamics*, 10, no. 3 (Winter 1982), 5–25.

Gardner, Howard. *Frames of Mind*. New York: Basic Books, 1983.

Gardner, William L., and Mark J. Martinko. "Impression Management: An Observational Study Linking Audience Characteristics with Verbal Self-Presentations," *Academy of Management Journal*, 31, no. 1 (March 1988), 42–65.

Georgiou, Petro. "The Goal Paradigm and Notes toward a Counter Paradigm," *Administrative Science Quarterly*, 18, no. 3 (September 1973), 291–310.

Gettleman, Marvin E. "Charity and Social Classes in the United States: 1874–1900," *American Journal of Economics and Sociology*, 22 (April, July 1963), 313–29, 417–26.

Gilbert, Neil. *Capitalism and the Welfare State*. New Haven: Yale University Press, 1983.

Gilbert, Neil, Armin Rosenkranz, and Harry Specht. "Dialectics of Social Planning," *Social Work*, 18, no. 2 (March 1973), 78–86.

Gilbert, Neil, and Harry Specht. *Dimensions of Social Welfare Policy*, 2nd ed. Englewood Cliffs, N.J.: Prentice Hall, 1986.

Gilligan, Carol. *In a Different Voice*. Cambridge, Mass.: Harvard University Press, 1982.

Glisson, Charles A., and Patricia Yancey Martin. "Productivity and Efficiency in Human Service Organizations as Related to Structure, Size, and Age," *Academy of Management Journal*, 23, no. 1 (March 1980), 21–37.

Goleman, Daniel. "Influencing Others: Skills Are Identified," *New York Times*, February 19, 1986, p. C1.

———. "Psychiatry: First Guide to Therapy Is Fiercely Opposed," *The New York Times*, September 23, 1986, p. C1.

Goodstein, Leonard D. "Getting Your Way: A Training Activity in Understanding Power and Influence," *Group & Organization Studies*, 6, no. 3 (September 1981), 283–90.

Gouldner, Alvin W. "Cosmopolitans and Locals: Toward an Analysis of Latent Social Roles—I," *Administrative Science Quarterly*, 2, no. 3 (December 1957), 281–306.

———. "Organizational Analysis," in *Sociology Today*, ed. Robert K. Merton, Leonard Bloom, and Leonard S. Cottrell. New York: Basic Books, 1959.

Greenhalgh, Leonard, Scott A. Nesline, and Roderick W. Gilkey. "The Effects of Negotiator Preferences, Situational Power, and Negotiator Personality on Outcomes of Business Negotiations," *Academy of Management Journal*, 28, no. 1 (March 1985), 9–33.

Gronn, Peter C. "Talk as the Work: The Accomplishment of School Administration," *Administrative Science Quarterly*, 28, no. 1 (March 1983), 1–21.

Gruber, Murray L. "A Three-Factor Model of Administrative Effectiveness," *Administration in Social Work*, 10, no. 3 (Fall 1986), 1–14.

Gummer, Burton. "Are Administrators Social Workers? The Politics of Intraprofessional Rivalry," *Administration in Social Work*, 11, no. 2 (Summer 1987), 19–31.

———. "Competing Perspectives on the Concept of 'Effectiveness' in the Analysis of Social Services," *Administration in Social Work*, 11, nos. 3, 4 (Fall and Winter 1987), 257–70.

———. "On Helping and Helplessness: The Structure of Discretion in the American Welfare System," *Social Service Review*, 53, no. 2 (June 1979), 214–28.

———. "Is the Social Worker in Public Welfare an Endangered Species?" *Public Welfare*, 37, no. 4 (Fall 1979), 12–21.

Gummer, Burton, and Richard L. Edwards. "The Enfeebled Middle: Emerging Issues in Education for Social Administration," *Administration in Social Work*, 12, no. 3 (1988), 13–23.

Hackman, Judith Dozier. "Power and Centrality in the Allocation of Resources in Colleges and Universities," *Administrative Science Quarterly*, 30, no. 1 (March 1985), 61–77.

Hall, Richard H. *Organizations*, 3rd ed. Englewood Cliffs, N.J.: Prentice Hall, 1982.

Hambrick, Donald C., and Phyllis A. Mason. "Upper Echelons: The Organization as a Reflection of Its Top Managers," *Academy of Management Review*, 9, no. 2 (April 1984), 193–206.

Handler, Joel F. *The Coercive Social Worker*. Chicago: Markham–Rand McNally College Publishing, 1973.

Hasenfeld, Yeheskel. "Citizen Encounters with Welfare State Bureaucracies," *Social Service Review*, 59, no. 4 (December 1985), 622–35.

———. "Power in Social Work Practice," *Social Service Review*, 61, no. 3 (September 1987), 469–83.

Heclo, Hugh. "Issue Networks and the Executive Establishment," in *The New American Political System*, ed. Anthony King. Washington, D.C.: American Enterprise Institute for Public Policy Research, 1978.

Herbert, Adam. "The Minority Administrator: Problems, Prospects, and Challenges," *Public Administration Review*, 34, no.6 (November-December 1974), 556–74.

Hermone, Ronald H. "How to Negotiate and Come out the Winner," *Management Review*, 63, no. 11 (November 1974), 19–25.

Hirschhorn, Larry. "The Stalemated Agency: A Theoretical Perspective and a Practical Proposal," *Administration in Social Work*, 2, no. 4 (Winter 1978), 425–38.

Hirschhorn, Larry, et al. *Cutting Back*. San Francisco: Jossey-Bass, 1983.

Holloway, Stephen, and George Brager. "Implicit Negotiations and Organizational Practice," *Administration in Social Work*, 9, no. 2 (Summer 1985), 15–24.

Hopps, June Gary, and Elaine B. Pinderhughes. "Profession of Social Work: Contemporary Characteristics," in *Encyclopedia of Social Work*, vol. 2, 18th ed., ed. Anne Minahan, et al. Silver Spring, Md.: National Association of Social Workers, 1987.

Howe, Elizabeth. "Public Professions and the Private Model of Professionalism," *Social Work*, 25, no. 3 (May 1980), 179–91.

Hutchinson, Elizabeth D. "Use of Authority in Direct Social Work Practice with Mandated Clients," *Social Service Review*, 61, no. 4 (December 1987), 581–98.

Ilich, John. *The Art and Skill of Successful Negotiations*. Englewood Cliffs, N.J.: Prentice Hall, 1973.

Jacobs, Mark D. "The End of Liberalism in the Administration of Social Casework," *Administration & Society*, 18, no. 1 (May 1986), 7–27.

Jansson, Bruce S., and June Simmons. "Building Departmental or Unit Power within Human Service Organizations: Empirical Findings and Theory Building," *Administration in Social Work*, 8, no. 3 (Fall 1984), 41–56.

———. "The Survival of Social Work Units in Host Organizations," *Social Work*, 31, no. 5 (September-October 1986), 339–43.

Jaques, Elliott. *A General Theory of Bureaucracy*. New York: Halsted Press, 1976.

Jones, Jr., Edward W. "Black Managers: The Dream Deferred," *Harvard Business Review*, 64, no. 3 (May-June 1986), 84–93.

Kanter, Rosabeth Moss. *Men and Women of the Corporation*. New York: Basic Books, 1977.

———. "Power Failure in Management Circuits," *Harvard Business Review*, 57, no. 4 (July-August 1979), 65–75.

———. "Some Effects of Proportions on Group Life: Skewed Sex Ratios and Responses to Token Women," *American Journal of Sociology*, 82, no. 5 (March 1977), 965–90.

Kaplan, Robert K. "Trade Routes: The Manager's Network of Relationships," *Organizational Dynamics*, 12, no. 4 (Spring 1984), 37–52.

Katz, Daniel, and Basil S. Georgopoulos. "Organizations in a Changing World," *Journal of Applied Behavioral Science*, 7, no. 3 (May-June 1971), 342–70.

Katz, Daniel, and Robert L. Kahn. *The Social Psychology of Organizations*. New York: John Wiley and Sons, 1966.

Keith-Lucas, Alan. "Political Theory Implicit in Social Case-Work Theory," *American Political Science Quarterly Review*, 47, no. 4 (December 1953), 1076–91.

Kelly, Charles M. "The Interrelationship of Ethics and Power in Today's Organizations," *Organizational Dynamics*, 16, no. 1 (Summer 1987), 5–18.

Kelman, Steven. "The Grace Commission: How Much Waste in Government," *The Public Interest*, no. 78 (Winter 1985), 62–82.

Kerson, Toba Schwaber, and Leslie B. Alexander. "Strategies for Success: Women in Social Service Administration," *Administration in Social Work*, 3, no. 3 (Fall 1979), 313–26.

Kipnis, David. *The Powerholders*. Chicago: University of Chicago Press, 1976.

Kipnis, David, Stuart M. Schmidt, and Ian Wilkinson. "Intraorganizational Influence Tactics: Explorations in Getting One's Way," *Journal of Applied Psychology*, 65, no. 4 (August 1980), 440–52.

Knapman, Shirley Kuehnle. "Sex Discrimination in Family Agencies," *Social Work*, 22, no. 6 (November 1977), 461–65.

Kochan, Thomas A., and Anil Verma. "Negotiations in Organizations: Blending Industrial Relations and Organizational Behavior Approaches," in *Negotiations in Organizations*, ed. Max H. Bazerman and Roy J. Lewicki. Beverly Hills: Sage Publications, 1983.

Kohlberg, Lawrence. *Stages in the Development of Moral Thought and Action*. New York: Holt, Rinehart and Winston, 1969.

Kotter, John P. *The General Managers*. New York: The Free Press, 1982.

———. *Power in Management*. New York: AMACOM, Division of American Management Association, 1979.

Kram, Kathy E., and Lynn A. Isabella. "Mentoring Alternatives: The Role of Peer Relationships in Career Development," *Academy of Management Journal*, 28, no. 1 (March 1985), 110–32.

Kravetz, Diane, and Carol B. Austin. "Women's Issues in Social Administration: The Views and Experiences of Women Administrators," *Administration in Social Work*, 8, no. 4 (Winter 1984), 25–38.

Krupp, Sherman. *Pattern in Organizational Analysis*. New York: Holt, Rinehart and Winston, 1961.

Ladd, Everett C. "The Reagan Phenomenon and Public Attitudes toward Government," in *The Reagan Presidency and the Governing of America*, ed. Lester M. Salamon and Michael S. Lund. Washington, D.C.: The Urban Institute, 1984.

Lane, Larry M. "Karl Weick's Organizing: The Problem of Purpose and the Search for Excellence," *Administration & Society*, 18, no. 1 (May 1986), 111–35.

Lasswell, Harold. *Power and Personality*. New York: Viking, 1962.

Levine, Charles H. "More on Cutback Management: Hard Questions for Hard Times," *Public Administration Review*, 39, no. 2 (March-April 1979), 179–83.

———. "Organizational Decline and Cutback Management," *Public Administration Review*, 38, no. 4 (July-August 1978), 316–25.

Levine, Charles H., Irene S. Rubin, and George G. Wolohojian. *The Politics of Retrenchment*. Beverly Hills: Sage Publications, 1981.

Levy, Charles. "The Ethics of Management," *Administration in Social Work*, 3, no. 3 (Fall 1979), 277–88.

Lincoln, James R., Mitsuyo Hamada, and Jon Olson. "Cultural Orientations and Individual Reactions to Organizations: A Study of Employees of Japanese-Owned Firms," *Administrative Science Quarterly*, 26, no. 1 (March 1981), 93–115.

Lindblom, Charles E. "The Sociology of Planning: Thought and Social Interaction," in *Economic Planning, East and West*, ed. Morris Bornstein. Cambridge, Mass.: Bollinger Publishing, 1975).

Lipsky, Michael. "Protest as a Political Resource," *American Political Science Review*, 62, no. 4 (December 1968), 1144–58.

———. "Standing the Study of Policy Implementation on Its Head," in *American Politics and Public Policy*, ed. Walter Dean Burnham and Martha Wagner Weinberg. Cambridge, Mass.: MIT Press, 1978.

———. *Street-Level Bureaucracy*. New York: Russell Sage Foundation, 1980.

Lorenz, Patsy Hashey. "The Politics of Fund Raising through Grantsmanship in the Human Services," *Public Administration Review*, 42, no. 3 (May-June 1982), 244–51.

Lowery, David, and Caryl E. Rusbult. "Bureaucratic Responses to Antibureaucratic Administrations: Federal Employee Reaction to the Reagan Election," *Administration & Society*, 18, no. 1 (May 1986), 45–75.

Lowi, Theodore J. *The End of Liberalism*. New York: W. W. Norton, 1969.

Maritain, Jacques. *Man and the State*. Chicago: University of Chicago Press, 1951.

Martin, Patricia Yancey. "A Critical Analysis of Power in Professional-Client Relations," *Aretê*, 6, no. 3 (Spring 1981), 35–48.

———. "Group Sex Composition in Work Organizations: A Structural-Normative Model," *Research in the Sociology of Organizations*, vol. 4. Greenwich, Conn.: JAI Press, 1985.

———. "Multiple Constituencies, Dominant Societal Values, and the Human Service Administrator: Implications for Service Delivery," *Administration in Social Work*, 4, no. 2 (Summer 1980), 15–27.

Mashaw, Jerry L. "Conflict and Compromise among Models of Administrative Justice," *Duke Law Journal*, 1981, no. 2 (April), 181–213.

Maslow, Abraham H. "A Theory of Human Motivation," *Psychological Review*, 50, no. 4 (July 1943), 370–96.

Mastenbroek, Willem F. G. "Negotiating: A Conceptual Model," *Group & Organization Studies*, 5, no. 3 (September 1980), 324–39.

McClelland, David C. *Power*. New York: Irvington, 1975.

McClelland, David C., Stephen Rhinesmith, and Richard Kristensen. "The Effects of Power Training on Community Action Agencies," *Journal of Applied Behavioral Science*, 11, no. 1 (January-February-March 1975), 92–115.

McSwain, Cynthia J., and Orion F. Wright, Jr. "The Case for Lying, Cheating, and Stealing—Personal Development as Ethical Guidance for Managers," *Administration & Society*, 18, no. 4 (February 1987), 411–32.

Meindl, James R., Sanford B. Ehrlich, and Janet M. Dukerich. "The Romance of Leadership," *Administrative Science Quarterly*, 30, no. 1 (March 1985), 78–102.

Melman, Seymour. *Profits without Production*. New York: Knopf, 1984.

"Membership Survey Shows Practice Shifts," *NASW News*, 28, no. 10 (November 1983), 6–7.

Meyer, Carol H. "What Directions for Direct Practice?" *Social Work*, 24, no. 4 (July 1979), 267–72.

Meyer, John W., W. Richard Scott, and Terrence E. Deal. "Institutional and Technical Sources of Organizational Structure: Explaining the Structure of Educational Organizations," in *Organization and the Human Services*, ed. Herman D. Stein. Philadelphia: Temple University Press, 1981.

Mintzberg, Henry. *The Nature of Managerial Work*. New York: Harper and Row, 1973.

———. *Power in and around Organizations*. Englewood Cliffs, N.J.: Prentice Hall, 1983.

———. "Power and Organization Life Cycle," *Academy of Management Review*, 9, no. 2 (April 1984), 207–24.

Mitchell, Terrence R., and William G. Scott. "Leadership Failures, the Distrusting Public, and Prospects of the Administrative State," *Public Administration Review*, 47, no. 6 (November-December 1987), 445–52.

Mitroff, Ian I. *Stakeholders of the Organizational Mind*. San Francisco: Jossey-Bass, 1983.

Moore, Mark H. "Anatomy of the Heroin Problem: An Exercise in Problem Definition," *Policy Analysis*, 2, no. 4 (Fall 1976), 639–62.

Moore, Scott T. "The Theory of Street-Level Bureaucracy: A Positive Critique," *Administration & Society*, 19, no. 1 (May 1987), 74–94.

Morgan, Douglas F. "Varieties of Administrative Abuse: Some Reflections on Ethics and Discretion," *Administration & Society*, 19, no. 3 (November 1987), 267–84.

Morley, Donald Dean, and Pamela Shockley-Zalabak. "Conflict Avoiders and Compromisers: Toward an Understanding of Their Organizational Communication Style," *Group & Organization Studies*, 11, no. 4 (December 1986), 387–401.

Morris, Robert, and Delwin Anderson. "Personal Care Services: An Identity for Social Work," *Social Service Review*, 49, no. 2 (June 1975), 157–74.

Murphy, Jerome T. "The Educational Bureaucratics Implement Novel Policy: The Politics of Title I of ESEA, 1965–72," in *Policy and Politics in America*, ed. Allan P. Sindler. Boston: Little, Brown, 1973.

Nakamura, Robert T., and Frank Smallwood. *The Politics of Policy Implementation*. New York: St. Martin's Press, 1980.

National Association of Social Workers. *Code of Ethics of the National Association of Social Workers*. Silver Spring, Md.: National Association of Social Workers, 1980.

Neale, Margaret A., and Max H. Bazerman. "The Effects of Framing and Negotiator Overconfidence on Bargaining Behaviors and Outcomes," *Academy of Management Journal*, 28, no. 1 (March 1985), 34–39.

Neustadt, Richard E. *Presidential Power*. New York: John Wiley and Sons, 1960.

Nielsen, Richard P. "Arendt's Action Philosophy and the Manager as Eichmann, Richard III, Faust, or Institution Citizen," *California Management Review*, 26, no. 3 (Spring 1984), 191–201.

O'Day, Rory. "Intimidation Rituals: Reactions to Reform," *Journal of Applied Behavioral Science*, 10, no. 3 (July-August-September 1974), 373–386.

Office of Personnel Management. *EEO Statistical Report on Employment in State and Local Government*. Washington, D.C.: Office of Personnel Management, 1977.

Olsen, Johan P. "Choice in Organized Anarchy," in *Ambiguity and Choice in Organizations*, ed. James G. March and Johan P. Olsen. Oslo: Universitetsforlaget, 1976.

Ouchi, William G., and Jerry B. Johnson. "Types of Organizational Control and Their Relationship to Emotional Well Being," *Administrative Science Quarterly*, 23, no. 2 (June 1978), 293–317.

Parsons, Talcott. *Structure and Process in Modern Societies*. Glencoe, Il.: The Free Press, 1960.

Patti, Rino J. "Patterns of Management Activity in Social Welfare Agencies," *Administration in Social Work*, 1, no. 1 (Spring 1977), 5–18.

———. "Who Leads the Human Services? The Prospects for Social Work Leadership in an Age of Political Conservatism," *Administration in Social Work*, 8, no. 1 (Spring 1984), 17–29.

Patti, Rino, et al. "From Direct Service to Administration: A Study of Social Workers' Transitions from Clinical to Management Roles—Part I: Analysis," *Administration in Social Work*, 3, no. 2 (Summer 1979), 131–151.

Pawlak, Edward S., Charles Jester, and Richard L. Fink. "The Politics of Cutback Management," *Administration in Social Work*, 7, no. 2 (Summer 1983), 1–10.

Pecora, Peter J., and Michael J. Austin. "Declassification of Social Service Jobs: Issues and Strategies," *Social Work*, 28, no. 6 (November-December 1983), 421–26.

Perlmutter, Felice Davidson, and Leslie B. Alexander. "Exposing the Coercive Consensus: Racism and Sexism in Social Work," in *The Management of Human Services*, ed. Rosemary C. Sarri and Yeheskel Hasenfeld. New York: Columbia University Press, 1978.

Perrow, Charles. "The Analysis of Goals in Complex Organizations," *American Sociological Review*, 26, no. 6 (December 1961), 854–66.

———. "Demystifying Organizations," in *The Management of Human Services*, ed. Rosemary C. Sarri and Yeheskel Hasenfeld. New York: Columbia University Press, 1978.

Perry, Lee T., and Jay B. Barney. "Performance Lies Are Hazardous to Organizational Health," *Organizational Dynamics*, 9, no. 3 (Winter 1981), 68–80.

Peters, Thomas, and Robert H. Waterman, Jr. *In Search of Excellence*. New York: Harper and Row, 1982.

Pfaff, William. "Aristocracies," *The New Yorker*, January 14, 1980, pp. 70–78.

Pfeffer, Jeffrey. "The Micropolitics of Organizations," in Marshall W. Meyers, et al., *Environments and Organizations*. San Francisco: Jossey-Bass, 1978.

Pfeffer, Jeffrey, and Alison Davis-Blake. "The Effect of the Proportion of Women on Salaries: The Case of College Administrators," *Administrative Science Quarterly*, 32, no. 1 (March 1987), 1–24.

Pfeffer, Jeffrey, and Gerald R. Salancik. "Organizational Decision Making as a Political Process: The Case of a University Budget," *Administrative Science Quarterly*, 19, no. 2 (June 1974), 135–51.

Polsby, Nelson W. *Community Power and Political Theory*. New Haven: Yale University Press, 1963.

Popple, Philip R. "Negotiation: A Critical Skill for Social Work Administrators," *Administration in Social Work*, 8, no. 2 (Summer 1984), 1–11.

———. "The Social Work Profession: A Reconceptualization," *Social Service Review*, 59, no. 4 (December 1985), 560–77.

Potuchek, Jean L. "The Context of Social Service Funding: The Funding Relationship," *Social Service Review*, 60, no. 3 (September 1986), 421–36.

Pressman, Jeffrey, and Aaron Wildavsky. *Implementation*. Berkeley: University of California Press, 1977.

Price, Don K. "Purists and Politicians," *Science*, 163, no. 3862 (January 3, 1969), 25–31.

———. *The Scientific Estate*. Cambridge, Mass.: The Belknap Press of Harvard University Press, 1965.

Pruger, Robert. "The Good Bureaucrat," *Social Work*, 18, no. 4 (July 1973), 26–32.

Pruitt, Dean G. "Achieving Integrative Agreements," in *Negotiating in Organizations*, ed. Max H. Bazerman and Roy J. Lewicki. Beverly Hills: Sage Publications, 1983.
————. "Kissinger as a Traditional Mediator with Power," in *Dynamics of Third Party Intervention*, ed. Jeffrey Z. Rubin. New York: Praeger, 1981.
————. *Negotiation Behavior*. New York: Academic Press, 1981.
Pulakos, Elaine D., and Kenneth N. Wexley. "The Relationship among Perceptual Similarity, Sex, and Performance Ratings in Manager-Subordinate Dyads," *Academy of Management Journal*, 26, no. 1 (March 1983), 129–39.
Rabinovitz, Francine, Jeffrey Pressman, and Martin Rein. "Guidelines: A Plethora of Forms, Authors, and Functions," *Policy Sciences*, 7, no. 4 (December 1976), 399–416.
Raelin, Joseph A. "An Examination of Deviant/Adaptive Behaviors in the Organizational Careers of Professionals," *Academy of Management Review*, 9, no. 3 (July 1984), 413–27.
Randall, Ronald. "Presidential Power and Bureaucratic Intransigence: The Influence of the Nixon Administration on Welfare Policy," *American Political Science Review*, 73, no. 3 (September 1979), 795–810.
Rapoport, Anatol. "Conflict Resolution in Light of Game Theory and Beyond," in *The Structure of Conflict*, ed. Paul Swingle. New York: Academic Press, 1970.
Reich, Robert B. *The Next American Frontier*. New York: Penguin Books, 1983.
Rein, Martin. "The Social Service Crisis: The Dilemma—Success for the Agency or Service to the Needy?" *Trans-action*, 1 (May 1964), 3–8.
Rein, Martin, and Francine F. Rabinovitz. "Implementation: A Theoretical Perspective," in *American Politics and Public Policy*, ed. Walter Dean Burnham and Martha Wagner Weinberg. Cambridge, Mass.: MIT Press, 1978.
Rich, Wilbur. "Special Role and Role Expectations of Black Administrators of Neighborhood Mental Health Programs," *Community Mental Health Journal*, 11, no. 4 (Winter 1975), 394–401.
Riesman, David. *The Lonely Crowd*. New Haven: Yale University Press, 1961.
Ripple, Lillian. "Motivation, Capacity, and Opportunity as Related to the Use of Casework Service: Theoretical Base and Plan of Study," *Social Service Review*, 29, no. 2 (June 1955), 172–93.
Rohr, John A. *Ethics for Bureaucrats*. New York: Marcel Dekker, 1978.
Roos, Jr., Leslie L., and Roger I. Hall. "Influence Diagrams and Organizational Power," *Administrative Science Quarterly*, 25, no. 1 (March 1980), 57–71.
Rosenberg, Janet. "Discovering Natural Types of Role Orientation: An Application of Cluster Analysis," *Social Service Review*, 52, no. 1 (March 1978), 85–106.
Rosenbloom, David H. "Public Administrative Theory and the Separation of Powers," *Public Administration Review*, 43, no. 3 (May-June 1983), 219–27.
Rubin, Jeffrey Z., and Bert R. Brown. *The Social Psychology of Bargaining and Negotiation*. New York: Academic Press, 1975.
Ruble, Thomas L., Renae Cohen, and Diane N. Ruble. "Sex Stereotypes: Occupational Barriers for Women," *American Behavioral Scientist*, 27, no. 3 (January-February 1984), 339–56.
Salancik, Gerald R. "The Effectiveness of Ineffective Social Service Systems," in *Organization and the Human Services*, ed. Herman D. Stein. Philadelphia: Temple University Press, 1981.
Salancik, Gerald R., and Jeffrey Pfeffer. "Who Gets Power—And How They Hold on to It: A Strategic-Contingency Model of Power," *Organizational Dynamics*, 5, no. 3 (Winter 1977), 3–21.
Salancik, Gerald R., Barry M. Staw, and Louis R. Pondy. "Administrative Turnover as a Response to Unmanaged Organizational Interdependence," *Academy of Management Journal*, 23, no. 3 (September 1980), 422–37.

Sarri, Rosemary C. "Effective Social Work Intervention in Administrative and Planning Roles: Implications for Education," in Council on Social Work Education, *Facing the Challenge*. New York: Council on Social Work Education, 1973.

Sarri, Rosemary C., and Yeheskel Hasenfeld. "The Management of Human Services— A Challenging Opportunity," in *The Management of Human Services*, ed. Rosemary C. Sarri and Yeheskel Hasenfeld. New York: Columbia University Press, 1978.

Schattschneider, E. E. *The Semisovereign People*. New York: Holt, Rinehart and Winston, 1960.

Schelling, Thomas C. *The Strategy of Conflict*. Cambridge, Mass.: Harvard University Press, 1960.

Schlesinger, Jr., Arthur M. *A Thousand Days*. Greenwich, Conn.: Fawcett Publications, 1965.

Schlesinger, Leonard A., and Barry Oshry. "Quality of Work Life and the Manager: Muddle in the Middle," *Organizational Dynamics*, 13, no. 1 (Summer 1984), 4–19.

Schorr, Alvin L. "Professional Practice as Policy," *Social Service Review*, 59, no. 2 (June 1985), 178–96.

Schramm, Sanford F. "Politics, Professionalism, and the Changing Federalism," *Social Service Review*, 55, no. 1 (March 1981), 78–92.

Sennett, Richard. *Authority*. New York: Vintage Books, 1981.

Shnit, Dan. "Professional Discretion in Social Welfare Administration," *Administration in Social Work*, 2, no. 4 (Winter 1978), 439–50.

Siegel, Sidney, and Lawrence E. Fouraker. *Bargaining and Group Decision Making*. New York: McGraw-Hill, 1960.

Simon, Herbert A. "On the Concept of Organizational Goal," *Administrative Science Quarterly*, 9, no. 1 (June 1964), 1–22.

Sims, Jr., Henry P. "Further Thoughts on Punishment in Organizations," *Academy of Management Review*, 5, no. 1 (January 1980), 133–38.

Smith, Catherine Begnoche. "Influence of Internal Opportunity Structure and Sex of Worker on Turnover Patterns," *Administrative Science Quarterly*, 24, no. 3 (September 1979), 362–81.

Smith, Dorothy E. "Front-Line Organization of the State Mental Hospital," *Administrative Science Quarterly*, 10 (1965), 381–99.

Smith, Howard R. "Who's in Control Here?" *Management Review*, 69, no. 2 (February 1980), 43–49.

Specht, Harry. "Managing Professional Interpersonal Interactions," *Social Work*, 30, no. 3 (May-June 1985), 225–30.

Steers, Richard M., and Daniel M. Braunstein. "A Behaviorally-Based Measure of Manifest Needs in Work Settings," *Journal of Vocational Behavior*, 9, no. 2 (October 1976), 251–66.

Stern, Mark J. "The Emergence of the Homeless as a Public Problem," *Social Service Review*, 58, no. 2 (June 1984), 291–301.

———. "The Politics of American Social Welfare," in *Human Services at Risk*, ed. Felice D. Perlmutter. Lexington, Mass.: Lexington Books, 1984.

Stewart, Lee P., and William B. Gudykunst. "Differential Factors Influencing the Hierarchical Level and Number of Promotions of Males and Females within an Organization," *Academy of Management Journal*, 25, no. 3 (September 1982), 586–97.

Strauss, Anselm, et al. "The Hospital and Its Negotiated Order," in *The Hospital in Modern Society*, ed. Eliot Friedson. New York: The Free Press, 1963.

Sundquist, James L. "The Crisis of Competence in Government," in *Setting National Priorities*. Washington, D.C.: The Brookings Institution, 1980.

Thomas, K. W. "Conflict Handling Modes in Interdepartmental Relations," Ph.D. diss., Purdue University, 1971.

Thompson, James D., *Organizations in Action*. New York: McGraw-Hill, 1967.

Thompson, James D., and Arthur Tuden. "Strategies, Structures, and Processes of Organizational Decision," in *Comparative Studies in Administration*, ed. James D. Thompson, et al. Pittsburgh: University of Pittsburgh Press, 1959.

Titmuss, Richard M. "The Social Division of Welfare: Some Reflections on the Search for Equity," in Richard M. Titmuss, *Essays on 'The Welfare State.'* New Haven: Yale University Press, 1959.

Tullock, Gordon. *The Politics of Bureaucracy*. Washington, D.C.: Public Affairs Press, 1965.

Turem, Jerry S. "Social Work Administration and Modern Management Technology," *Administration in Social Work*, 10, no. 3 (Fall 1986), 15–24.

Turner, Francis J. "Theory in Social Work Practice," in *Social Work Treatment*, 3rd ed., ed. Francis J. Turner. New York: The Free Press, 1986.

Tversky, Amos, and Daniel Kahneman. "The Framing of Decisions and the Psychology of Choice," *Science*, 211, no. 4481 (January 30, 1981), 453–58.

Ugalde, Antonio. "A Decision Model for the Study of Public Bureaucracies," *Policy Sciences*, 4, no. 1 (March 1973), 75–84.

U.S. House of Representatives, Committee on Government Operations. *Mismanagement of the Office of Human Development Services*. Washington, D.C.: U.S. Government Printing Office, 1987.

Van Meter, Donald, and Carl Van Horn. "The Policy Implementation Process: A Conceptual Framework," *Administration & Society*, 6, no. 4 (February 1975), 445–88.

Wakefield, Jerome Carl. "Psychotherapy, Distributive Justice, and Social Work— Part 1: Distributive Justice as a Conceptual Framework for Social Work," *Social Service Review*, 62, no. 2 (June 1988), 187–210.

Walton, Richard E., and Robert B. McKersie. *A Behavioral Theory of Labor Negotiations*. New York: McGraw-Hill, 1965.

Walzer, Michael. "Political Action: The Problem of Dirty Hands," *Philosophy & Public Affairs*, 2, no. 2 (Winter 1973), 160–80.

Weatherley, Richard, et al. "Accountability of Social Service Workers at the Front Line," *Social Service Review*, 54, no. 4 (December 1980), 556–71.

Weaver, Charles N. "Sex Differences in the Determinants of Job Satisfaction," *Academy of Management Journal*, 21, no. 2 (June 1978), 265–74.

Weber, Max. "Politics as a Vocation," in *From Max Weber*, ed. and trans. H. H. Gerth and C. Wright Mills. New York: Oxford University Press, 1958.

———. *The Theory of Social and Economic Organization*, trans. A. M. Henderson and T. Parsons. New York: The Free Press, 1964.

Weick, Karl E. "Educational Organizations as Loosely Coupled Systems," *Administrative Science Quarterly*, 21, no. 1 (March 1976), 1–19.

———. *The Social Psychology of Organizing*, 2nd ed. Reading, Mass.: Addison-Wesley, 1979.

Weil, Marie. "Preparing Women for Administration: A Self-Directed Learning Model," *Administration in Social Work*, 7, no. 3/4 (Fall-Winter 1983), 117–32.

Whetten, David A. "Coping with Incompatible Expectations: Role Conflict among Directors of Manpower Agencies," *Administration in Social Work*, 1, no. 4 (Winter 1977), 379–93.

Wilbern, York. "Types and Levels of Public Morality," *Public Administration Review*, 44, no. 2 (March-April 1984), 102–08.

Wildavsky, Aaron. "Budgeting as a Political Process," in *The International Encyclopedia of the Social Sciences*, vol. II, ed. David L. Sills. New York: Crowell, Collier and Macmillan, 1968.

————. *The Politics of the Budgetary Process*, 3rd ed. Boston: Little, Brown, 1979.

Wilson, Woodrow. "The Study of Administration," *Political Science Quarterly*, 2 (June 1887), 197–222.

Wright, Paul H. "A Model and a Technique for Studies of Friendship," *Journal of Experimental Social Psychology*, 5, no. 3 (1969), 295–309.

Yankey, John A., and Claudia J. Coulton. "Promoting Contributions to Organizational Goals: Alternative Models," *Administration in Social Work*, 3, no. 1 (Spring 1979), 45–55.

Yates, Jr., Douglas. *The Politics of Management*. San Francisco: Jossey-Bass, 1985.

Zald, Mayer N. *Organizational Change*. Chicago: The University of Chicago Press, 1970.

————. "Who Shall Rule? A Political Analysis of Succession in a Large Welfare Organization," *Pacific Sociological Review*, 8, no. 1 (Spring 1965), 52–60.

Zaleznik, Abraham. "Power and Politics in Organizational Life," *Harvard Business Review*, 48, no. 3 (May-June 1970), 47–60.

Zeitz, Gerald. "Hierarchical Authority and Decision-Making in Professional Organizations: An Empirical Analysis," *Administration & Society*, 12, no. 3 (November 1980), 277–300.

Index

217

Conflict
  managers and line workers, 75–78
  negotiators and constituents, 178–80
  over organizational goals, 10–11, 19–20,
    115–16, 154–56, 162–63
  professionals and bureaucrats, 101–03
  realistic and nonrealistic, 154–56, 181
  over social policies, 34–38, 101–04, 198
  See also Political behavior in organizations
Consensus, lack of in organizations, 10, 12,
    19–21, 37–38
Constituents, role in negotiations, 178–80
Constitutions, organizational, 146
Cooper, M. R., 6, 28
Cooper, Terry L., 199, 202
Coser, Lewis A., 154, 183
Coulton, Claudia J., 114
Cournoyer, Barry R., 149
Crocker, Jennifer, 87, 90, 91
Crosby, Faye, 80–81, 83, 90
Crossman, Richard H. S., 145, 152
Crow, Richard T., 67
Crozier, Michael, 27
Cutbacks in social service spending, 7–8, 31–
    34, 60–61
  management of, 60–65
  resistance to, 65
  uneven distribution, 31
Cyert, Richard M., 9, 26

Dachler, H. Peter, 179, 184
Davis-Blake, Alison, 87, 91
Davis, Kenneth, 95, 112
Davis, Liane V., 96, 112
Deal, Terrence E., 114
Decision making and organizational power,
    21, 137, 138–39, 146–47
Demone, Jr., Harold W., 31, 47
Denhardt, Robert B., 6
Department of Health, Education, and Wel-
    fare, 56
  reorganization under Nixon administra-
    tion, 57, 60
Department of Health and Human Services,
    102, 103
Derthick, Martha, 57, 58, 66, 113
Deutsch, Morton, 178, 184
Discretionary decision making
  ethics of administrator's, 197–200
  and line social workers, 9, 104–07, 189–90
  and New Federalism, 57–58
  strategies for managing, 110–11

and weak legislation, 97–98
Discrimination. *See* Racial minorities;
    Women
Dissent in organizations, 24, 128–29
Distributive justice, 188–89, 195, 199
Domestic violence, politics of, 96–97
Donnison, David D., 10, 26
Drake, Bruce H., 201
Drake, Eileen, 201
Drucker, Peter, 65, 67
Dukerich, Janet M., 151
Durkheim, Emile, 18, 27

Easton, David, 6
Economic Opportunity Act (1964) as weak
    legislation, 93
Edwards, Richard L., 150
Ehrlich, Sanford B., 151
Eisenberg, Eric M., 184, 192, 201
Elmore, Richard F., 113
Emerson, Richard M., 27
Emery, F. E., 88
Environment, organizational, 42, 111
Ethics
  content and process approaches to, 194–95
  and managerial work, 186–87
  manager's personal, 191–97
  and policymaking, 197–200
  and public professions, 189–97
  and social work practice, 187–89
Ewing, David W., 6
Expert power, 132–34, 148, 165
Ezell, Hazell, 85, 90

Fabricant, Michael, 67
Fanshel, David, 89
Feld, Allen, 149
Fink, Richard L., 67
Fisher, Roger, 157, 164, 167, 183
Ford, Henry, 8
Forester, John, 143, 152
Fouraker, Lawrence E., 172, 184
French, Jr., John R. P., 126, 151
Friedson, Eliot, 105, 113
Friendship and influence networks, 144–45
"Front-line organization," 9, 105
Funding of social services
  and agency power, 32
  conservative bias of funders, 34
  iron triangles and, 56–57
  politics of, 55–56, 58–59
  rational approach to, 31–32